Concerning

Tongues

By Curry R. Blake

General Overseer of

John G. Lake Ministries

and

Dominion Life

International Apostolic Church

Published by
CHRISTIAN REALITY BOOKS
P.O. Box 742947
Dallas TX 75374
1-888-293-6591

Cover Design by John E. Blake.

Unless otherwise noted, all Scripture quotations are taken from the King James Bible.

Printed in the United States of America.

This teaching was taken from Sunday Broadcasts and 2012 Diversities of Tongues Seminar, presented by Curry R. Blake.

DEDICATION

First and foremost, I dedicate this book to The Father and The Son and The Holy Spirit.

> To The Father because of His love toward us, who so little deserve it and for His willingness to send His Son on our behalf.

> To The Son because of His willingness to suffer the humiliation and death that He suffered on our behalf, and for His identifying with us, so that we could be identified with Him, and for sending us this great "Comforter".

> To The Holy Spirit because of His willingness to be so closely united with us, so that we can speak God's will through our lips and know the things that are freely given to us by our Heavenly Father.

Secondly, I dedicate this book to my mother-in-law, Marie Stewart. She has had to put up with me for as long as my wife has, and she has done it with grace and "class." Without her (and her amazing team of transcribers) this book, as well as all the others that are now being read around the world, would still be just a desire in my heart.

A book of this size, coupled with the monumental task of "Englishizing" my Texan verbiage, would easily overwhelm most, but she and her merry band of transcribers and editors completed the work in record time, because they understood the vital importance of the topic and this information. I pray they all know that they receive the same credit and blessing from Heaven for every good that comes from this book.

Thirdly, and far from last or least, I dedicate this book to my daughter-in-law, Stephanie Blake. As with everything she does, she had the "gumption" to pick up the book publication aspect of this ministry and push it through into reality. (I'm sure she heard me complain about not having books in print until she just got fed up and decided to make it happen.)

Readers may never know how difficult it can be to get me to sit still long enough to answer questions that must be answered before a book can go to print. Stephanie had the grit to take on the job and see it through.

To all the above:
All that is being done to advance the Kingdom of God through this ministry could never be done without each and every one of you. Every person that benefits from these books owes a tremendous debt of gratitude to you.

Curry R. Blake

TABLE OF CONTENTS

READ THIS!

This book is the accumulated knowledge, wisdom, insight and revelation concerning the spiritual activity commonly known as "speaking in tongues", that I have gathered/received in over 40 yrs of personal Bible study (with over 30 of those years as an experiential practitioner).

Over the last 20 years as a Bible teacher, the topics of "tongues" and "healing" have brought the most questions from Christians and non-Christians alike. I have never wanted to write books just for the sake of having books out in the market.

There has to be a real reason, a real need, and I have to believe that I have insight that can't be found elsewhere. Otherwise, why write another book?

After reading literally every book in print concerning "tongues" (both for and against), I realized that there was not a book available that clearly, concisely, and Scripturally covered this extremely misunderstood topic.

So...Here it is!

This book should answer the most common questions, give simple Biblical direction and instruction concerning how to utilize one of the basic weapons of our (spiritual) warfare.

Should you, the reader have questions or comments after reading the book and putting the instructions into practice, please feel free to contact us at publishing@jglm.org. Future editions are planned to include specific questions and answers.

Blessings,

Curry R. Blake

PROMISE OF THE FATHER

BAPTISM IN THE HOLY SPIRIT

Sermon given by Curry R. Blake

Father, I thank You for this day that we can gather up and hear Your Word. Father, I thank You for the Word that You're going to bring forth this morning. Father, I fully expect this to go forth, both here locally and to those who are listening and watching by Internet. Right now, Father, we bless them and we say, in the name of Jesus, your understanding will be enlightened, and that, Father, You will greatly and more greatly fulfill Your will in their lives, throughout their lives. Father, right now in the name of Jesus, I bless those who are under the sound of my voice. Father, I say right now, my desire is that You take pleasure in what takes place here today. In the name of Jesus, Amen.

There's an old saying among charismatic circles: "The Word without the Spirit will cause you to dry up, the Spirit without the Word will cause you to blow up, but the Word and the Spirit together will cause you to grow up." One of the things that we have noticed is that in JGLM, as God brings things in, it's almost like He's fixing things. When there have been certain errors in the Body of Christ, then He seemed to promote a ministry or a message to fix that problem.

As a historian, I've done a lot of research, and it's almost like Solomon said, "There's nothing new under the sun." A lot of things that occur are simply cycles.

Look at the last 10, 15, or 20 years and you can see where the Prophetic Movement came in and then you can see what was called the Apostolic Movement. We look at these things as though they're new, saying something like, "Oh, this is what God is doing right now," when, in reality, it started as early as 1885-1888. John Alexander Dowie actually believed in apostolic ministry and was considering his ministry to be apostolic. Many people considered him an apostle and, eventually at one point, he even called himself an apostle. Apostolic ministry or recognizing the apostolic ministry is nothing new, and it was beginning to be accepted back in the late 1800s and early 1900s.

Today people say, "Oh, this is a new thing that God is doing." It's not that God is doing anything new; it's just that every now and then the Church seems to catch up with what God wants done.

That's one of the reasons I have a problem sometimes when people say, "Well, God is restoring this to the Church or He is restoring that." It's not that He's restoring; it's already been here. It's that the Church is finally waking up to it. If we say that God is restoring it, then we have to also say that it was God's fault that we didn't have it before because He didn't give it to us. The reality is this: He's given us everything that pertains to life and godliness. He gave us that with Jesus, so it's been here. It is up to us to awake to that.

Now, in the Church world—I'm not talking about in the dead religious church world, I'm talking about the living Church world—the Church usually bounces from one wall to the other. It's almost like it's on this path and it bounces from one side to the other. I could even say it in Biblical terms: "It goes from one ditch across the road to the other ditch." The key is staying out of the ditch, but the Church hardly ever does that. It seems to run to extremes.

My early days, when I was first coming into a lot of this, were almost 40 years ago. Back then, the big thing was teaching. Everything was teaching, because there had been so little teaching. In the group that I was with, there was a lot of in-depth teaching. They got me to studying the Word. They also got me to using Strong's Concordance and doing research.

Many times, when you sit under a teacher, it can be very dry. That is the normal situation; there isn't much Spirit activity. Usually what happens next is that you'll have this teaching or this particular ministry and then, at some point, the people will get fed up with that and say, "There's got to be something more." Then they will rebound from that to the opposite. Again, it goes from one ditch to the other.

Well that's what happened back in the late '80s and into the '90s. There was a rebound from the emphasis on teaching and from the teaching ministry, so to speak, over into the prophetic. It went from just teaching the Word and not much Spirit, to the other extreme where it was all Spirit; everything was prophetic. Every person was a prophet, and everything was a prophecy. People were waiting for that. They wanted that "live" aspect and the spiritual life; they wanted it back in the church. They went from the teaching emphasis over into the other ditch of the prophetic aspect.

As with the teaching, there are excesses. Any time you focus on one thing too much, you're usually going to get away from the Word. What happens is that you exhaust that subject in the Bible and then you tend to get off into an area that is not Bible. That leads into error. Usually what happens is that people will begin to gravitate. They did the same thing with the prophetic.

Just as there were extremes and wrong teachings in the movement of the '70s and '80s, whenever it started being the prophetic and apostolic, people got into it. At first, it was new. There were a lot of things to explain. There was a lot of movement going on but then, it got to a point where they had exhausted all the basics and the fundamentals and the truth, and started getting over into the weird. They started doing things that weren't biblical. It got to the point where, "The Word without the Spirit will cause you to dry up; the Spirit without the Word will cause you to blow up." That's kind of what happened.

During that time, God really started bringing us to prominence and started giving us some influence. We started going out, actually around the world. We are better known in other countries than we are even here in the United States. Usually, whenever I go overseas, we will have thousands in our crowds and here in the States, hardly anybody knows us.

That's the same thing that happened to T.L. Osborne at first. He had crowds abroad but when he came back to the United States, they didn't know who he was.

What we've done in JGLM came from that movement and from just teaching. We've brought in some correction, and we've kept it from going into extremes. We haven't gotten off onto some tangent or something.

People would say, "Healing is your tangent." It's not that I always try to teach on healing. It is just what the people usually ask us to teach on. There are a lot of other things that I really study and that God brings out to me, but it's healing that people usually ask for. They ask, "What about healing?" I could teach on any topic and then say, "Okay, now we're going to take questions," and I guarantee you that 90 percent of the questions are going to be about healing. That's just the way it goes. I'm not against that; we love healing. I can pick up the Bible and read anywhere in it and find something about healing. It's easy.

What we've done is kept from going off into a ditch. We have been able to maintain balance, Biblical balance, and so we've been able to continue to move forward with it, to take ground from the enemy, and to establish truth.

Turn to Luke chapter 11. We're going to lay some foundations.

I always start by asking, "Okay, God, what do you want me to bring to the people?" I always ask Him, "What do they need, and what do You want me to bring out?" I can honestly say that the things that God definitely presses on me are what I bring out. Other times, it's more like, "Okay, this is what the people need, this is what they want, and this is what they're asking me to teach on so I can do that." Of all the times that I've been teaching, I believe this teaching is setting something up. We may be doing a series of teachings on this topic. I felt more of a push of the Spirit to lay this foundation and to really dig into this and establish it. That's what we're going to be doing.

We're going to be talking about the Promise of the Father. They did a study about Spirit-filled ministry and said, "If something doesn't change, it's going to die." Well, I don't believe it's going to die. I believe that the Word of the Lord will live forever, and I believe that God has raised this up specifically in many areas to do just that.

This is Jesus speaking in Luke 11, starting in verse 9. He says,

9 And I say unto you, Ask, and it shall be given you; seek, and ye shall find; knock, and it shall be opened unto you.

10 For every one that asketh receiveth; and he that seeketh findeth; and to him that knocketh it shall be opened.

11 If a son shall ask bread of any of you that is a father, will he give him a stone? or if *he ask* a fish, will he for a fish give him a serpent?

12 Or if he shall ask an egg, will he offer him a scorpion?

13 If ye then, being evil, know how to give good gifts unto your children: how much more shall *your* heavenly Father give the Holy Spirit to them that ask him?

Notice it said, "…to them that ask Him." The first point in the promise of the Father and understanding what that promise means is that you have to know that there is a Holy Spirit and you have to request Him. You have to ask the Father for Him.

Only born again people can receive the Spirit of God and can receive the promise of the Father the way that it's talking about here. The Father wants to give you the Holy Spirit. He wants to give Him to you even more than you want Him.

Go to John chapter 7. Again, we're laying some foundation here.

> 37 In the last day, that great *day* of the feast, Jesus stood and cried, saying, If any man thirst, let him come unto me, and drink.

> 38 He that believeth on me, as the scripture hath said, <u>out of his belly</u> shall flow rivers of living water.

Notice where it is coming from — out of the belly. He's talking about the seat of the Spirit. This is where the Spirit abides, and He's saying, "In your inner most being, in the very depths of your being, the Holy Spirit will flow out of you."

There comes a point where He comes into you. After that, He comes out of you. If you're going to be ministering the Spirit of God to people (which is what makes New Testament ministry different than Old Testament ministry: we are ministering life by the Spirit), then it is going to be coming out of your spirit.

The scriptures say that the Holy Spirit is going to flow out of you. He's not going to be poured out from somewhere else. He's going to pour out of you; out of your belly will flow rivers of living water. Here's a little sub note: notice it says "rivers," plural. Not a river, but rivers. If you look up "rivers" in the Bible you'll see that when it talks about water and different things like that, it's always in reference to the Holy Spirit.

The Bible also gives reference to the voice of God, the sound of God's voice being as the sound of many waters. The work of the Holy Spirit coming out of you is going to have more purposes, not just one purpose, but many purposes.

You can tell that I'm trying to get everybody ready for the Diversities of Tongues Seminar. If you're not filled with the Spirit and have not received or spoken in other tongues, then you need to experience that and be operating in that. The seminar on the Diversities of Tongues will help you to receive it. The purpose of that seminar is going to be teaching you how to operate and be fluent in other tongues. We will be teaching you why there are diversities or differences.

Notice here, in verse 39 it says,

> 39 (But this spake he of the Spirit, which they that believe on him should receive: for the Holy Ghost was not yet *given;* because that Jesus was not yet glorified.)

"But this spake he of the Spirit, which they that believe on him should receive…" Remember that word, "receive." We're going to look at that in just a minute.

It says, "…for the Holy Ghost was not yet given; because that Jesus was not yet glorified." You'll notice that this was all future. He was talking about what would happen. Here, He was talking about the Spirit. He was talking about the Spirit of God (the Holy Spirit, the Comforter). He was talking about how, when the Spirit comes inside of you, He will start to pour out of you. He will be poured into you and then He will be poured out of you, and "out of your belly will flow rivers of living water."

Look at the word "*receive*" and remember that I told you to take note there. In the Greek it's the Greek word "*lambanō*" and it means *to take; to get hold of.* I want to differentiate something here, and this is very important.

There are three types of words for *"receive"* in the Greek:

1. *"Receive"* is passive. It means *to have offered to one.*

2. *"To receive"* means *to be more violent, or more aggressive.* It means *to seize, to take hold of and remove.*

3. The word receive that's used here is where it talks about *"receiving"* so as *to accept as an owner.* It's also the word for *"receive"* in Acts 1:8.

> 8 But ye shall receive power, after that the Holy Ghost is come upon you: and ye shall be witnesses unto me both in Jerusalem, and in all Judaea, and in Samaria, and unto the uttermost part of the earth.

Notice, in the third definition here, *"receive"* means *to accept as an owner.* It's not passive. You don't just sit and say, "Okay, God, if you want to give it to me, I'll take it." It's not aggressive in the sense that you take it from God and you pull it down. However, it is the third aspect, which is *to accept as an owner; you own it.* Notice that this is also from an area of believing, where you believe that you receive. You believe and by that, you accept it as an owner and you have it.

Let's go to John 14:8.

> 8 Philip saith unto him, Lord, shew us the Father, and it sufficeth us.
>
> 9 Jesus saith unto him, Have I been so long time with you, and yet hast thou not known me, Philip? he that hath seen me hath seen the Father; and how sayest thou *then,* Shew us the Father?

10 Believest thou not that I am in the Father, and the Father in me? the words that I speak unto you I speak not of myself: but the Father that dwelleth in me, he doeth the works.

Notice, Jesus didn't even claim to do the works; He said it was the Father in Him. You can't even claim any glory in doing anything that God does through you because He is the One who does it.

11 Believe me that I *am* in the Father, and the Father in me: or else believe me for the very works' sake.

12 Verily, verily, I say unto you, He that believeth on me, the works that I do shall he do also; and greater *works* than these shall he do; because I go unto my Father.

The only reason we are given why we can do the same works as Jesus did (heal the sick, raise the dead, cast out devils, preach the gospel, multiply food, calm storms, whatever needs to be done), is because He went to the Father. In that sense, it is absolutely and totally by grace. However, you still have to step out and put your hands on the sick. You still have to speak words to people, and you still have to speak to the storm. There are still things that you do, but it is the Spirit of God working in you. It's all because Jesus went to the Father.

Did He go to the Father? Of course; the answer is, "Yes." What's the result? We can do the same works. It's that simple.

Then, He said,

13 And whatsoever ye shall ask in my name, that will I do, that the Father may be glorified in the Son.

14 If ye shall ask any thing in my name, I will do *it*.

Notice: He repeats Himself there. Then in verse 15,

15 If ye love me, keep my commandments.

He didn't say keep the Law and He didn't even say keep the Ten Commandments. He shouldn't have to say that because, technically, if you love God with all your heart, mind, soul and strength (which is the great commandment) and your neighbor as yourself, you will automatically do those things.

He says in verse 16,

> 16 And I will pray the Father, and he shall give you another Comforter, that he may abide with you forever;

Notice this Comforter. In the Greek it's the word *"paraklēt"* or *"paraklētos"* which means literally, *an advocate, a counselor, a consoler*, but it is also our word *"Helper."* It means *one called alongside to help.* He said, "I will pray the Father, and he will give you another *Helper.*" He will give you someone to come along beside you to help you.

> 17 *Even* the Spirit of truth; whom the world cannot receive, because it seeth him not, neither knoweth him: but ye know him; for he dwelleth with you, and shall be in you.

"Even the Spirit of truth; whom the world cannot receive..." The world cannot receive the Spirit. You have to be born again first, then you receive the Spirit. "Because it seeth Him not, neither knoweth Him, but you know Him..."

There are some people who say, "Well, saying that He is in us means He's just in union or in agreement." No. Jesus made a distinction right here. He said, "He dwells with you and shall be in you." The Holy Spirit desires to dwell within you.

In verse 18, He says,

> 18 I will not leave you comfortless: I will come to you.

"I will not leave you comfortless." You could also say that the word "comfortless" means "helpless." He was saying, "I will not leave you helpless, but I will come to you."

> 19 Yet a little while, and the world seeth me no more; but ye see me: because I live, ye shall live also.

> 20 At that day ye shall know that I *am* in my Father, and ye in me, and I in you.

At this point in Scripture, these promises were all future tense, but you have to realize this: He lives in you.

> 21 He that hath my commandments, and keepeth them, he it is that loveth me: and he that loveth me shall be loved of my Father, and I will love him, and will manifest myself to him.

> 22 Judas saith unto him, not Iscariot, Lord, how is it that thou wilt manifest thyself unto us, and not unto the world?

> 23 Jesus answered and said unto him, If a man love me, he will keep my words: and my Father will love him, and we will come unto him, and make our abode with him.

Notice, He said, "If a man loves me, he will keep my words: and my Father will love him, and we will come unto him, and make our abode with him." Look at verse 24,

> 24 He that loveth me not keepeth not my sayings: and the word which ye hear is not mine, but the Father's which sent me.

> 25 These things have I spoken unto you, being *yet* present with you.

> 26 But the Comforter, *which is* the Holy Ghost, whom the Father will send in my name, he shall teach you all things, and bring

all things to your remembrance, whatsoever I have said unto you.

The Holy Spirit is only going to say what Jesus has said and bring to your remembrance the things that Jesus has said. Notice it is saying here, "This is a Comforter, a Helper; He is the One who the Father is going to send, and He is going to come to live in you."

We just brush over this so many times and we move past it very quickly, but you have to realize how awesome this is! The third Person of the Godhead, God the Holy Spirit, will live in humans. What an honor that is because under the Old Covenant, that never happened.

If you are a born again, Spirit-filled Christian, you are in a position that no other being was ever in before Jesus went to the cross. It is so radically different from how it was before. Sometimes we get used to how it is now, and we don't think about and appreciate the difference.

Had you had lived at the time before Jesus was crucified or shortly thereafter, during the early days of the Book of Acts, everything would have been different. Back then the Spirit would only come upon people. Now, He comes to dwell within. That dwelling is constant. He abides within you and He stays with you. He doesn't come and go.

I'm trying to emphasize this because I want you to get a real consciousness of the Spirit's presence and His abiding presence within you. This is such good news because what it means is that you are never helpless; you are never without help. There is nothing that you can't do and even Paul said, "I can do all things through Christ who strengthens me." We know of course that with God all things are possible and that nothing is impossible. All of this is because of that Spirit who lives in you.

My goal in teaching this is to get you stirred up in the Spirit of God, to get the Spirit of God—who is within you and abiding with you—stirred up within you. God has really been pushing this on me; He's really been bringing it to my remembrance. I have noticed that, even in my own life, it's sometimes easy to just get into cruise control. That's when you're just going through, living life, and doing what you've got to do.

We pray for people every day. We minister to people, and we get results. The fact is that there are times to do as Paul told Timothy, "Stir up the gift that is in you." Timothy was doing the work, he was out there ministering, and he was left to put things in order. I firmly believe that he was doing what he was supposed to be doing. Yet, at the same time, Paul said, "Don't neglect the gift that's in you. Stir up the gift that's in you, rekindle it, and fan it into a flame." Apparently even Timothy had gotten into cruise control. It's easy, especially if, in just normal life, you're working a "9 to 5" job. You're paying bills and just living a normal life. It's so easy to get into that normal cruise control in the spiritual life.

What I'm hoping to do, and what I believe is the goal of the Spirit of God, is to get us all back on course and get us into a place where the Spirit of God literally stirs up what is within us.

Over the last couple of weeks, when someone would start to talk to me, I would almost answer in tongues. I'm not even spending more time in tongues; I've always prayed extensively in tongues.

That's what happens when you start to stir up the gift that's in you. We'll talk about that a little later on, too. When I say, "Gift," I'm not talking about a particular gift. I'm not talking about "the nine gifts of Spirit." The gift that you stir up is "the gift of the Holy Ghost."

I will prove that to you. You can activate other gifts and you can actually stir up other gifts, but what Paul was talking about was stirring up the Holy Spirit within you. That means to bring it to fruition. It means to rekindle that flame that's there.

Now the Holy Spirit is always "on." It's you that needs to be awakened to it. As you start to draw your attention to it, it's as if He moves closer. I'm not saying that He does move closer, because He can't really move any closer than abiding within you. What I am saying is that you are more conscious of it and you get to where you live in that realm. Like I said, it's really easy to move in and out of that and fluctuate.

During the course of this teaching I will be giving you several examples, experiences, and testimonies. If you have been baptized in the Spirit, if you have received the promise of the Father, and if you have spoken in other tongues, it needs to be stirred up; it needs to be an ongoing thing. Perhaps you've been told by some people, "Well, you do it once and that's all you need." That's not true. Paul said, "I thank my God, I speak in tongues more than you all." If it's good enough for the Apostle Paul, we probably need it just as much.

What I want to do is to stir up the Spirit of God in you, and even as I speak, the Spirit of God in you, right now, agrees with this. What we should begin seeing is a stirring and a moving of the Spirit among us so that we should have more of the Spirit of God actually permeating every aspect of our lives, every second of our lives. Every minute of our day should be in closer contact with Him, in the sense that we are even more conscious of His presence.

When you get more conscious of His presence, it is you're going to feel like He just moved in. You say, "His presence is here." His presence was always there; it's just that you weren't paying attention. All I'm trying to do is draw your attention to it because He is in you, and He dwells in you. As you give Him more leeway, He will use you more and more and He will become more in union with you. When I say more in union, I am saying that He will actually be functioning through you more fluently. He can't be more in union with you than He is.

Like I said, lately it's actually easier for me to speak in tongues. When someone talks to me, I'm either praying in tongues out loud, or under my breath, or even in the Spirit without saying a word vocally that you could hear. It's almost as if when someone interrupts, they are interrupting a conversation between God and me. Rather than switch to English, sometimes it's easier just to open my mouth and speak in tongues. Now, that wouldn't be technically biblical, but what I'm saying is that He's right there and whenever He is so stirred up inside of you like that, it just becomes normal.

I'll be driving down the road and not even thinking about praying in tongues and it just comes out. I'm not saying He takes control or anything like that; it's not that at all. It's that I have yielded; I'm available. I want God to speak through me, and I want Him to speak to me.

Whenever you're praying in other tongues, it is almost like what happens with fiber optics. Fiber optics enables information to go both ways at the same time. That's exactly what goes on when you speak in tongues. You are praying to God and He is also downloading into you; He is talking through you, yet at the same time, you're in union with Him. There is this perfect communion going on. Again, we will talk more in detail about this as we go along, but right now, I just want to emphasize that the promise of the Father is that the Spirit of God can and will dwell within you.

LEVELS OF INFILLING OF THE SPIRIT

Many people have received an infilling or have received the Holy Spirit to a degree but have not received the Baptism of the Spirit. The Baptism of the Holy Spirit is not just speaking in tongues; it is much more than that. Speaking in tongues is just the overflow of what takes place at the Baptism of the Spirit.

I really want to get this founded into you and get you to understand this. We are going to become a fully functioning Spirit-filled church, a fully functioning Spirit-filled body, to where the Spirit of God is in union with us and is moving in us on a regular basis.

It should get you to a place where you start participating and joining with us in Spirit and mind. If you begin praying in other tongues and speaking in other tongues during your week, especially on Sunday mornings, then when you come in here, you will have an idea of what I'm going to say before I say it. Why? The Holy Spirit will get you ready for it. He will prepare you for it.

Many of you have been crying out to God about this very thing, which is why He is bringing it out now. That's what the Holy Spirit does: He knows the needs of those that are listening, and He knows their cry, their hunger. Their desire actually brings Him up and causes Him to meet that need. I fully believe that what I am putting out here is an answer to what has been going on inside of you and that God has been dealing with you on this.

> 26 But the Comforter, *which is* the Holy Ghost, whom the Father will send in my name, he shall teach you all things, and bring all things to your remembrance, whatsoever I have said unto you.

27 Peace I leave with you, my peace I give unto you: not as the world giveth, give I unto you. Let not your heart be troubled, neither let it be afraid.

28 Ye have heard how I said unto you, I go away, and come *again* unto you. If ye loved me, ye would rejoice, because I said, I go unto the Father: for my Father is greater than I.

He was saying, "If you could understand when I say that I go to my Father, and if you love me, you would rejoice." Why? It is a two-fold answer. Number one, "I get to go be with my Father." Love rejoices, not in evil, but love rejoices whenever someone else gets something good from God. Here Jesus was saying, "I get to leave this place. I get to go back to be with my heavenly Father. I've been parted from Him, for 33 years. I've been parted from Him and now I get to go back. You ought to be throwing me a going-away party because this is exciting." Number two, He said, "Not only that, but if I go, then I get to send the Holy Spirit back. If I don't go, I can't send Him back."

He was saying, "It's better for you. If you know me and love me and you know I am going to the Father, you should rejoice, because when I go to the Father, I get to send the Spirit back to you. You will have everything I have and you will have it within you."

We read this sometimes in King James and we read right over it. We think, "Well, that's just Jesus being religious or being spiritual." He said, "No, if you love me, you would rejoice that I get to be with my Father."

He goes on in verse 29 of John chapter 14,

29 And now I have told you before it come to pass, that, when it is come to pass, ye might believe.

30 Hereafter I will not talk much with you: for the prince of this world cometh, and hath nothing in me.

He was saying, "I'm not going to talk with you much after this." Remember that.

In John chapter 15 verse 26, it says,

> 26 But when the Comforter is come, whom I will send unto you from the Father, *even* the Spirit of truth, which proceedeth from the Father, he shall testify of me:

"But when the Comforter is come..." Who is that? He is the Helper, the One who will fill you, live in you, and abide in you. When He is come, the One "whom I will send unto you from the Father, even the Spirit of truth..." We know that the Holy Spirit, the Comforter, the Helper, is the Spirit of truth, "which proceeds from the Father." Then it says, "He shall testify of Me." Now, you'll notice that this is all future tense.

John 16:7, He says,

> 7 Nevertheless I tell you the truth; It is expedient for you that I go away: for if I go not away, the Comforter will not come unto you; but if I depart, I will send him unto you.

"Nevertheless I tell you the truth; It is expedient for you that I go away: for if I go not away, the Comforter," your Helper, "will not come unto you; but if I depart, I will send Him unto you."

In John chapter 16, He says,

> 12 I have yet many things to say unto you, but ye cannot bear them now.

"I have yet many things to say unto you..." Now, do you hear that? Notice, right back there in chapter 14, verse 30, He was saying, "I'm not going to talk with you much after this because the wicked one is coming."

13 Howbeit when he, the Spirit of truth, is come, he will guide you into all truth…

He said, "I'm not going to talk with you," but then just two chapters later, He said, "I have yet many things to say to you, but you cannot bear them now. Howbeit when he, the Spirit of truth, is come, he will guide you into all truth."

13 …for he shall not speak of himself; but whatsoever he shall hear, *that* shall he speak: and he will shew you things to come.

Notice that He is putting all of the things He wants to say into a time after He has sent the Spirit back, which we know took place on the day of Pentecost. He says, "…for He shall not speak of Himself; but whatsoever He shall hear, that shall He speak: and He will show you things to come."

Back in John 14:30, He said, "Hereafter I will not talk with you much." Remember, I told you to make a note of that. I'm just going to give you a quick list. This all happened very quickly from John 15 to John 21.

- John 15 - Jesus preaches about being the vine. He's the vine, we are the branches, and He gives us a new commandant.
- John 16 - He prophesies persecution and talks about the Holy Spirit.
- John 17 - The whole chapter basically is Him praying to the Father.
- John 18 - His arrest and trial.
- John 19 - His crucifixion.
- John 20 - His resurrection.
- John 21 - His post-resurrection appearances.

John 15 to John 21 happened within a matter of days and even hours. He said, "I'm not going to talk much with you, but when the Holy

Spirit comes, I'm going to share these things with you through the Holy Spirit and He's going to tell you everything I've said."

The Holy Spirit is going to tell what He hears and He's even going to be talking about the things that Jesus couldn't say at that time. He's going to bring those things through the Holy Spirit to us in this time.

Let's go to Acts chapter 1, starting with verse 1. This was Luke writing and he said,

> 1 The former treatise have I made, O Theophilus, of all that Jesus began both to do and teach,
>
> 2 Until the day in which he was taken up, after that he through the Holy Ghost had given commandments unto the apostles whom he had chosen:
>
> 3 To whom also he shewed himself alive after his passion by many infallible proofs, being seen of them forty days, and speaking of the things pertaining to the kingdom of God:
>
> 4 And, being assembled together with *them,* commanded them that they should not depart from Jerusalem, but wait for the promise of the Father, which, *saith he,* ye have heard of me.
>
> 5 For John truly baptized with water; but ye shall be baptized with the Holy Ghost not many days hence.

This is just before the day of Pentecost. He says, "You are going to get the promise of the Father." He now relates the promise of the Father to the Baptism of the Spirit; He relates that it is to happen on the day of Pentecost. We know that the promise of the Father was to receive the Spirit and we know that it initially happened at the day of Pentecost.

You've got to get the picture; put yourself there. You're standing around and Jesus is talking to them and Jesus tells them, "John baptized with water, but you will be baptized with the Holy Ghost in just a couple of days."

It says,

> 6 When they therefore were come together, they asked of him, saying, Lord, wilt thou at this time restore again the kingdom to Israel?

Things went right over their heads. They were still thinking about natural, earthly matters.

> 7 And he said unto them, It is not for you to know the times or the seasons, which the Father hath put in his own power.

> 8 But ye shall receive power, after that the Holy Ghost is come upon you: and ye shall be witnesses unto me both in Jerusalem, and in all Judaea, and in Samaria, and unto the uttermost part of the earth.

Jesus said, "But you shall receive *power*." He was saying, "Did you not hear what I'm talking about? I'm telling you that you're going to be baptized with the Holy Ghost in just a couple of days." Then they said, "Oh, we're going to get a kingdom?" He wanted them to get their heads out of the natural. He was telling them, "You're going to receive *power*. I'm going to send you what I have. You're going to be walking around this earth just like I do."

He said, "You shall receive *power*." The Greek word for *power* here is "*dunamis*" and it literally means "*miraculous ability*." Notice it didn't say, "And you shall receive tongues." He said, "You will receive *miraculous ability*." When you receive the Holy Ghost, when you receive the promise of the Father, and when you get baptized in the Holy Ghost you have received. "*Received*" means *to own*. Remember, I told you what it meant here in Acts 1:8: "You shall *receive*," which means that you shall have *ownership of miraculous ability*.

That was the whole point of Jesus' coming: it was to get the Spirit back into the people so that the people could go into the world and give signs and wonders to the world and get them converted. The purpose was to produce signs and wonders.

"After that the Holy Ghost is come upon you, and you will be witnesses unto me..." Notice what the purpose of this miraculous ability was: it was to produce signs as seen in Mark 16 and Matthew 28. The purpose was to produce signs so that you could be a witness and so that you could win the world.

You have to realize this: God was trying to put His Spirit into a people so that the people with His Spirit could evangelize the world. That was the whole point of Jesus' coming. It was to get the Spirit back into the people so that the people could go into the world, give signs and wonders to the world, and get the world converted.

It wasn't just so we could be a clique. It wasn't just so we could be Pentecostal or could be Spirit filled or could be Charismatic. No, it was so that we could win the world. The purpose was to produce signs and wonders.

I'm going to be talking about praying in tongues over the next few weeks and in the Diversities of Tongues seminar. We're talking about this because almost every major miracle that we have seen in our lives came after an extended time of praying in other tongues. Each miracle was amazing!

As we put this into practice more and more here in this church, and we're going to do that, then you're going to see more and more of this. I'm not just talking about healings. Healings come, but I'm talking about the miraculous; I'm talking about more displays of the power of God.

They are going to be coming through me, and they're going to be coming through you. Why? That's because there's no difference in the Spirit. God is not a respecter of persons; what He does through one, He will do through any. The difference is—and it's amazing—God has made all of this available.

Then He says, "Now, who wants it? Who wants it?" If you want it, you can step into it, but to step into the miraculous, you have to step out of the natural. It is that simple.

Go down to verse 13. It says,

> 13 And when they were come in, they went up into an upper room, where abode both Peter, and James, and John, and Andrew, Philip, and Thomas, Bartholomew, and Matthew, James *the son* of Alphaeus, and Simon Zelotes, and Judas *the brother* of James.

"And when they were come in, they went up into an upper room." Notice, "They went in." It was speaking of the disciples and it said they were staying there.

Then in Acts chapter 2, it says,

> 1 And when the day of Pentecost was fully come, they were all with one accord in one place.

> 2 And suddenly there came a sound from heaven as of a rushing mighty wind, and it filled all the house where they were sitting.

> 3 And there appeared unto them cloven tongues like as of fire, and it sat upon each of them.

> 4 And they were all filled with the Holy Ghost, and began to speak with other tongues, as the Spirit gave them utterance.

"And they were all..." Notice the word, "all." It says that their number was about 120. You will see that in a minute. It says, "And they were all filled with the Holy Ghost, and began to speak with other tongues, as the Spirit gave them utterance." They were all filled and they all began speaking in other tongues. There was not one exception. They all were filled and they all spoke in other tongues.

If you go on through this whole passage here, you'll see that they began speaking in other languages that the people actually understood. We will be talking about that. I can give you several examples that I know of personally where that took place.

Look down at verse 15. Remember that some onlookers said, "Ah, these men are drunk" and then Peter stood up and he said,

> 15 For these are not drunken, as ye suppose, seeing it is *but* the third hour of the day.

> 16 But this is that which was spoken by the prophet Joel;

Then, he quotes Joel and says,

> 17 And it shall come to pass in the last days, saith God, I will pour out of my Spirit upon all flesh: and your sons and your daughters shall prophesy, and your young men shall see visions, and your old men shall dream dreams:

"And it shall come to pass in the last days, saith God, I will pour out of my Spirit upon all flesh: and your sons and your daughters shall prophesy." When it says, "They will all prophesy," it could very well also include speaking in tongues and interpreting. It says, "...and your young men shall see visions, and your old men shall dream dreams:"

> 18 And on my servants and on my handmaidens I will pour out in those days of my Spirit; and they shall prophesy:

Understand, we're talking about the Spirit. We're talking about the promise of the Father, we're talking about the Spirit of God dwelling within, and we're talking about something much greater than just saying, "Oh yes, I've got the Spirit of God, I'm born again, and I'm set for heaven; I'm good." I'm talking about a specific union with God to the place where you give Him the right of way to be able to use your vocal chords. You're going to be using them, but He's going to be speaking through you. The very language of God Himself, the language of heaven, is going to come through you. If that has never happened to you, it will. We're going to minister to you and we're going to do it biblically. I will show you what the biblical practice is, and we will go from there.

PROMISE OF THE FATHER

SPEAKING IN OTHER TONGUES

Sermon given by Curry R. Blake

We are still talking about the Promise of the Father and that it is the Holy Spirit coming, not only to dwell within, to live within, but also to flow out from. That is the key. Peter has actually preached all the way through verse 33, and there are some good things in there. You definitely should go back and read them.

He says in Acts 2:33,

> 33 Therefore being by the right hand of God exalted, and having received of the Father the promise of the Holy Ghost, he hath shed forth this, which ye now see and hear.

"Therefore being by the right hand of God exalted, and having *received...*" There is that word *received* again. Notice that he is tying this in. It says, "Therefore being by the right hand of God exalted, and having received of the Father the promise of the Holy Ghost:"

First of all, He is seated at the right hand of the Father, and secondly, He has received the promise of the Holy Ghost from the Father Himself.

"He hath shed forth this, which you now see and hear." He is tying in this receiving of the promise of the Holy Spirit: He received it and He shed it forth just like He told them. It is just like we showed you earlier. He said, "If I don't go, I can't send the Holy Spirit back, but if I go, I will send the Comforter back to you."

He said, "He received that Spirit and now He is shedding it forth, which you now see and hear." By the shedding forth (as it says here), the sharing, the sending back of the Spirit as Jesus promised, there will be things that you can see and hear.

That is a key: when the Holy Spirit comes forth, it is something that you can see and hear.

Acts 2:34-35:

> 34 For David is not ascended into the heavens: but he saith himself, The LORD said unto my Lord, Sit Thou on My right hand,
>
> 35 Until I make Thy foes Thy footstool.

Jesus is going to be seated until His foes, His enemies, are made His footstool.

Acts 2:36-38:

> 36 Therefore let all the house of Israel know assuredly, that God hath made that same Jesus, Whom ye have crucified, both Lord and Christ.
>
> 37 Now when they heard *this*, they were pricked in their heart, and said unto Peter and to the rest of the apostles, Men *and* brethren, what shall we do?
>
> 38 Then Peter said unto them, Repent, and be baptized every one of you in the name of Jesus Christ for the remission of sins, and ye shall receive the gift of the Holy Ghost.

"Then Peter said unto them, repent and be baptized every one of you in the name of Jesus Christ for the remission of sins (or because of the remission of sins), and you shall receive the gift of the Holy Ghost." We are going to explain this in detail as we go along.

Throughout church history, we have seen that as humans we want to categorize things. We want things to work linearly. I really want to move you away from that because back in the early days (I am talking about before the Pentecostal Movement even), during the Holiness Movement, they talked about the first blessing, the second blessing, and the third blessing. They talked about the blessings of God's grace or God's gifts of grace. They talked about the new birth as being the first gift of grace, and the second gift of grace as sanctification or separation from sin.

They started saying (during the early days of the Pentecostal Movement in the early 1900s), "Oh, there is now a third blessing. There is the new birth, there is sanctification, and now this third blessing is this Baptism of the Holy Spirit." We divide these things up. I really believe it will help you immensely if you get hold of this. Rather than thinking of it like that, think about the Baptism of the Holy Spirit, speaking in other tongues, and gifts as experiences.

I don't want to call them "events," but they are events, and they should be part of your lifestyle; they should be a common event. I want you to realize, though, that they are experiences. I don't want you to think of them in terms of, "I have to get this; then I have to get this; then I have to get that." It is not about chronological steps. It is not that at all. I want you to think more in terms of the raising of a child.

If you think in terms of a child growing, it is not a matter of saying, "Okay, my child is eight years old or ten years old. Let me see. Today, the lesson I want to teach will be this." It is not like that. You teach them, yet at the same time, they learn from life experiences. There are experiences they can learn from, but it is life.

It is not a get born again, get sanctified, and get baptized in the Spirit where you have these events. There will be events, but it is not a matter of 1-2-3. It is part of the growing up process. From the time you get born again, you are moving toward maturity. The separation from sin is part of maturity; it is part of the growth of maturity. Being filled to overflowing, baptized in the Holy Spirit, is part of that process of maturity. It is an event and it is an experience, but don't think of it as a 1-2-3 event. Think of it in terms of growing up, as you start to move into these things.

If you think of it in terms of 1-2-3, you could start to think: 1 this year, 2 next year, and 3 the next. No, it is not like that. It doesn't have to be that way. Even in the Book of Acts, when He said, "Wait until you receive the promise of the Father," they didn't wait long.

They had to wait until the day of Pentecost when it was first poured out. They spent 50 days there. Fifty days from the time of Jesus' resurrection until the day of Pentecost was a set time. The Holy Spirit could not be given until that day of Pentecost. They had to wait until then, but you will see after that, while they preached, the Holy Spirit fell on them.

When a person gets born again, they can get filled and baptized in the Spirit of God instantly. It doesn't have to be, "Well, I have to wait and tarry, go down to the altar and spend time there for the next nine months." Historically, many people do, but biblically they didn't. Biblically it is very rapid.

Historically, John Lake did wait. From the time he heard and believed the message of the Baptism of the Spirit and speaking in other tongues, it was over nine months before he actually received the Baptism of the Spirit. J. Roswell Flower, who was one of the founders of the Assemblies of God, waited for over two years. (I am actually a descendant of his.) He believed it, preached it, but he waited two years before he actually saw any evidence (as they would call it) of speaking in other tongues.

Do you think it is God telling people to wait that long? No, it usually has to do with a person being open to God. Many times you see in the

New Testament and even in examples of early Pentecostal history in the 20th century that people would get born again, and then they would get baptized.

When they got baptized, it was usually in a river or a big body of water. When they came up out of the water, they would be speaking in other tongues. Nobody even laid hands on them; nobody prayed for them. Many times they weren't even expecting it, but they just wanted all of God. They wanted all that God had for them, and they were open.

Many times our doctrines shut us off to the things that God would have us experience. It is not that we don't believe in them. It is the fact that because we believe against them, it shuts us off from experiences.

All I am saying is that if you have not received the Baptism of the Spirit, and if you have not spoken in other tongues, don't think that you have to wait.

In Luke 11:13, it says,

> 13 If ye then, being evil, know how to give good gifts unto your children: how much more shall *your* heavenly Father give the Holy Spirit to them that ask him?

He said, "How much more will He give the Holy Spirit to them that ask?" The key is just simply to ask and then to understand that if you ask and you believe that you will receive. It's the typical answer to prayer. Honestly, this is something that God does. It's not something that you do. The key is to understand, know, and be willing for God to move through your life in that way. You watch: things are going to happen.

If you have not received the Baptism of the Holy Spirit, we're going to pray for you. Then, God is going to fill you with the Holy Spirit, with the evidence of speaking in other tongues. I don't always use that term, but it is something that you can see and hear.

I want to go back to verse 38.

Acts 2:38-39

> 38 Then Peter said unto them, Repent, and be baptized every one of you in the name of Jesus Christ for the remission of sins, and ye shall receive the gift of the Holy Ghost.

> 39 For the promise is unto you, and to your children, and to all that are afar off, *even* as many as the Lord our God shall call.

When Peter talked about the promise of the Spirit right there, he was still talking about how the people saw and heard them speak in other tongues. He said, "This is the same promise." They said, "What do we have to do?" He said, "Repent, be baptized in the name of Jesus, and you will receive this."

He says, "Because the promise is for you and for your children," and then he said, "…for as many as God shall call." In other words, he was saying, "You don't have to worry about not being special and thinking that God doesn't want you to have it." There are groups that actually teach that saying, "Well, some people are special and God gives it to them, but there are other people who aren't, and He doesn't give it to them." That is not true. The promise of the Spirit, the Baptism of the Spirit with speaking in other tongues, is for every person. God wants every person to have it.

I know there are different groups, and I don't want to say something controversial. Have you heard of F.F. Bosworth who wrote "*Christ the Healer*?" He is well known. He was one of the founders of the Assemblies of God. He was with Dowie. He also was with John Lake in the early 1900s. He then moved to Dallas in 1910. He was at Azusa Street with John Lake and William J. Seymour. (There are pictures of them together.) He helped found the Assemblies of God in 1914.

By 1916 the Assemblies of God had established a standard: "Speaking in tongues is the single evidence of being baptized in the Spirit." He actually broke away from the Assemblies because he did not agree with that. He said he did believe that if you were baptized in the Spirit you would speak in tongues, but he didn't believe that speaking in tongues was the only evidence. He said any of the gifts should be evident.

That is somewhat true, but there are groups in the church today that will say, "Well, as long as you have any of the gifts of the Spirit, then that is proof you have received the Baptism of the Spirit." That is just not true.

The truth is that there is a special reason why God ordained tongues. The two things that have been fought for the hardest in Christianity are healing and tongues. Those two have brought the devil's attacks more than any other doctrines. The enemy is always working to try to stop those two. If the devil could stop the healings then people would die sooner and the world wouldn't be evangelized as quickly. He also hates speaking in other tongues. There are several reasons why, and we will get into that at another time. It is too long a list to go into, but he tries to fight it.

God Himself has set tongues as a sign. It is really one of the few signs in Mark 16 that is mentioned. It also carries over into 1 Corinthians, when it talks about the gifts. He talks about how they shall speak in new tongues. People say, "Well, I am good with healing but I just don't want anything to do with tongues." God will let you walk just so far with Him, and He will say, "Okay, I brought you this far; now believe this."

Many times people say, "I cannot go with that." They just stop. Usually, when they stop, they find a group that stopped in that same place and started a church around that. It then ends up being a denomination of some sort, or a group, or fellowship, or something. You can always find those kinds of camps where people went so far with God and then stopped and said, "This is as far as we are going." God Himself set tongues to signify the Baptism of the Holy Spirit.

We are going to talk about why this is. We are going to get into these details and we are going to analyze this thing and explain it. However, the reason I am talking about it is that I am trying to stir up the gift that is in you. The Spirit of God is already in you so that you receive the overflowing abundance of the Baptism of the Holy Spirit.

You say, "Well, I prayed. I asked God, and I don't speak in tongues. I have never spoken in tongues, so it must not be for me." That is not true. This Scripture, verse 39, says, "The promise is to you. It is to as many as God shall call." It is, therefore, for you. You say, "Well then, why? What is the problem?" We will get into that. Don't worry about that at this point. Sometimes it is just a matter of someone laying hands on you and imparting it to you. There is an impartation of the Spirit.

As a matter of fact, you don't see any references in the New Testament of people laying hands on people and giving them a specific gift. What you do see is the laying of hands (especially in the Book of Acts) on people and those people receiving the gift of the Holy Ghost, the Holy Spirit, Himself. There is that.

Acts 2:40-47

40 And with many other words did he testify and exhort, saying, Save yourselves from this untoward generation.

41 Then they that gladly received his word were baptized: and the same day there were added *unto them* about three thousand souls.

42 And they continued stedfastly in the apostles' doctrine and fellowship, and in breaking of bread, and in prayers.

43 And fear came upon every soul: and many wonders and signs were done by the apostles.

44 And all that believed were together, and had all things common;

45 And sold their possessions and goods, and parted them to all *men,* as every man had need.

46 And they, continuing daily with one accord in the temple, and breaking bread from house to house, did eat their meat with gladness and singleness of heart,

47 Praising God, and having favour with all the people. And the Lord added to the church daily such as should be saved.

This is where there has been a lot of confusion in the church. We bounce around between these because we talk about the reception of the Holy Spirit, and about people being filled with the Spirit. We talk about people speaking in other tongues.

In the Scripture it talks about how people were speaking in other tongues and others understood the tongues they spoke as being in their own language.

It says here that God added to the church there. Then toward the end in verse 47, it says, "The Lord added to the church daily such as should be saved." It is almost like, "Okay, what are we talking about? Are we talking about salvation? Are we talking about getting born again? Are we talking about being baptized in the Spirit?" Yes, we are talking about all of that.

Remember, you don't want to think in terms of categorizing: born again, Spirit-filled, speaking in tongues, and gifts. Don't think like that. Think in terms of maturity, of growing and having more experiences in God to where He is filling your life more and more, and you are experiencing more and more of Him in your daily life. Don't think of it as, "Well, I received the Baptism on February 15, back in 1980. I spoke in tongues then, but I never have since." Well, that is a shame. You should speak in tongues every day; you need to speak in tongues every day.

As a matter of fact, in the Sunday services and in the Diversities of Tongues seminar this month, we are going to be detailing those things. I am telling you that if you get this, your life will be radically changed. Radically changed! I am talking about God giving you understanding. I am talking about revelation. I am talking about things just happening around you and testimonies of these things.

I could give you testimonies of speaking in tongues that would literally fill up a book. They are testimonies of speaking in other tongues, for what I consider an extended period of time (more than just an hour a day), and what we have seen God do every time we have ever done that. There is an aspect of the Holy Spirit, God Himself, living in you. He is talking through you and working with you.

As we look at this, I am going to give you a couple of things:

1. The promise of the Father is the promise of the Holy Spirit coming to dwell within men and women. That is the promise of the Father. When you receive the promise, you will begin to speak with other tongues, and it should not be a one-time thing, but it should be a constant ongoing thing.

2. There are diversities of tongues—that means differences. The King James says diversities. It also says divers kinds of tongues, or as we would say, diverse kinds of tongues.

There are different reasons for speaking in tongues. There are tongues for edification; they are to build you up. There are tongues for maintenance that just keep your life good. You can avoid a whole lot of problems just by praying in tongues every day. There is wisdom that will come out; you will make the right decision, and you won't even know why you are doing it. You will not even realize what is happening when people start talking to you and saying, "Wow, that was good. That was a good call." You don't even know that it came because you were praying in tongues. He gave you the wisdom to make the right choices.

There are tongues of intercession for when you start to intercede for others and sometimes, you don't even know who you are interceding for. I can give you an example.

When I was in Africa in 1997, I got picked up. I was in a restricted area. Government troops were there and a lot of things were happening. I will give you more details as we get into it, but at one point, they were taking people out of their cars and shooting them. They were just leaving their cars there and going through all their belongings and stealing things. These were government troops. They were taking people over past a couple of hills and just shooting them. You could hear the gunshots.

At one point, they caught me and a pastor who was with me. They put us in this truck and started driving us off into this area, and we did not know where we were going. For all we knew, they were going to take us out and shoot us because they had already done that to several other people. I had about $3,000 in U.S. currency on me. The average person at that point there made about $300 a year, so I would have been a 10-year pension plan for somebody if they had known I had that money on me. When they grabbed us, however, they did not even search me.

They put us into the back of this truck and started driving off with us. I assumed that meant they were going to take us somewhere else, then search us, and then kill us. They put us in the truck. As they were driving, this pastor and I just started praying in tongues. We were praying in tongues really loud. I mean forcefully.

The amazing thing is that it was daytime there, but it was nighttime here. My wife was awakened here at exactly that time. We know it was the exact time because when I got to where I was going, I actually wrote this down. She began praying for me in other tongues. My time schedule showed right when she and I were both praying in tongues at the same time. At that point, the truck turned from one road onto another road, and they took me to the airport. They dropped me off at the airport, and said, "Now, get out of the country!"

I firmly believe that if the pastor and I had not been praying in tongues and if my wife had not awakened and prayed in tongues, I would have been killed. She knew she was praying for me but had no idea what it was about. You say, "Well, if you had not prayed in tongues, you would have been killed?" That's possible, but maybe her speaking in tongues had done it for me, who knows? All I know is that we were all working together. You are going to find some things in Scripture that refer to this, but most people never tie them in. They never see them. We are going to go through these and show them to you.

John Lake said, "Tongues were the making of my ministry." If you look at the ministry he had, you will see that there were several hundred thousand healings. Miracles, literally, that have not been talked about or seen since the days of the Book of Acts with the early apostles. He credits every bit of his ministry to speaking in other tongues.

As a matter of fact, I do know that the vast majority of his sermons came by his walking around and praying in other tongues. He would go for a walk and he would pray in other tongues and then on the way back, he would pray for God to interpret that through him. Then he would interpret it out. When he got home, he would write down the interpretation he got out of tongues. Most of his sermons that you read were tongues that were interpreted. That's one of the things about John Lake's sermons. People say, "Whenever I read his sermons I find that they are different from this person's or that person's."

Smith Wigglesworth had some amazing things happen. He prayed in tongues a lot. I don't know if he got his sermons by praying in tongues and then interpreting them.

When you read John Lake's sermons, there is something different about them—it is that light. I firmly believe it is because they were Spirit-birthed in tongues and interpretation. You can interpret your own tongues. You can interpret tongues in church, in a message to the church, and you can also interpret your own tongues. Again, we will talk more about that as we go.

John Lake said that tongues were the making of his ministry. He said, "Speaking in other tongues is the dynamo of the Spirit." Back in his day, electricity was just coming into full fruition, and they had dynamos that would turn. As they would turn, you could see the electrical sparks transferred into a battery, where it would be charged up. Lake said that that was what tongues were.

At the 1893 World's Fair in Chicago, where Dowie had his church and where healing was going on, they had Buffalo Bill's Wild West Show. They also had an electrical work there. They had completely wired the entire exposition center with a particular type of electricity. By this time, Thomas Edison had electricity, but there was electricity by another guy named Nikola Tesla. Nikola Tesla was a genius. He had a particular type of electricity he brought in that actually replaced Thomas Edison's type of electricity. Thomas Edison was using direct current, whereas Tesla showed an alternating current, which is what we use now. That was being used at the exposition. Well, that drew John Lake.

Dr. Lake had gone to the World's Fair and had seen these demonstrations where they would turn these things, the sparks would start to fly, and electricity would be transferred into this battery. This was in 1893, so he did not know about the Baptism of the Spirit or any of that. John Lake was standing there, looking at this and saying, "That is what the Spirit of God is; it is that dynamo inside." He at that time, however, had no idea about the Baptism of the Spirit, speaking in tongues, or any of that.

Later on, he referred back to that event and said that speaking in tongues, specifically, was the dynamo of the Spirit of God. The way he explained it was that you could begin to pray in other tongues, and it would be like turning that dynamo, which created and generated energy and power. Then, if it was not needed right then, it would be transferred and stored in your spirit like a battery so that when you needed it, it was there, and you could release it at will.

This is where Dr. Lake got the idea. It was the foundation of his idea that a man or woman of God should be able to minister the Spirit of God at will, and that it was not something that should just happen, but it should be a way of being able to minister and to release the power of God.

Smith Wigglesworth said one time, "I may start in the flesh, but I end up in the Spirit." He said, "If the Spirit doesn't move me, I move the Spirit." He believed that the way to move the Spirit was to begin praying and speaking in other tongues.

At some point, we are going to differentiate between tongues used in two different situations: (1) Tongues used in a congregational situation in a church: giving a message in tongues and then having it interpreted. (2) Tongues in your private spiritual life.

We are going to be talking about the two of those. We are going to show in the Bible where they were differentiated, but most of the time, it was not just to differentiate. There were a lot of similarities, but they were just for different purposes.

We are going to talk a little about stirring up the Spirit of God. We are actually going to show you how to stir up the Spirit of God. Go with me to Acts chapter 1, starting in verse 4.

Acts 1:4

> 4 And, being assembled together with *them,* commanded them that they should not depart from Jerusalem, but wait for the promise of the Father, which, *saith He,* ye have heard of Me.

Jesus said, "Wait for the Promise of the Father, which you have heard of me."

> 5 For John truly baptized with water; but ye shall be baptized with the Holy Ghost not many days hence.

I know I have already read this, but we are looking at it again.

Acts 1:8

> 8 But ye shall receive power, after that the Holy Ghost is come upon you: and ye shall be witnesses unto me both in Jerusalem, and in all Judaea, and in Samaria, and unto the uttermost part of the earth.

"But you shall receive power, after that the Holy Ghost is come upon you and you shall be witnesses unto Me." Go with me to 2 Timothy. The Apostle Paul was writing to Timothy.

In 2 Timothy 1:5 and 6 it says,

> 5 When I call to remembrance the unfeigned faith that is in thee, which dwelt first in thy grandmother Lois, and thy mother Eunice; and I am persuaded that in thee also.

> 6 Wherefore I put thee in remembrance that thou stir up the gift of God, which is in thee by the putting on of my hands.

He is not talking about a particular gift. He is talking about the gift of the Holy Spirit. Notice he said, "I am reminding you that you stir it up." It is not up to God, therefore, to stir up the gift of God; it is up to you to stir up the gift of God. If the gift of God, the Holy Spirit, is not stirred up within you, it is not God's fault. It is your fault for not stirring Him up. We are going to talk about how to do that. We are going to talk about the key to stirring up "the gift that is in you."

I have already said this: there are no examples of spiritual gifts being given by the laying on of hands. There is not one example. Every example, where someone laid hands on someone other than for healing, is that of imparting the gift of the Holy Ghost. It was for imparting the Baptism of the Spirit, not for imparting a gift of healing, or a gift of the word of knowledge, or a gift of faith. It was not for specific gifts; it was for getting the gift of the Holy Ghost.

In 2 Timothy 1:7, it says,

> 7 For God hath not given us the spirit of fear; but of power, and of love, and of a sound mind.

"For God has not given us the spirit of fear." The word used here for *fear* is the Greek word *deilia*, pronounced *di-lee'-ah*. *Deilia* means *timidity*. "God has not given us a spirit of timidity."

Listen carefully: if you consider yourself part of this fellowship here, either here locally or worldwide, I want you to know right now what is in store for you. Anybody is welcome to attend, anybody is welcome to watch by Internet, watch our DVDs, and listen to our CDs. We will help you as much as we can, but if you are going to be an active member of this fellowship, locally, or internationally, I can tell you right now, I am going to get the spirit of timidity out of you.

The spirit of timidity is not going to remain. It will not remain. Why? That's because people are going to come here, or they are going to come to you. They will be watching by video or by Internet in other countries and they will be expecting you to be able to help them. If you have the spirit of timidity, you don't have the Spirit of God.

The spirit of timidity has not been given by the Spirit of God. He says here, "God has not given us the spirit of timidity, but of *power*." There is that word for "*power*" again. It is the Greek word *dunamis*. We have already seen it before. *Dunamis* means *power; specifically miraculous power.*

"He has given us the spirit of miraculous ability, not timidity, but miraculous ability and the spirit of *love*." That word "*love*" is the Greek word *agapē*, which we know means *sacrificial love that gives without expecting to receive back.* He has not given us a spirit of timidity, nor has He given us a spirit of fear. He has given us a spirit of miraculous ability.

He has given us a "can-do" spirit. He has given us the spirit of ability: "We can do all things through Christ who dwells in us." He has given us the spirit of love that gives without thinking of getting back. Usually, the reason people withhold love is because they don't think it is going to be reciprocated. They think, "Well, if I do this, they aren't going to like me back, or they aren't going to love me back, so I am just not going to do it." No, the agape love of God is that you give regardless of how you even think people are going to respond. Unless you can read minds, you don't know how they are going to respond.

Many people have the hardest shell, but once you minister to them in love, that shell breaks, and all that love in them is able to come out. Before it was behind a shell; it had been locked in. All you were seeing, judging with your eyes, was them being locked in. You saw that shell, that hardened crust, and you thought, "Well, I am not going to be nice to them because they sure aren't very nice to me." However, as soon as you give them that soft word, their wrath melts away and that shell breaks open. All of a sudden, they become gentle and can love the way they want to because you were able to break through. They cannot break through from the inside, but you can break through from the outside. You minister that love first.

That is what you have been given. You have not been given a spirit of timidity; you have not been given a spirit of fear. You have been given a spirit of miraculous ability that can love without expecting to get back. Let us read the verse again. It says,

> 7 For God hath not given us the spirit of fear; but of power, and of love, and of a sound mind.

You have been given *"the spirit of a sound mind."* The word for *"sound mind"* in the Greek is a long one; it is *sōphronismos*, pronounced *so-fron-is-mos*. He has given us the *spirit of a sound* mind, *sōphronismos*, meaning, *a spirit of discipline and self-control.*

We have not been given a spirit of timidity. We have been given a spirit of miraculous ability. We have been given a spirit of love that gives without thinking of getting back. We have been given a spirit of self-control and discipline. That is why you are a disciple; it is because you have discipline.

Remember, in 2 Timothy 1:6 it said,

> 6 Wherefore I put thee in remembrance that thou stir up the gift of God, which is in thee by the putting on of my hands.

He says, *"...that you stir up."* In the Greek, the word for *"stir up"* is *anazōpureō* and it is pronounced *an-ad-zo-poor-eh'-o*. It means *to re-enkindle; to fan embers into flame.* It means *to stir up*, and you are going to do that. You! God doesn't do it for you—you do it.

Jude, verses 17-19:

> 17 But, beloved, remember ye the words which were spoken before of the apostles of our Lord Jesus Christ;
>
> 18 How that they told you there should be mockers in the last time, who should walk after their own ungodly lusts.
>
> 19 These be they who separate themselves, sensual, having not the Spirit.

It says that these mockers are going to separate themselves. They are going to be *sensual*, and that means *sense oriented*, "having not the Spirit."

Jude, verse 20 says,

> 20 But ye, beloved, building up yourselves on your most holy faith, praying in the Holy Ghost,

He was saying, "But you," in contrast, "aren't going to be that way. You aren't going to be sense oriented. You do have the Spirit." He said in verse 20, "But you, beloved, building up yourselves on your most holy faith (building up), praying in the Holy Ghost." This was a direct reference to praying in other tongues.

In Isaiah chapter 28, it says at one point, "This is the rest wherewith He gives rest to the weary." He said, "With stammering lips and other tongues will I give this rest to people." Isaiah was talking about in the last days.

Here in verse 20, Jude was referring to praying in the Holy Ghost, by praying in other tongues, and *building yourself up*, meaning *to edify, to build up, and to strengthen.*

Jude, verse 21 says,

21 Keep yourselves in the love of God, looking for the mercy of our Lord Jesus Christ unto eternal life.

He was saying, "By building yourselves up and by praying in the Holy Ghost, you keep yourselves in the love of God." Praying in the Holy Spirit and praying in other tongues helps keep you in the love of God, "Looking for the mercy of our Lord Jesus Christ unto eternal life."

22 And of some have compassion, making a difference:

23 And others save with fear, pulling *them* out of the fire; hating even the garment spotted by the flesh.

24 Now unto Him that is able to keep you from falling...

"Now unto Him that is able to keep you from falling." He is talking about Jesus being able to keep you from falling, and He is doing it in reference to you or in connection to you being able to build yourself up by praying in the Holy Spirit or praying in other tongues.

I am going to be very blunt here. Praying in other tongues is the language of heaven. Praying is the language of the Spirit realm. I will give you an example. Let me finish reading this Scripture here.

24 ...and to present *you* faultless before the presence of His glory with exceeding joy,

25 To the only wise God our Saviour, *be* glory and majesty, dominion and power, both now and ever. Amen.

Notice again in Jude, verse 20:

20 But ye, beloved, building up yourselves on your most holy faith, praying in the Holy Ghost,

"*Building up yourselves*" means *to edify; to charge up*. It means, literally, *building layer upon layer*. It is almost like you are putting bricks into a building. Praying in other tongues builds you in the Spirit, layer upon layer.

The Apostle Paul said, "I travail in birth for you again until Christ be formed in you." Paul was praying for Christ to be formed in them. When you pray in the Spirit it helps Christ to be formed in you. He has placed, in you, all the components for you to be conformed to His image and to look like Him, but a large portion of that is the renewing of your mind and another large portion is praying in the Spirit, and praying in other tongues. As you pray in other tongues, it starts to put all of this together.

As you pray in other tongues, you build yourself up; you are laying brick upon brick. As you pray in tongues today, you will add upon the brick that you laid yesterday by praying in tongues. What you lay today is the brick and the mortar, and when you pray in tongues tomorrow, you are putting another layer of brick on top of the brick you laid today. The more you do that, the more in the Spirit you get built up and strengthened so that the enemy cannot get you to crack, so to speak. That is how vital praying in other tongues is.

In Isaiah, he was talking about other tongues that He would bring out. No one spoke in other tongues until the New Covenant because the Spirit did not dwell within people until the New Covenant. They were not changed. He worked in union with them, but He did not dwell in them to work within them the way He does us. We are made new creations.

As you begin to pray in these other tongues, understandings are going to come forth. As you are read the Scriptures, there will be things that you don't understand, but you can pray in other tongues and all of that will fall into place.

Many times while I am driving down the road, God will share things with me. I can't make notes; I don't want to take out my phone and try to make notes to myself. I don't want to pull over and write the notes down, but I don't want to lose them. God will speak something to me, and I will want to grab it and hang on to it. Because I can't always stop and pull over to write a note, I started developing the ability to begin praying in other tongues instead. As soon as God would give me that idea, that thought, or that teaching, right then I would think, "Okay, if I don't do something, if I don't jot this down, I am going to lose it." Immediately, I would begin praying in other tongues.

When I pray in other tongues after getting a download like that, or whenever God gives me a message, I will pray in other tongues and that will seal it. It is like it keeps it. Then later, when I get to my motel room when I am traveling or when I get back home I will say, "Okay, what was that?" Sometimes I will find that it is gone, so I will just sit there for a few seconds, start praying in other tongues, and as I pray in other tongues, that thing will come back, "Oh, yeah, that is what I heard." I will just write it down. It is almost like a retrieval system.

What I did was I linked it with the tongues so that when I started praying in tongues, it stirred up the gift that reminded me that the Holy Spirit's job is to bring to my remembrance everything that Jesus has said and is saying, so as I began to pray in other tongues, that came back out.

There are a lot of different uses for tongues and different purposes for tongues. Again, I will give you many examples.

Let us go back to Jude, verse 20.

> 20 But ye, beloved, building up yourselves on your most holy faith, praying in the Holy Ghost,

It says, "Building up yourselves on your most holy faith," and then it says, "…praying in the Holy Ghost." That word *"praying"* is the Greek word *proseuchomai*, pronounced *pros-yoo'-khom-ahee,* and it means *to pray to God; to supplicate,* or *to worship.*

When you start looking at other tongues, it always says that they were glorifying, magnifying, or worshiping God. On the day of Pentecost, when they began speaking in other tongues, all of these people from other lands said, "We hear them in our own languages, glorifying and magnifying God," but they weren't talking to them.

Here is something I want to throw out at you. I know it has been said, "Speaking in tongues is the evidence of the Baptism of the Spirit." I agree with that to a degree. I want you to realize, though, we have changed it to where we use tongues as a sign to ourselves that we have received it. When you read the Book of Acts, however, tongues was never a sign to a person that he or she had received it. It was always a sign to someone else that that person had received it. In other words, when the Apostle Peter was preaching and the Spirit fell on Cornelius and his group, they began speaking in other tongues. You can see the Scriptures that show what they were doing.

Then Peter said, "Well, who can prevent these guys from getting baptized, seeing that God has shed the Holy Ghost on them as He did us at the beginning." It wasn't a sign to the Gentiles. It was a sign, at that point, to the Apostle Peter that the Gentiles could be saved and filled with the Spirit.

Some people say, "Well, you will know that you are baptized in the Spirit when you speak in other tongues." I don't like using that. Does that generally happen? Yes, but I don't like using that as an evidence. Personally, I think that spiritual things don't need physical evidence for a believer. A believer should believe because he says it, and the tongues shouldn't be proof of that. It should be the result of believing.

I am going to give you some testimonies.

Most of the time, we have lived in this area. I grew up in Wylie. My dad was a policeman in Wylie, a few miles east from here, and he was a policeman in Balch Springs, a few miles south from here. Then we went up to Howe, Texas, which is north of here. My dad was Chief of Police in Howe for a short time and then they moved back to east Texas.

My dad was a policeman from the time I was 10 years old. As long as I lived at home with my parents, he was a policeman. My mother was raised very Pentecostal. From early on, my dad worked nights.

I can remember situations where I would be asleep. My mom would come into my room and say, "Curry, wake up! You have to wake up." I would have to go to school the next day; I was 10 or 11 years old. She would say, "You have to get up." I would say, "Why? Why do I have to get up?" She would say, "It's your dad. There is something the matter with your dad." I would say, "Okay, what?" She would say, "I don't know. I just know that something is wrong with your dad."

I would get up and we would get down by my bed or go into the living room, and kneel down by the couch, and we would just start praying. My mom would start praying in tongues. At that time I did not pray in tongues. I had not received the Baptism of the Spirit. She would pray in tongues, and I would just agree with her and say, "Father, please take care of my dad. Protect him from whatever is going on," because I had no clue.

She would start praying in other tongues and there would be times when she would start crying. Then all of a sudden, the tongues would change from crying to almost laughing. Sometimes it would go from crying into groaning, and then it would go from that back into crying and then sometimes from that into laughing. Usually, by the time it got to the laughing stage, I knew we were almost done because I knew she had beaten that thing, whatever it was.

I really don't know why she needed me to be there because I was not much help. Maybe it was for moral support; it was probably the best I could do at 10 or 11 years old. Invariably, within a short period of time, we would get a phone call. I can give you specifics.

We were in Port Arthur, Texas, where my dad was a policeman. It was in the middle of the winter; it was very cold, even down there on the coast. My dad was coming home from work that night, and he went off a bridge; it was icy. He went off into a 30-foot water canal. He was fully dressed in uniform. He had the gun belt on, the boots, the uniform, the heavy jacket, everything; it was the full uniform. He went off into this canal and went 30 feet to the bottom. In order to get out, he had to roll down the window and let the car fill up with water.

Once the car filled with water (this is ice cold water in the middle of winter), he had to get out of the car and then swim 30 feet to the top in full uniform with the gun, the gun belt, the boots, and the heavy jacket. Then, when he got to the top of the water, he crawled out of the canal, crawled to the middle of the highway, and got onto the median in the middle of the highway. There he collapsed and passed out.

It was in the middle of winter; he was completely wet. He was passed out and would have probably frozen to death, but some people came by, saw him, and called the police. They could not tell who he was, but they said, "There is some guy lying out here in the middle of the median." The police went out, and found out that he was one of their own. They took him to the hospital. (Incidents like this happened on at least two occasions where he totaled police cars.) When they got him to the hospital, they put him in traction. He was complaining about his neck and later on, we found out that he had broken his neck.

When they found him, it was at the time that my mother and I were praying; it was the exact time. Then, when she got the victory on that thing, we started laughing about it. By this time, it was morning, so I just stayed up and started getting dressed to go to school. Within a matter of less than 30 minutes before time to go to school, we got the call from the police department saying they were sending a car to pick us up and take us to the hospital. They said my dad had been in that wreck. That was just one incident.

There was another incident, where we were doing the same thing on Christmas morning in 1972. It was in Balch Springs, right here by Dallas. My dad was on patrol, and as I said, it was Christmas morning. There was a van that was driving very slowly, and it had its flashers going, so he pulled them over. When he pulled them over, he pulled up behind them. He got out and started walking up to the van, and as he passed the back of the van toward the front door, the guy opened the door, got out, and started acting like he was stretching his back.

My dad said, "Do you have problems?" The guy said, "Well, no, but you do," and he took out a gun and stuck it in my dad's stomach. My dad pushed it down, and when he did, the gun went off and the bullet went through his finger. It blew out part of the bone in his finger. The way my dad grabbed the gun made it jam, so it couldn't shoot again. Another guy came out of the back of the van with a knife and started trying to cut him. He cut through his shirt and his T-shirt but never touched his skin.

At that exact time, my mom came into my room. We were still living in Wylie. She came into the room and said, "Curry, get up! We have to pray for your dad." By this time, I was pretty used to this, so I got up and went in and started praying, "God protect him." Again, I still had not received the Baptism of the Spirit, but she started praying in tongues. She started crying out to God and going into these things.

Then as she went into these tongues, the phone rang. We were still praying. She answered the phone first and then handed it to me because when she answered the phone, they told her, "Johnny has been shot in the hand." She thought they said "head," so she screamed and dropped the phone. I picked it up and started talking to them. They said, "Tell your mom he was shot in the hand, not the head, in the hand, and there is a police car waiting outside. They just got there, and they are waiting to take you to Parkland Hospital." At that time, I was 13.

I finally got my mom calmed down, we got into the car, and they took us to Parkland Hospital. By the time we got there, my dad was actually walking around with a rag tied around his hand, dripping blood in the middle of the hall, because there were other people there in much worse condition.

During that time, and this is the amazing thing, we went back over the time, and at exactly the time my mom woke me up was just a few minutes before the attack actually took place. What had happened was that my dad had taken the gun and stopped the first guy from shooting. The other guy tried to cut him through the T-shirt, but it never touched his skin. My dad went backward toward the police car, pulled out his gun and shot toward the vehicle. The driver got back into the driver's side of the vehicle and the other guy was getting into the back of the van. That is when my dad actually shot him. The guy fell into the van, and then the van took off.

By this time, my dad had lost a lot of blood and was going into shock. He made it back to the police car and sat down. The door was open, and he sat down on the ground, and he didn't even get to the radio. About that time, a highway patrolman showed up and walked around the car.

This is what was strange: he was in full uniform as a highway patrolman, and he walked around the car to my dad. My dad was still sitting there holding his gun, and he said, "Johnny, you have to call them, and let them know where you are." My dad agreed. He reached over into the squad car, got the radio, and gave his location.

Within a matter of minutes, of course, all the other policemen in the city were there. When they got there, there was no highway patrolman. First of all, if a highway patrolman had come on the scene, he would not have left the scene until help arrived, but there was no one there. Secondly, we found out later on that that was exactly when my mother and I were still praying. Then we found out that when they started trying to find out who that highway patrolman was, there was no highway patrol in that area that night at all, at that time. Obviously, that was not a highway patrolman.

At that time, my dad would have claimed to be saved, but his life wouldn't have shown it. He was moving in that direction, though. The amazing thing was that I talked with my dad about the incident later, and he knew God had protected him as He had so many other times before. We talked about this, and he said he had figured it out. He said, "It had to be an angel that showed up because God knew that if anybody else, even an angel, had just walked up looking like a man, I wouldn't have let him get near me. I wouldn't have listened to him, but God knew that if I saw that uniform I would listen to him." He said, "And that is what it was." My dad knew that God had actually sent an angel to take care of him.

Later on, the man who did the shooting was caught and ended up going to prison for a long time. They never found the other man, and the word was that he had died and that his partner had buried him.

That was just another example of how praying in tongues saved my dad. There was another incident that was almost identical to the previous one. My dad was hit in the head. He was doing a burglary investigation. He went into a building there in Balch Springs, Texas. A guy was hiding and hit him on the head with a tire iron and literally crushed his skull. Again, that was another time that my mother was awakened, and then she came and got me, and we began praying.

A backup went and actually found my dad much faster than they would have found him because they weren't going to send backup at that point. I could go on and on and tell you a lot more stories of amazing things that happened. We saw them.

You need the Baptism of the Spirit. It is not just an add-on. It is not just something where you say, "Well, we do that because this is part of the group we are with, or I do that to fit in." Jesus died so that we could receive His Spirit. Receiving His Spirit includes being born again.

There is not a whole lot taught in the New Testament or the Gospels about getting born again. He just mainly talked to Nicodemus about it. He talked a little bit about being born of water and being born of the Spirit, but the emphasis was on the Spirit.

It is almost like you have got to get the Spirit. To get the Spirit, you have to be born again, so we are going to take care of that, but the emphasis is on the Spirit. In the church, we have done the opposite: we put the emphasis on being born again and not much on the Spirit. The reality is that we have almost made it to where it is like we get our ticket punched, and then we are ready to go to heaven. That is not God's plan.

God's plan is for you to be useful and to be effective for the Kingdom of God here. To do that, you must have the same equipment that God gave Jesus. That equipment includes the Spirit of God dwelling in you. You have to realize that the Spirit of God is God, Himself, coming to dwell within you. This gives you access to all that is God so that you can know all that God knows. At any given time, God can pour through you, so if there needs to be a dead-raising, He can do it. If there needs to be a healing, He can do it. If there needs to be a tongue, or an interpretation, or wisdom, or understanding, or you need something, or whoever is in front of you needs something, you can do whatever the need is because God Himself dwells in you.

What will make that more or less applicable is how much you pray in tongues. I say that with no hesitation. The more you pray in tongues, the more fluent you will get in sharing the things of the Spirit realm even in your normal language. You will begin to share the things of the Spirit. It will become fluent.

You need to think of tongues like this: tongues are the language of the Spirit realm and tongues are the language of the Kingdom of God. There are different dialects; there are different kinds of languages in tongues.

Next year I am going to the Netherlands, to France, Spain, Denmark, and to Germany. I don't speak any foreign languages. I tried to learn Spanish and know very little, not enough to get by at all, just because I haven't focused on it. I know nothing in French. With English, I can go to any English speaking country and fit right in and know what is going on around me. I can fit in, I can negotiate, I can maneuver, I can do what I need to do in that country; no one can fool me because I can understand what is going on.

I have gone into several foreign countries where I did not speak the language. If you don't speak their language, you are at the mercy of someone to interpret for you what others are saying. You might think something is going to cost $10, and they will say, "Oh, it is going to cost $100." I will say, "Okay, here is a $100; give it to him." Then they keep it. You are at the mercy of someone else. If I know the language, then I am not at the mercy of anybody else, because then I can understand what is going on.

In other words, once I know the language of a country, that country opens up to me. If I know Spanish, any Spanish speaking person becomes accessible to me. Their culture becomes accessible to me. The people become accessible to me. If I don't know that language, however, there is a barrier between us and sometimes to break that barrier, I need an interpreter. Even then I am only at the mercy of how good that interpreter is. Maybe the interpreter is not a good interpreter and they won't get it.

What I am saying is this: tongues are the language of the Spirit realm. You can function; you can be a visitor. You can even have your citizenship.

Here in Texas and along the southern states there are a lot of Hispanics who don't speak English even though English is the official language. It is not a matter of trying to be harsh toward somebody and saying, "You learn this or else." On my part, if I were to tell a Hispanic person, "Learn English," it would be so that people couldn't take advantage of them. It would be so that they could understand and so that they could function freely. All of the culture would become accessible to them; they could start to partake in the activities of this country. That would be the purpose.

You may be a person born of the Spirit, but perhaps you don't speak in other tongues. You are born of the Spirit; you are there. You have some of the benefits, but there are benefits of the Kingdom of God, and benefits of the Spirit realm that you will never experience. You will never be fluent in them. You will never truly experience the culture of heaven because there are things that the Spirit of God wants to get across to you, but He can't because you don't speak in other tongues and interact with the Spirit. That is why when you speak in other tongues, it opens up the culture to you.

Many of you know me and you know the ministry. You have watched us and you have listened to us over time. You know I am always very careful about staying very true to Scripture and in context. We are always going to do that. That is my focus. When we start teaching on a subject like tongues or even healing, everything that I teach is right there in the Bible. There are things that I have also learned by experience that help people minister healing. They are in tune and they are in line with the principles of the Bible. They are biblical, but they aren't necessarily written down in the Bible.

It is the same thing when we get into the realm of the Spirit. When we talk about tongues, interpretation, and diversities of tongues, we are going to see that more than ever. There are going to be principles which are biblical, but at the same time, we are going to get into some things that are deeper than just surface level.

We will talk about how to operate in these things: they will be experiential. We always have to remember that if we are going to be experiential, it will not be within the confines of Scripture because Scripture doesn't confine. Scripture equips. It has to be within the equipage of Scripture.

If you aren't used to this, grab hold, hang on, and go with us on this trip. I promise you that when we are finished here and when you begin to function in tongues the way we are going to teach it and show you from Scripture, your spiritual growth will accelerate like it has been turbo charged. That is what is going to take place.

If you have not received the Baptism of the Spirit, the promise of the Father, the infilling of the Spirit of God, and you would like to do so, then I am going to minister to you. You are going to ask, and I am going to agree. I am going to lay hands, and God is going to give. That is what He does.

For those of you who are watching by Internet or listening by CD or watching by DVD, I am going to pray for you right now. I am going to do the same thing for you that I am doing for the people who are here. The only difference is I will not be able to lay hands on you, but that is okay. Jesus said His Words are Spirit, and they are life. If I lay hands on you, we are going to transmit the Spirit, but we can transmit the Spirit by words, also.

For those of you who are here, just begin. If you want to receive the Baptism of the Spirit, ask Him. You don't have to have my hands. You don't have to have anybody's hands. It is a New Covenant. There is nothing between you and God except Jesus. Amen?

Right now let us just ask Him. If you want to, you can even repeat this after me. To those who are watching and want to repeat this after me.

"Father, in the name of Jesus, I thank You that You said that if we ask, You will give us the Holy Spirit. Father, we thank You, and we ask right now for Your Holy Spirit, to be baptized in Your Spirit, to receive the promise of the Father, and to be filled to overflowing to the point, Father, where You are able to speak through us in other tongues. We receive that right now, in the name of Jesus. Father, we thank You for it. We praise You for it, and we receive it now.

"I say in the name of Jesus, right now, right where you are, whether you are seated here, seated at home, listening by CD, watching by DVD, even now, in the name of Jesus, there is no time in the Spirit realm; there is no distance in the Spirit realm. In the name of Jesus, receive the Holy Spirit. Receive Him, in the name of Jesus; receive the promise of the Father. It is a gift to you and to as many as the Lord our God shall call. Receive it now in the name of Jesus, and just breathe in the Spirit of God and allow that Spirit to flow up and through you, even in other tongues, in the name of Jesus. Amen."

If you have already received the Baptism of the Spirit, and you already speak in other tongues, begin to do that even now. Right where you are, begin to speak in other tongues. Right now in the name of Jesus, begin to speak in other tongues.

Those who are watching by Internet, even now, receive the Holy Ghost. Right now in the name of Jesus, begin to worship Him and thank Him for it. Don't do it in your own language. Just allow the Spirit of God to rise up within you and come out of your mouth.

You are going to speak the words out, but He will give you the words. Don't wait until you hear a word. Just begin: open your mouth and let it just flow. In the name of Jesus, right now, just begin to flow.

"Father right now, if there are any in this congregation or watching or listening who need to receive Jesus Christ as their Savior and as their Lord, Father, I say right now, in the name of Jesus, by Your Spirit, begin to move in them."

If you are listening and you have never been born again, right now is the time to receive. Right now is the time to take Jesus as your Lord. It is very simple. You just tell Him what you want. You just tell Him, "I make you the Lord of my life. I accept that You died for my sins and were raised again and when You were raised, I was raised, so in the name of Jesus, I receive You as my Lord." You just tell Him that. It is not a formula; it is just you connecting with Him and telling Him you want Him to be your Lord and Savior, and at that moment, you are born again.

If you have been listening to this message, you might as well go ahead and receive the promise of the Father right now and be filled with the Spirit, baptized in the Holy Ghost, and begin to speak in other tongues.

"In the name of Jesus, we thank You for it. So be it. Amen."

God bless you.

WHY TONGUES?

Sermon given by Curry R. Blake

One of the ways that God has used John G. Lake Ministries has been to bring emphasis back to the Spirit of God in the areas of the Baptism of the Spirit and speaking in other tongues.

Dr. John G. Lake made the statement that tongues were the making of his ministry. If you look at the scope of the ministry he had, you will see that tongues were obviously a pretty big deal. Therefore, we will be looking at this subject in depth.

There are three areas the devil and those who are aligned with him, whether they are religious or not, have fought the hardest against: healing, tongues, and kingdom finances (or prosperity to some degree in some areas).

We have pretty well destroyed most of the sacred cows concerning healing. More than anything else, we have been used by God to push into the forefront the truths of the Bible about healing, how to receive healing, and how to minister healing. In the process of doing that, we have noticed that the enemy also works against tongues. He always likes to work against some things that God has promised you, which are usually the biggest blessings to you.

Why should we speak in other tongues? Why should we talk about tongues? Why are we even dealing with this?

TONGUES ARE A SIGN

Jesus said, "A wicked and an adulterous generation seeks after a sign." He said, "These signs will follow the believer." He is telling us to give this wicked and adulterous generation a sign, and one of the signs we are supposed to use is tongues.

People say, "Well, you know unbelievers. They don't understand tongues." That is right. Generally they will not. The idea is that there are tongues, and we will be talking about some of the details.

There are degrees in tongues. There are times when tongues are tongues of men and sometimes when they are tongues of angels. You see it in Acts 2. It was actually the tongues of men that the multitude could hear being spoken in each of their own languages. The apostles had gained languages that they had never learned. The men knew it was some type of supernatural occurrence because these disciples were, as they said, ignorant and unlearned men, yet here they were all speaking in different languages.

Here is something I want you to think about: when Jesus died and then arose, He appeared to 500 followers at one time. In Acts 2, His followers were all in the upper room on the day of Pentecost and only 120 were there. One hundred twenty are still better than the 11 He left here. When Jesus left, He had the 11 who were His main disciples; however, He had shown Himself to 500, and apparently, He had told everybody to go to the upper room.

Jesus said to them, "Go and wait until you receive the promise of the Father," which was the Baptism of the Spirit. There was a particular way they would know that they had actually received this promise and one of the ways they would know was by the speaking in other tongues.

The reality is that out of 500 people, only 120 were able to wait the full 40 days, which was around 50 days from Jesus' resurrection. It took only 40 days for the vast majority to fall away or at least not be there and not be found waiting. Had they waited, who knows how many would have been there.

The Bible says the upper room was a large place. I am assuming Jesus knew how many were going to be there, so I am assuming that He knew it was a large enough place to hold the number of people who were there. By the time the day of Pentecost was fully come, only 120 were left and out of that 120, of course, were the 11 and Mary. We know that Jesus' family was there, so there were groups there, but it is just amazing how many fell away!

I wonder how many were there on day 35. How many were there on day 37? For whatever reason, little by little, they started dropping off so that by day 50, when the day of Pentecost had come, there were only 120 left. You have to wonder: if the day of Pentecost had come three months later instead, would there have been anybody left?

There is an aspect to this. As we are talking about tongues, about the Baptism of the Spirit, and about a Spirit-filled church, I want to show you something that even Dr. John Lake saw back in 1927, and if anything, we have seen it more now. I really want us to see this because I want us to be looking at our own lives. I want us to "examine ourselves" to make sure whether we are in the faith.

We know that tongues are a sign. Mark 16:17 says,

> 17 And these signs shall follow them that believe; In my name shall they cast out devils; they shall speak with new tongues;

"And these signs shall follow them that believe." It goes on to say, "In my name shall they cast out devils; they shall speak with new tongues." Whether you like it or you don't, there it is.

Some people have said, "Well, yes, but that is Mark 16 and with Mark 16 there is some controversy about whether or not it was in the original text." I have news for you! All of the early apostolic fathers, the disciples (both the disciples of Jesus, Himself, and the disciples of the disciples) all quoted Mark 16. Every one of them quoted it, showing that it was in the Bible that they read. Therefore, if the first and second generations quoted it, then it is good enough for us.

Jesus said, "These signs shall follow them that believe." If you are a believer, you should be speaking with new tongues.

The group I was in originally would say, "Well, new tongues meant that before you got saved, you probably cursed and said all kinds of things, but when you got saved, you quit doing that. You got a new tongue." That is not the new tongues the Bible is talking about. That should be true, but that is not what it is talking about.

Then Jesus goes on in verse 18:

> 18 They shall take up serpents; and if they drink any deadly thing, it shall not hurt them they shall lay hands on the sick, and they shall recover.

Notice, laying hands on the sick is right there in the same passage with speaking in new tongues. If you are going to lay hands on the sick and if you believe that it is biblical doctrine for today, then you should also be speaking in new tongues. If you are going to do one, then you must do the other. You do not get to pick and choose.

TONGUES ARE A DIRECT COMMUNICATION BETWEEN YOU AND GOD

William Booth, a British Methodist preacher who founded The Salvation Army, said at one point that he was really concerned that Christianity (in the next century after him, beginning in the 1900s and going into the years after 2000) would be a religion without Christ, and it would supposedly be a spiritual endeavor without the Spirit of Christ. In other words, he was saying, "I am afraid that we are going to end up with a form but not the actual functioning of the Spirit." That is one of the situations the church is in today. We can see that over and over again.

You need to realize that the standard human trait is that if you do not rise to the level of any certain standard, then over a period of time, you will grow weary in trying to rise to that standard. You will generally bring the standard down to your level of experience rather than raising your experience up to that level. We can see that happening.

We see people who struggle against sin repeatedly and keep on struggling and never beat it. Usually, when that happens, they end up lowering the standard of sin by saying one of two statements: "That is not sin anymore," or "It does not matter." I can tell you sin always matters! It mattered enough to cost Jesus His life. It always matters, but people have this tendency to bring the standard down.

As I travel, I see a lot of people in the church world doing a whole lot of things. They would say, "It is by the Spirit," but most of the time, it is nothing more than what human energy can produce. Many times it is just excitement. It is an emotional facet rather than the real thing. That is what Dr. John Lake referred to in his letter, which I will read to you later.

I know what Dr. Lake's material did within me, but it is amazing to hear what other people say when they read Dr. Lake's material. I hear over and over again that there is something different about what he wrote, especially if you compare it to what people write today. There is a depth in his writings that came from experience. In the DHT there is a letter that Dr. Lake wrote, and in it he said that the secret was that he taught his workers that when they received the Baptism of the Spirit, they received the power of God!

So many times I think we have negated the actual depth of the Spirit of God in meetings. I am not talking about getting far off into one ditch so that Scripture is not even mentioned and it is all by the Spirit, supposedly, or you get off into the other ditch where everything is so legalistic, so formal, and just so much by the letter that you end up being legalistic and bashing people over the head with Scripture.

I am not talking about either ditch. I am talking about the Spirit and the Word working together in balance and bringing a depth that, as I travel around, I do not see in the Body of Christ.

When I read some of Dr. Lake's letters and sermons or some from the early Pentecostal pioneers, I see that they had such a depth there, and sometimes I just yearn for that in my own life. I ask, "Why do we not have that? Why do we not see that anymore?" Usually, whenever I say that, I have to turn right back to myself and say, "Why is that not in me the way it was in them? What is different?"

I read something that Dr. Lake said that really surprised me. He talked about a woman named Miss Emma Wick, who was his secretary at one time. He said she had a real knack for getting people to speak in tongues without the Baptism of the Spirit. When I first read that, I said, "Whoa, that's totally contrary to teaching I have heard. I didn't think that was possible." He then explained some things, and we will be talking about those.

That is why I am saying there needs to be a depth. It is not just a matter of receiving. It is not just a matter of, "Well, I spoke in tongues once, and that is all that counts, so you know that is good enough." No, speaking in tongues should be a daily occurrence. Paul said, "I thank my God, I speak with tongues more than you all."

I firmly believe that there is supposed to be an ongoing relationship with the Spirit that increasingly takes us into greater depths of the Spirit. That is what we want. What I always tell everybody is that we have this theology today that is usually an inch deep and a mile wide. We do not want to have that. It should be a mile wide and a mile deep. We should delve into the things of the Spirit.

Tongues are a direct communication between you and God. In 1 Corinthians 14:2, it says:

> 2 For he that speaketh in an *unknown* tongue speaketh not unto men, but unto God: for no man understandeth *him*; howbeit in the spirit he speaketh mysteries.

No man understands it, and that is the whole idea of 1 Corinthians 14. Paul is talking about the difference between prophecy, or prophesying, and speaking in other tongues. He is talking about predominately in a church setting or in an assembly setting. He talks about the depths of the Spirit of God. He talks about how when you speak in other tongues, you are not speaking to men but unto God, and that it is the Spirit of God in you motivating that speech. Know this: tongues are a direct communication between you and God.

For those of you who have not been baptized in the Spirit, have not received the Spirit, and have not spoken in other tongues, we want to give you that desire to ask God for the speaking in other tongues. He said if you ask He will give you the Holy Spirit, and you can and should speak in other tongues.

TONGUES CONFOUND THE WISE

Tongues confound the wise. This is always one that is fun. God always chose the foolish things of the world to confound the wise.

People say, "Well, that just sounds gibberish." You would say the same thing about a foreign language. If I took you somewhere into Africa or into India or into South America, there would be a dialect that sounds like gibberish. It does not sound like a language, but to the people speaking it and to the people who understand it, it is clear communication. If you do not speak it, you are the ignorant one.

It is not that the people who speak that language are ignorant because it sounds strange. It only sounds strange to you, but once you learn the language, it no longer sounds strange. Then it makes sense to you.

That is one of our problems. The things we do not understand we automatically push out and say, "Well, that does not make sense, so it must not be true." I know that many think they are the sum total of all wisdom, and therefore, if it does not make sense, then it must not be sensible. The fact is that the Spirit of God knows more than you do.

I love what Dr. Sumrall said one time when we were up there. He said, "People talk about tongues and how tongues do not make sense. They call tongues gibberish and all these different words.

"The fact is that you can go anywhere in this world where you may not know the language, and can say one sound, and that sound is a word to somebody. There is not a sound you can make that is not a word somewhere to somebody. All you would have to do is find out where they speak that and you would already have one word in their language.

"Whenever you say that speaking in other tongues is just gibberish, and tongues do not make any sense, it shows your ignorance, not their ignorance." I have always remembered that.

We are going to look at this because Isaiah prophesied about this. Many people say, "My language, when I pray in tongues, does not really sound like a language." That is okay. I will show you exactly what to do to allow God to grow that within you.

Tongues confound the wise. In 1 Corinthians 14:23 it says,

> 23 If therefore the whole church be come together into one place, and all speak with tongues, and there come in *those that are* unlearned, or unbelievers, will they not say that ye are mad?

Paul was saying, "If you are all there in church, and all you do is speak in tongues, and people come in, and they do not understand it, they are going to think you are mad (crazy) because they do not understand it." He did not say it was wrong to do it, and he didn't say don't do it because they won't understand it. He just said that they would not understand it.

Tongues confound even the wise in the world.

TONGUES REQUIRE FAITH

Speaking in tongues requires faith. That is one of the primary reasons you can prove it is of God because anything that is going to please God is going to require faith. Now listen carefully: anytime you decide to use your faith, you are pleasing God.

Hebrews 11:6 says,

> 6 But without faith *it is* impossible to please *him*: for he that cometh to God must believe that he is, and *that* he is a rewarder of them that diligently seek him.

Without faith it is impossible to please Him. When you use faith, it pleases Him. If it requires faith for you to speak in tongues (and it does and even after you receive the Baptism of the Spirit and even after you have spoken in tongues before), then every time you open your mouth to speak in tongues, it requires faith and because of that, at that moment, you are pleasing God. If there was no other reason to speak in tongues than that alone, that is enough.

It is amazing to me the number of people who think that doing good is not its own reward and that it is not enough for them. You should do things because it is right to do so and not because of what you are going to get back from it. The fact that you are doing it because it is right should be enough reward in itself. If you could do something to please

God, then that should be enough right there. You do it because God said it.

Mark 11:22-24 says,

> 22 And Jesus answering saith unto them, Have faith in God.

> 23 For verily I say unto you, That whosoever shall say unto this mountain, Be thou removed, and be thou cast into the sea; and shall not doubt in his heart, but shall believe that those things which he saith shall come to pass; he shall have whatsoever he saith.

> 24 Therefore I say unto you, What things soever ye desire, when ye pray, believe that ye receive *them*, and ye shall have *them*.

Half of the people in the Charismatic world think Kenneth Hagin wrote that because he taught on it so much. The fact is that Jesus said it, and a lot of people don't like it.

People do not like the fact that Jesus said, "You can have what you say." As a matter of fact, He even went further than that and said, "You will have what you say." People don't like that. The reason they don't like it is because they don't like to watch what they say. They don't like to tame their tongue, so they would rather discount the whole thing and say, "Oh, that is excess or that is wrong." No. Are there excesses in it? Yes. Is there still wrong in it? Yes. It is just like anything else. Still, regardless of whether we like it or whether we don't, Jesus said it.

By the same token, He said in Mark 16,

> 17 And these signs shall follow them that believe; In my name shall they cast out devils; they shall speak with new tongues;

© 2012 Curry R. Blake – John G. Lake Ministries

Jesus was saying that if you believe on Him, you will speak in other tongues. If for no other reason than that, it is enough. You are being obedient and following Him. Usually what happens with those who have thought that before and have not received it, eventually they will say, "Well, it must not be important." No, it is important, and if there is anything that you ask for and you are not seeing the benefit of it, it is usually because it is so important that the devil is fighting tooth and nail to keep you from getting it.

In that case, if it is a clear promise from God, you ought to push right on through and say, "No, I am not moving until I get it." Why? "It was promised to me, and Jesus said I need to speak in other tongues." We are getting into more of the "why" as we go along. Regardless, you should still get it.

What do we have so far? 1. Tongues are a sign. 2. Tongues are a direct communication between you and God. 3. Tongues confound the wise. 4. Tongues require faith.

TONGUES ARE A REST AND A REFRESHING

Isaiah 28:9-10 says,

> 9 Whom shall he teach knowledge? and whom shall he make to understand doctrine? *them that are* weaned from the milk, *and* drawn from the breasts.

> 10 For precept *must* be upon precept, precept upon precept; line upon line, line upon line; here a little, *and* there a little:

That word "*precept*" is the Hebrew word which means *commandment or an injunction*. "For precept (commandment or injunction) must be upon precept, precept upon precept; line upon line, line upon line, here a little, and there a little." He was saying, "You do not get it all in one sitting." He brings it piece by piece. It is like building a house. You have to lay the bricks and put in the mortar before you can lay another line of bricks. That is how the house is built—line upon line, layer upon layer. You will not understand it all at one time even if you try. If you wait until you think you understand it all before you start moving in the things of God, you will never do a thing.

At the church I started in 30 years ago, there were people who were (in their own words), "Waiting for God to open doors." They were waiting for this thing or that thing. They were waiting for a sign of some sort. Whenever they would make comments of that nature, I would ask them, "How do you even know they are shut? How do you know they are locked?" Then I would tell them, "The doors are open; just go and push on them and step out."

I have been around the world a dozen times now, and some of those people are still sitting there waiting for God to show them where to go. Well, the answer is easy: go anywhere in the world. We are commanded, "Go into all the world." Anywhere you go is going to be the right place.

That is what we have done, and we have gone around the world.

Every time I go around the world, I come back and go to visit that church. Guess what? People are still sitting there waiting on God. I tell them, "Do you want to see God move? Come and go with me. Travel with me." Why? That's because we are not waiting on God; God is waiting on us!

Isaiah 28:11 says,

> 11 For with stammering lips and another tongue will he speak to this people.

"For with stammering lips and another tongue will he speak to this people." He is referring to the Hebrew people, of course, but notice here that he has stated two things: (1) stammering lips and (2) another tongue. These were to be a sign, and we are going to look at the purpose of them here. It is important to note that some people say, "You know my tongues don't sound like a language. If tongues are a language, then my tongues would be baby talk." Okay, that is good enough. You are still in Scripture, though, because he said, "With stammering lips." He did not say, "With clear fluency." This is obviously what God wants you to move in but He said, "With stammering lips."

There has been such a lack of teaching in the church on tongues, and there are only a couple of ministries I know of that even deal with tongues to any degree at all. When you look at this, you can see why most people's tongues are still in stammering lips. If they do not develop their tongues by practicing regularly, or if tongues are not a common part of their lives and they do not move into them, then their tongues will not be fluent and will not flow. Their tongues will sound like (as we would say in modern language) stuttering; it is like the same word being spoken over and over.

In the many Pentecostal churches I have been in, I have heard people praying in tongues, and it sounded like they are stuttering. I am not making fun of their tongues. That is just the level of their speech toward God. What that shows is that they have not spent very much time speaking in other tongues. It usually is because they speak in tongues only when they are in church. If that is all they are going to do, like anything else, they are not going to be very good at it because they cannot get much practice in an hour on Sunday.

Usually, what they do in church is sit and they don't do anything, so they are not even practicing there. Usually, the only practicing in tongues in churches is done for 20 minutes, maybe, during the worship time.

Well, we are not going to do that here. We are going to be practicing this. We are going to be getting this to develop in you, on purpose. I have never intended for this to be church as usual. When we were talking about a name for the church, we were talking about calling it "World Outreach Training Center." The idea is that we want to train believers—not just teach and not just share—but actually get you activated to actually move into these things. That's what we are going to be doing here. You are coming here to be trained, so we can go out and change our world. That is the plan.

Isaiah 28:11 and 12,

> 11 For with stammering lips and another tongue will he speak to this people.

> 12 To whom he said, This is the rest *wherewith* ye may cause the weary to rest; and this is the refreshing: yet they would not hear.

"To whom he said," remember he is still talking about tongues, "This is the rest wherewith you may cause the weary to rest; and this is the refreshing: yet they would not hear." Notice, when tongues were first brought to the Jews, they did not receive them. Tongues were passed over, but we have accepted them. We will hear this even though they will not. We have heard tongues, we have received them, we believe them, and we agree with them. That is the number one reason that tongues are "a rest and a refreshing."

Peter told us not to grow weary in well doing but to continue doing. When people grow weary in well doing, it is just before they get their breakthrough. It is just before they actually get their miracle. They quit just before they get to what they are trying to get to. That is why I talked about how many people went to wait for the promise of the Father in the upper room but fell away little by little. Why? They grew weary in well doing and ended up with only 120 there. Speaking in other tongues is "a rest and a refreshing."

Let us read Isaiah 28:12 again. He says,

12 To whom he said, This is the rest *wherewith* ye may cause the weary to rest; and this is the refreshing…

What is the refreshing? It is speaking with stammering lips in another tongue. That is the refreshing. It came with the Spirit.

One of the best times to pray in other tongues is when you don't feel like it. There are things you need to do and you need to do them, even when you don't feel like doing them. That's one of the proofs that you need to do them.

When you get tired and ready to give up or when you don't see the use of getting up and making confession, that's when you need to start confessing what the Word of God says about you. (When I say confession, I am talking about confessing the Word of God. I am not talking about confessing sins. You should automatically take care of that.) Whenever you feel that it just doesn't seem like it is working, then you get tired because you don't see any change.

That is like a farmer planting seed and then going out every day for the first two weeks and saying, "I don't see anything, so I'm not going back out to the field again." No, there is a time of harvest. There is a time when you plant the seed of the Word of God and a time when you confess the Word of God.

There is a time between the time you plant and see it, and the time you start to harvest it. It is during that time that we always call the "meantime." The "meantime" is between the time you pray and the time you start to receive. That is when it is rough on you. If you are going to grow weary in well doing, that is when it is going to be.

I talk with people all of the time and they say, "Well, I have been believing for my healing for a long time. I'm tired, and I just don't see it." Well, if you see it, you don't need faith. Faith is for what you don't see. Anybody can believe it when they see it.

There is a time when you can grow weary. You can keep on going and keep on going and eventually you get tired and worn out. Usually, people who get weary in well doing are not speaking in other tongues very often. As you begin to pray in other tongues and speak in other tongues, it begins to lift you. You can start to go down, but then you begin praying in tongues again and tongues will build you back up. They just help carry you on. Again, you have to lay precept upon precept, line upon line so that you will be able to get deeper and deeper as you go along with this.

A reason to speak in other tongues, to be praying in other tongues, is because tongues give you a rest. They give you a refreshing. Praying in tongues refreshes you.

So many times I hear churches talk about looking for a time of refreshing and how they are waiting for the Holy Spirit to come and refresh them. Right there He says, "If you want refreshing, pray in tongues." If you pray in tongues, you will be refreshed. He did not say, "Wait until you are refreshed." He said, "This is the refreshing." Praying in tongues is the refreshing. If you want a refreshing, if you want a time for God to move freely in your midst, begin praying in other tongues.

There are times, when praying in tongues, where you are doing it. What I mean by that is that you can stop anytime you want, and it is almost like a push to do it. However, there comes a point after praying in tongues, when all of a sudden, there is a breaking through the flesh, and at that point, it is easier to continue praying in tongues than it is to stop. Tongues just keep carrying on.

Many times you will be going along and not thinking about anything, and tongues just burst out. You can be driving, thinking about something else, and all of a sudden, tongues will burst out.

There are other aspects of this. There is praying with tongues, which is called praying in the Spirit, and there is praying with your understanding. The very fact that Paul said, "I will pray with my spirit, and I will pray with my understanding," proves that whenever you pray with your spirit in other tongues, you do not understand what you are saying. If you did, you would be praying with the understanding. The Bible says, "If you pray in other tongues, also pray that you can interpret." That is why you should be interpreting your tongues. Interpreting is not just for church services. It is for your private life, also.

Oral Roberts built ORU (Oral Roberts University) based on praying in other tongues and interpreting them. Dr. Lake did the same thing. Almost every sermon of his was first prayed in tongues. He then interpreted them, made notes, and then preached the sermon. That is where the flow of the Spirit was, and that is why he said that tongues were the making of his ministry.

There is praying with the understanding and there is praying with the Spirit. Paul also said, "I will sing with the spirit, and I will sing with the understanding, also." That means there is a time for singing in other tongues, too.

He said, "This is the rest and this is the refreshing." Do you want to be refreshed? Pray in other tongues. I will tell you a good time to pray in tongues. Well, all the time is a good time to pray. There is never a wrong time. When you are busy, you get tired, and you get weary. Just stop and start praying in tongues. You will get refreshed and rejuvenated. Some say, "It is like getting my second wind." Exactly!

The second wind of the Spirit is the Greek word *pneûma*. It literally means *breath, wind*. It is akin to *pneîn* which means *to breathe*. You are getting your second *pneûma*. Why? Tongues are a refreshing; they are a rest. They bring peace.

Tongues shake all of the garbage off of you during the day, so you can actually stay focused. Pray in tongues. I cannot emphasize it enough. If you don't, you should.

I will tell you two facts: (1) you are never too young to do it, and (2) you are never too old to do it!

Back in the early 1900s, I think it was before 1914 or right around then, there was a group of Pentecostal believers in Armenia. They began praying in other tongues as they normally would do. Their children, as young as six and seven years old, were speaking in other tongues. They were having dreams and visions, and bringing out these tongues. As the elders would pray, the children would speak in other tongues and then would interpret them. They warned the group about this invasion that was going to happen.

Here was a group of people whose children were praying in tongues and they had begun interpreting them. When the children interpreted, they said that there was going to be an invasion, and this army was going to come in and kill a lot of people. The adult Pentecostals so believed that it was the Spirit of God in these children speaking, that they packed up their belongings, and moved into an area that was not inhabited. It was out in the wilderness.

When the army did invade within just a couple of months after that, it almost totally wiped out the civilian populace in Armenia. Most of the people who were left were the Pentecostal Christians who had hidden in the hills. It was all because of the children who at six, seven, and eight years old prophesied it through tongues and interpretation.

TONGUES WERE CHOSEN BY GOD

God chose them. God was the one who decided to use tongues as a sign. We do not always understand every reason that God has for doing something, but that is where faith in God comes in. If we have faith in God, then we know that He is our heavenly Father. If He has commanded us to do something, it is for our benefit as well as for the outcome of whatever the thing was that He commanded.

If you are going to follow God, you have to do what He says just because He said to do it. Later, you find out why. It is like being in the military. If I yell, "Duck!" I do not have time to explain why you should duck. If you wait for an explanation, you will probably get killed. Therefore, when someone yells, "Duck!" you just do it. You find out later why you did it. Most people do not have that concept. God said to speak in tongues. That is what He said, and we should just do it. It's as simple as that.

The language of heaven is knowing, but the communication of the Spirit is in tongues. Many who have testimonies of going to heaven said that while there, they would have conversations with people without talking. In other words, they knew what the other person was saying. "That is like mental telepathy," someone said. Yes, in a way it is, but it is just the fact that you know what they are saying, without words. Why? If you are of the same Spirit, and you both have the same Spirit, then there should be no difference in communication. It is ongoing conversation and it is as if you are talking to yourself, but you already know what you are going to say. Why? The same Spirit lives in both of you.

That type of communication is what is in heaven, but the communication of the Spirit here is through tongues. Speaking in tongues is almost like fiber optics, in the sense that it goes both ways. Information travels both ways at the same time. The Bible says that while you pray in tongues, you are talking not to men but to God, but He also said pray that you may interpret.

It is not just a matter of you talking to God. Every time we read about this in the Book of Acts, it talks about magnifying God, praising God, and worshiping God. The tongues you speak magnify God, but at the same time, you cannot magnify God without having that same power working in you to encourage you and to build you up. If you are magnifying God, the power you are using to magnify Him is building up your spirit at the same time.

Go to 1 Corinthians, chapter 2. I want to read some verses to you that you may not be used to, and you may not have seen them this way, but I want you to think about them. In 1 Corinthians, chapter 2 Paul says,

> 1 And I, brethren...

Remember that he was writing to the Corinthians, and they were sinful, and carnal, and had all kinds of things going on. They were not a spiritual church, yet they were the only group to whom he ever explained the gifts of the Spirit. That tells you something. Paul says,

> 1 And I, brethren, when I came to you, came not with excellency of speech or of wisdom, declaring unto you the testimony of God.
>
> 2 For I determined not to know any thing among you, save Jesus Christ, and him crucified.
>
> 3 And I was with you in weakness, and in fear, and in much trembling.
>
> 4 And my speech and my preaching *was* not with enticing words of man's wisdom, but in demonstration of the Spirit and of power:

Why was it in demonstration of the Spirit and of power? Verse 5 says,

> 5 That your faith should not stand in the wisdom of men, but in the power of God.

Notice the word "wisdom" in verse 6:

> 6 Howbeit we speak wisdom among them that are perfect: yet not the wisdom of this world, nor of the princes of this world, that come to nought:

Verse 7 says,

> 7 But we speak the wisdom of God in a mystery, *even* the hidden *wisdom*, which God ordained before the world unto our glory:

"But we speak the wisdom of God in a mystery…" If you read in 1 Corinthians 14, it says that if you speak to God, you are speaking mysteries to God. Think about these mysteries as tongues. He says, "We speak the wisdom of God in a mystery, even the hidden wisdom…"

> 8 Which none of the princes of this world knew: for had they known *it,* they would not have crucified the Lord of glory.

In verse 9, he is quoting out of Isaiah 64,

> 9 But as it is written, Eye hath not seen, nor ear heard, neither have entered into the heart of man, the things which God hath prepared for them that love him.

There are things that God has prepared strictly for people who love Him. They are not for everybody; they are for people who love Him.

Verse 10 says,

> 10 But God hath revealed *them* unto us by his Spirit: for the Spirit searcheth all things, yea, the deep things of God.

"God hath revealed them unto us by His Spirit." How do you learn them? You learn them by the Spirit. "For the Spirit searches all things, yea, the deep things of God." You say, "I thought the Spirit was God."

That is true, but it is the Spirit who works in between God and us and connects us to God. The things we can learn of God, we get by the Spirit. We do not bypass the Spirit. The Spirit brings these things to us. The things that God has prepared for us, He brings to us by His Spirit.

Verses 11-13:

> 11 For what man knoweth the things of a man, save the spirit of man which is in him? even so the things of God knoweth no man, but the Spirit of God.

> 12 Now we have received, not the spirit of the world, but the spirit which is of God; that we might know the things that are freely given to us of God.

> 13 Which things also we speak, not in the words which man's wisdom teacheth, but which the Holy Ghost teacheth; comparing spiritual things with spiritual.

> 14 But the natural man receiveth not the things of the Spirit of God: for they are foolishness unto him: neither can he know *them*, because they are spiritually discerned.

I am absolutely convinced that in this particular passage of Scripture, when Paul was talking about the things of the Spirit, about being given things by the Spirit, and speaking in wisdom that the Spirit teaches, he was talking about speaking in other tongues and drawing out the wisdom of God and then interpreting it. I really believe that was, in part, how Paul wrote his letters to his disciples. I also believe that most of what he was talking about here did refer to speaking in other tongues.

Go with me to Romans chapter 8. Remember: Paul wrote Romans 8, also. We are talking about tongues. We were looking at tongues in 1 Corinthians 2, and bringing these things by the Spirit of God. We know the things of the Spirit, by the Spirit that is in us, and we do not learn these by the wisdom which man teaches but by the wisdom which the Holy Ghost teaches, comparing spiritual with spiritual. Look at all of these things, and put them with Romans 8.

Let us read Romans 8, beginning with verse 1:

> 1 *There is* therefore now no condemnation to them which are in Christ Jesus, who walk not after the flesh, but after the Spirit.

Then he goes on:

> 2 For the law of the Spirit of life in Christ Jesus hath made me free from the law of sin and death.

I am not going to read the whole chapter, but you can go back and read it. Notice verse 4:

> 4 That the righteousness of the law might be fulfilled in us, who walk not after the flesh, but after the Spirit.

Again, he is talking about walking after the Spirit.

> 5 For they that are after the flesh do mind the things of the flesh; but they that are after the Spirit the things of the Spirit.

"For they that are after the flesh do mind the things of the flesh." How do you know if you are of the Spirit or of the flesh? What do you think about? Do you think about the things of the flesh? Do you think about the things of the Spirit? Where is your head all of the time? Is it on the flesh, on things in the world, or is it on the things of the Spirit of God? "But they that are after the Spirit [mind] the things of the Spirit."

> 6 For to be carnally minded *is* death; but to be spiritually minded *is* life and peace.

7 Because the carnal mind *is* enmity against God: for it is not subject to the law of God, neither indeed can be.

8 So then they that are in the flesh cannot please God.

If you are always thinking of the things of the flesh, walking in the flesh, acting like flesh, living like the world, talking like the world, living in the things of the world, you cannot please God. Why? The love of the Father is not in you if you love the things of the world.

9 But ye are not in the flesh, but in the Spirit, if so be that the Spirit of God dwell in you. Now if any man have not the Spirit of Christ, he is none of his.

"But you are not in the flesh, but in the Spirit, if so be that the Spirit of God dwell in you." If the Spirit of God dwells in you, then you are not in the flesh but in the Spirit. If the Spirit of God dwells in you, your mind is going to be on the things of the Spirit. "Now if any man have not the Spirit of Christ, he is none of His." You either are or you are not.

10 And if Christ *be* in you, the body *is* dead because of sin; but the Spirit *is* life because of righteousness.

11 But if the Spirit of him that raised up Jesus from the dead dwell in you, he that raised up Christ from the dead shall also quicken your mortal bodies by his Spirit that dwelleth in you.

Watch what he is talking about here again, "But if the Spirit of Him that raised up Jesus from the dead dwell in you…." Remember: we are still talking about the Spirit and speaking in other tongues. He was saying, "If that Spirit that raised Jesus from the dead dwells in you, it is that Spirit in you who is speaking in tongues out of your spirit."

If that Spirit that raised Jesus from the dead dwells in you, "He that raised up Christ from the dead shall also quicken your mortal bodies by

His Spirit that dwells in you." How is He going to quicken your mortal body? It is by His Spirit that dwells in you, not by the Spirit that dwells in somebody else.

I am not saying that we do not lay hands on people. We do. We will lay hands on you. I am saying that God's desire is that you get things directly from Him, and you don't have to go to somebody else to get it. That is His desire.

Now, in the meantime, if you are suffering, don't hold out. Get help. Work toward getting it for yourself. Work together with the Body. The Body is here to minister to you, to help you, and sometimes you just need some help getting over the hump, so to speak. Help is always there, but God's desire is that you work through His Spirit in you to bring healing and anything else you need.

His real desire, though, is that He will not have to heal you, even by His Spirit. His real desire is that you live in divine health and walk in divine health. The way you live in that divine health is you learn how to let the Spirit of God emanate from you so that sickness and disease can't even get to you.

Go down to verse 16. Remember: we are talking about the Spirit of God that dwells in us. He is the One who speaks in these other tongues. It is His coming into us that brings a refreshing and brings the rest.

Romans 8:16 says,

16 The Spirit itself beareth witness with our spirit, that we are the children of God:

When it says, "The Spirit itself," it should say "Himself;" it is the same difference. "The Spirit [Himself] beareth witness with our spirit, that we are the children of God."

Go to verse 26 of Romans chapter 8. It says,

> 26 Likewise the Spirit also helpeth our infirmities: for we know not what we should pray for as we ought: but the Spirit itself maketh intercession for us with groanings which cannot be uttered.

"Likewise the Spirit also helps our infirmities." That word "infirmities" does not always mean sickness. It can mean any type of frailty. It can mean a problem. It can be physically, emotionally, or mentally. It could be any area where you have a lack or a need. That is an infirmity. "Likewise the Spirit also helps our infirmities: for we know not what we should pray for as we ought: but the Spirit itself [Himself] makes intercession for us with groanings which cannot be uttered."

I want you to realize that this is talking about the Spirit of God dwelling in you. You do not always know how to pray, and you do not know how to pray the right prayers, so when you do not know how to pray, then automatically the Spirit in you can pray correctly. However, if He is going to pray correctly for you, He is going to pray through you.

It is the Spirit of God energizing you, inside, to speak in other tongues. That is why he says you do not speak to men, but you speak to God. The Holy Spirit will make intercession for you for the infirmity you have. It may not be sickness. It may be that you don't know which job to take, you don't know which contract to sign, or you don't know certain things. Because of that, you can pray in other tongues, and as you pray in other tongues, the Spirit of God praying through you will intercede on your behalf.

Do you realize that many times you are not interceded for because you won't pray in other tongues, and let the Spirit work through you? You say, "Why is God not doing something?" He says, "I am waiting for you to let the Spirit pray through you." Why? There is an aspect on this earth where men have to ask to bring the things of heaven to this earth. That is why Jesus said, "Pray that His will be done on earth as it is in heaven."

If you want to pray the perfect prayer, pray in tongues. It is the perfect prayer. How do we know that? Notice, it says, "He will make intercession." It is the Spirit that "makes intercession for us with groanings which cannot be uttered." In other words, "The groanings are inside." You cannot make these words. It is the Spirit of God that makes the words.

Notice verse 27. It says,

> 27 And he that searcheth the hearts knoweth what *is* the mind of the Spirit, because he maketh intercession for the saints according to *the will of* God.

"And he that searches the hearts," the Spirit of God, "knows what is the mind of the Spirit because He makes intercession for the saints according to the will of God." As He speaks through you, you are the one giving the Spirit the ability to speak through you on your behalf, praying the perfect will of God, and praying God's will for the saints (us) at that moment.

I hesitate to say this, but unfortunately this is what motivates some people, so I am going to say it anyway: "Strictly from a selfish level, if you don't pray in tongues for any other reason, you ought to pray just so God can do things for you." Again, I wish I didn't even have to say that, but if that is what motivates somebody, eventually he or she will move out of that and move into the things of God.

Romans 8:28 says,

> 28 And we know that all things work together for good to them that love God, to them who are the called according to *his* purpose.

You always hear this verse, but most people don't ever read it in its full context.

There are a couple of things here:

First of all, it says, "And we know that all things work together." What things? They are the things that the Spirit of God is praying through you in tongues and intercession. As you pray in other tongues, the Spirit of God is praying those things through you, and those are the things that He is praying that work together for your good. People say, "Well, you know, all things work together for the good," and that is as far as they go. They say, "Did you hear about so and so? They were in a car accident." "Well, all things work together for the good." They are not saying that car accidents work together for the good.

The Bible says that all things work together for the good but it is based on the Spirit of God making intercession for you by the Spirit with "groanings that cannot be uttered." Therefore, all things do not work together.

Secondly, all things do not work together for the good for everybody. The Bible says that all things work together for the good to those who are the called according to His purpose, to those who love God. It is not always based on just everything that happens.

I want you to get the idea of the Spirit of God working through you. If I could just get this across to you! This is the big thing. I really want to get you to see it.

It is amazing how little the Bible talks about being born again. Yes, it mentions it; it talks about it. Obviously, it is the connection of God. It is important, but the overwhelming evidence of the Bible from all of the disciples, Jesus, God, and the Old Testament prophets and what they taught was more about the incoming of the Holy Spirit and the Spirit dwelling within us more so than it did the result of us being born again. Being born is pretty important because a person can't be here without being born.

That is the same way Paul talked in Galatians 4:6.

> 6 And because ye are sons, God hath sent forth the Spirit of his Son into your hearts, crying, Abba, Father.

Yes, it is great that you are born again, but don't just stop there. Be filled with the Spirit. Why? The purpose of His coming was to give us the Spirit. It was to bring the Spirit of God into union with us.

I think too often that we minimize the interaction of the Spirit of God with us. In the training we have done before, we tried to bring this out. Too many people today look at the Spirit of God the way we used to look at the old scuba diving tanks. They had two tanks on the back, and they had to get the mixture perfect between the two, but they always had two tanks. Most people still look at that interaction the same way today. "Well, here I am, and there is the Holy Spirit. I am over here, and the Holy Spirit is over there." They think of it just like the two tanks on the scuba divers.

Then they figured out, "We could mix these two gases and get a perfect mixture so that nobody would have to mess with the mixture. It would be perfect, and we could just put them together in one tank." Now, when you see the scuba divers, instead of having two tanks, they have one tank because the mixture is perfect, and they don't have to mess with it. In the church, they still talk about the Spirit of God as being separate from us, whereas we have this element and that element. I am telling you, "If you have a person and then you have the Spirit of God separately, you still don't have a Christian."

T.L. Osborn said, "The Spirit of God in a person makes a Christian." You don't have the Spirit of God and a Christian separately.

In 1 Corinthians 6:17 it says,

> 17 But he that is joined unto the Lord is one spirit.

You have the Spirit of God. He that joins himself to the Lord is one spirit with the Lord. This was the revelation that John Lake had, and this is what the Church still does not have. One hundred years later, they still do not get it.

I say that it has been 100 years, but it has been 2,000 years because Paul said it first. He said, "He that is joined to the Lord is one spirit with the Lord." However, we still have this idea of, "Well, there is the Spirit of God and then there is me." No! We are one!

There is a union that God has brought us to where His Spirit literally has permeated our spirit to where you cannot tell us apart. That is what it is supposed to be in our spirit.

I have always used this example when people asked me, "Brother Curry, how shall we do this? What should I do?" I tell them what they should do. They stop, and they say, "Okay, I can see that now, but when you said that, was it you or the Lord speaking?" I would say, "Yes." They would look at me strangely. "No, you did not understand, Brother Curry. Was it you or was that the Lord?" I would say, "Yes, it was." Why? If I speak by the Spirit, I am speaking and the Lord is speaking. We are one.

To the degree that my mind is renewed to the Word of God and by the Spirit of God, we can operate as one.

Whether I operate as if we are one or not, we are still one. People are walking around with the Spirit of the Living God. We are talking about the Spirit of God who created everything. Here is the real tragedy: they are walking around with Him living in them, joined to them, in union with them, having total access to all the wisdom of God, total access to literally all the power of God, yet they are walking around like orphans. Jesus said, "I will not leave you as orphans. I will not leave you comfortless. I will send another comforter. And He was with you, and He shall be in you."

You have people walking around with the Spirit of the Living God in them, and they walk around acting like, "Oh, what am I going to do? I don't know what I am going to do? You know, we just can't pay our bills. We can't do this, and we can't do that. I just don't know where to turn." For a Christian to say that is a tragedy!

A Christian should never have to say, "I do not know." If anything he or she should say, "Hang on just a second. Yes, here is what you should do." Why? They draw on the wisdom of God, but I will tell you this: When you do that, it is going to be because you have spent so much time praying in other tongues. Praying in other tongues draws out the counsel of God, and it literally imbeds itself into you to be used whenever you need it. Dr. Lake said, "Praying in other tongues is the dynamo of the Spirit of God."

A lot of people today wouldn't know what a dynamo is, but in the old days they had these cranks and they would use those to turn this dynamo. As they cranked it, it would generate electricity. Then that electricity would go into a line and into a battery, and it would charge up the battery. The thing is that when they stopped charging, that is not when the electricity stopped. The electricity was stored for later use. You did not have to stand there and say, "Well, as long as we want electricity, and as long as we want lights, we will have to stand here and turn this thing." No, you turned it and then you could stop.

Remember the old telephone? Maybe you have seen it in movies. It was mounted on the wall, and it had the speaker sticking out of the front and the earpiece was on the side. They had to pick up the earpiece and hold it to their ear. However, they had to crank it before they could talk. Why? They had to generate some power to send out, and it would generate enough to talk. They didn't have to stand there the whole time talking and cranking. They could crank and then stop, and it would generate power and store it to be used.

That is what speaking in other tongues does. You don't have to do it right then. That is why I tell people if they want to pray the perfect prayer, pray in other tongues. That does not mean you have to pray the perfect prayer right then. When a person comes to me, many times I don't know exactly what to pray. I don't know what to say, but what comes out is a result of my spending time praying in tongues. The Holy Spirit knew who was coming, knew those people would be standing in front of me, and knew what they needed.

I didn't know anything about them, but as I prayed in other tongues, He put in and brought up inside me what they needed. When I got in front of them was not the time to pray in tongues. I had already prayed in tongues. That was the time to use the power that was stored in the battery. When I released it, I drew on the wisdom of God that was imparted to me through the praying in other tongues.

There are different aspects of this, and this is walking in the realm of the Spirit.

While in Houston, Texas, Dr. Lake wrote to Charles Parham, who founded the Pentecostal Movement in 1901. The letter is dated March 24, 1927. I am not going to read the whole letter, but I do want to read some parts.

"Dear Brother Parham:

I've been waiting to write to you for a long time, but have been so very unsettled, and when things around me get unsettled I don't write to anybody until they begin to shape again.

It would be difficult for me to explain to you how or why I am in Houston. A something grew up in my soul that I wanted to see and talk with Carothers [W A. Carothers was one of the founders of the Assemblies of God], and he kept grinding in me so long that eventually I found myself here.

While at San Diego, I was in the habit of meeting with a few of the brethren in Los Angeles. Dr. Kenyon [that is E.W. Kenyon], Cannon, Wallace, myself, and others. We would get together once in awhile and talk things over.

We did not discuss just the interests of the Pentecostal movement only, but whether or not there was anything that a group of sane men could do that would be of real value to Christianity."

Now, think about that. These guys got together, and they asked, "What can we do to help Christianity?" It was not just to help their group."

Dr. Lake continues in his letter:

"The consensus of opinion was that what the Christian world is suffering from more than anything else is a lack of the ideal of Christianity." In other words, people didn't know where they were going. They didn't have the "ideal." They did not see what Christianity was supposed to be.

He said, *"The world does not know what real Christianity is. Pentecost should have exemplified it. In that, it has failed in my judgment about 93 percent."*

Think about that. This is a man who saw a quarter million healings in a ten year period; he saw amazing miracles! He said, "For the most part, for about 93 percent, we have failed to show the world what real Christianity is." If he said that, imagine what his ideal of Christianity was. Most people would have been pleased to have walked in what he did.

He says: "*However, it has done this much. It has demonstrated that there is such a thing as the baptism of the Holy Ghost. That men may enter into God if they will. That some have, in a slight degree. That none have in an outstanding way that would make their life or revelation comparable with the apostles or the leaders of Christianity in the first centuries.*"

It was amazing for him to be able to say that.

Dr. Lake goes on, "*We have rather been an order of cheap evangelism, with a rather cheap evangelistic message that is not worthy in the high sense of being called Pentecostal.*"

He was saying that everything they had done had been this "cheap evangelistic" type of thing. He was saying, "We have not yet really seen real Christianity."

This letter was written in 1927. He passed away in 1935. Up until that time, 1927, he had already done all of his South Africa mission trips, his Healing Rooms in Spokane, and the Healing Rooms in Portland. All of that was already done and over with at that point. It was amazing that he said, "We still have not seen real Christianity, yet." He said, "We have this ideal. We got together, and we talked about it."

He says:

"*Next, my own idea was that if I were going to undertake to do for Christianity the thing that seems to me would be the greatest blessing, and to present to the world the ideal that it needs, I would like to do it through a sort of Bible University, that first taught the full rounded life of Christ in man.*

"Second, this Bible University would send into the world a group of men to give that ideal to the public. How my own soul has longed to see yourself [Charles Parham], *above every other man measure up in God to the stature of the need of this hour.*

"And while I take my hat off to you and recognize in you a humble servant of God who has labored hard, and while you have been an amazing propagandist of the truth that God revealed to you, yet brother, like myself and all the others I see, there has been an utter failure to measure up to the stature of fatherhood in God that would mark you as the real father and leader of the Pentecostal forces. [He was pretty blunt.]

"Now brother I'm not scolding and I'm sure that you know my deep love for the men who bear this Gospel, especially for yourself, so that you'll be ready to conceive that my aim is not only to help you, but to help my own soul and the souls of those about us to rise up in God, to be and do and give the real Pentecostal life and vision to the world."

What I am saying is that Dr. Lake said, "We have not yet recognized it. We have not yet seen this, but it is there. If we will push on into it, we will walk in the things of the Spirit."

Then he goes on and says,

"The great mass of independent churches in the Pentecostal faith have a local status." [In other words, they are not really impacting the world.] *"They're all trying to do something. One of the things we're all compelled to admit is that so far as real Pentecost is concerned, it is rapidly dying out in the world."*

That was in 1927. He said, "Most of what we have seen is dying out." Why? People have gotten too concerned and too satisfied with form and just going through the motions rather than actually experiencing the depths of God. Everything now has become an outward show rather than an inward growth into the things of God.

He said,

"If this is the real Pentecost, there must come out of it eventually the thing that Pentecost produced in the early Church and that was the real Body of Jesus Christ. A group of Holy Ghost baptized souls in which dwell and through which is manifest the life of the Lord."

There is a lot here. I am not going to read all of it, but it is amazing because he talks about some personal things with Charles Parham and what he should have seen and what they should have done.

The key here and what I really want to get across to you is this: it is time for us to really settle down into the things of God. I am not talking about moving away from healing. What we have to see as a Christian is that a Christian is made up of three major traits.

THE THREE MAJOR TRAITS OF A CHRISTIAN

Number One: The gifts of the Spirit. When I say number one, I am not talking about the main thing. I am just giving you the parts. We should have the gifts of the Spirit operating in our lives or at least the manifestation of the Spirit in these areas. That should be there.

Number Two: We should manifest the fruit of the Spirit. Now gifts are given, but fruit is grown. Gifts usually come instantly, but fruit has to be grown, and it takes time for it to grow.

In the church world right now, I see a lot of people, typically young people, who get ahold of power, yet they don't have fruit. They have gifts of power and they operate in power, but they don't have the fruit of the Spirit. The fruit of the Spirit is what gives them the character to carry the gifts of the Spirit for any length of time.

What you end up seeing are people who burned out and got off into weird things, or they got led astray because they didn't have the stability of the Spirit to be able to walk it out and stay straight with God. Instead, they got off on some tangent and over into some weird doctrine that stole what they had.

Remember: the enemy of our souls, the devil himself, is not concerned about getting you to go to hell. All he is trying to do is make sure that you are not effective here and now. In order to do that, all he has to do is get you off just a little bit. People that do that will soon have the form, and will be doing things that look right, yet there will not be any real life.

People will see them and because it looks like they are doing the right thing, they will ask, "Do you want to see the sick healed?" They will show someone how to lay hands without first asking, "Are you born again?" People learn how to lay hands on the sick, and then they go out and do that, yet they are not even born again. You wonder, "How can that happen?"

Jesus said, "They are going to come to Me and say, 'Lord, Lord, have we not prophesied in Your Name? Have we not done all these mighty works in Your Name? And I will say, 'I never knew you.'" Why? You can preach to people and get them healed even though you yourself are not saved. You can get people healed, and you can do these mighty works, yet not have the Spirit of God dwelling in you. You would still be working to help people.

I am really concerned about the next generation where they are seeing power, but they are not seeing character, they are not seeing growth, and they are not seeing the fruit of the Spirit.

Number one, we have the gifts. Number two, we have the fruit.

Number Three: We have the nature and the character of God. All of these traits together make a Christian; it is not any one by itself. Together they build up into a Christian so that a Christian can be a living, true example of the Son of God, walking in the power of God, and walking in the knowledge of God. That is what is going to come forth, and that is where we are going.

A lot of that comes about by giving the Spirit more control in you, and most of that comes through praying in other tongues. There is going to be emphasis on speaking in tongues, and you are going to see more and more of it as we go along. We will go into it in depth.

THE BENEFITS OF BEING SPIRIT FILLED

Sermon given by Curry R. Blake

"Father, we thank You for this day. We thank You that we can gather together. Right now, we know that Your presence, Your Spirit, is with us because You said You would never leave us nor forsake us. Father, we thank You that right now by Your Spirit we are able to learn and to grow in the knowledge of Your will and Your Word. Father, we thank You for this. In the name of Jesus, we bless You. Amen."

In this sermon we are looking at some of the benefits of being Spirit filled. Over the last couple of weeks, we have been talking about unknown tongues, the Baptism of the Spirit, and the promise of the Father. This teaching goes along with those, but this one will take you to the next step. I want you to realize that I am trying to head you in a direction. This is not haphazard; I am regularly praying about what to bring out and how to bring it out. I can see how things are starting to take shape. It is good to see how God puts things together.

We are going to start in verse 25 of Mark 5. First, you have to remember this: Jesus was a Spirit filled person. Would you agree? Believe it or not, there might be some people who would argue with you on that, but we firmly believe Jesus was Spirit filled. We want to look at some things here: some of the benefits of being Spirit filled— what happens to you and what should be the norm when you are Spirit filled. Turn first to Mark chapter 5.

Mark 5:25-28

25 And a certain woman, which had an issue of blood twelve years,

26 And had suffered many things of many physicians, and had spent all that she had, and was nothing bettered, but rather grew worse,

27 When she had heard of Jesus, came in the press behind, and touched his garment.

28 For she said, If I may touch but His clothes, I shall be whole.

Notice her words here: "If I may…" She said, "If I may touch but His clothes," then she says, "I shall be made whole."

The first part says, "If," but in the last part, there is no "if." The last part says, "I shall be made whole." It was not a matter of where the power was. She knew where the power was. Her whole key was, "If I can get to it, I can get it." "If I may touch but His clothes, I shall be whole."

Mark 5:29,

29 And straightway the fountain of her blood was dried up; and she felt in *her* body that she was healed of that plague.

Notice that it happened instantly. That is what we want. We always push for the instant. I always tell everybody, "We will take it any way we can get it." If it takes a while to get someone healed, we will take that; we do not like it, though. That is why we keep pushing. We believe for the instant, but once we attach our faith to a person and to that situation, we do not let go until it is done. That is the key.

A lot of people have problems with that. (This is parenthetical here.) They say, "Well, you know Jesus' healings were all instant." Technically they were not, but they happened fairly quickly. Most of them were within a day or within the time they left. About the one boy it was said, "He began to amend from that hour," so he was getting better from that time; he was recovering. All of Jesus' healings were not instant, but people did not stand around believing for 10 or 20 years, so in that case, we would say it happened quickly.

The main thing here is if you look at healing as being instant, it is always good, and we always want that. If, however, you look at the very fact that John Lake had Healing Rooms and had people agree to come back every day for 30 days, you see that even John Lake's healings, as miraculous as many of them were, were not all instant.

John Lake himself, the people who worked with him, and the people I have talked to who worked with him said at the height of his ministry, when he was seeing the most people healed, his success rate was only 76 percent. I say "only," but the average church has less than 10 percent. Even back then 76 percent was still a pretty good rate. We are now seeing 94 to 97 percent as I just testified to you a few minutes ago; we are seeing more and more cases of 100 percent.

Proverbs 4:18 says,

> 18 But the path of the just *is* as the shining light, that shineth more and more unto the perfect day.

It is not wrong to surpass past days; it is right. We are supposed to grow stronger and stronger and be more and more like Jesus, not less and less. We should learn from the old days, but we should never be stuck there. We should never reverence them to the point where we are afraid to show them up: not the people but the days. Do you understand what I am saying? In other words, we should be growing. "The path of the righteous grows brighter and brighter unto the perfect day." We should be growing and getting more like Jesus, looking more like Him.

People say, "Let us get back to the Book of Acts." The Book of Acts church is not the church you want to go back to. It is the church in the Book of Ephesians that you want to go back to—the glorious, overcoming church. The Book of Acts church was awesome, but they were just figuring things out, and unfortunately, that is where we are right now. Most of the churches are still trying to figure things out, and most are at least 100 years behind where Dr. Lake was 100 years ago. It is time to move forward.

If you do not believe that you can do more today than they could yesterday, then I guarantee you will never do more today than they did yesterday. There comes a point where you have to realize that the purpose of the previous generations is for us to climb up on their backs and go to the next level.

Going back to verse 29, it says, "She felt in her body that she was healed of that plague." Notice, this is called a "plague" in the Bible. It was a plague; it was wrong. It was not of God. God was not in agreement with it.

Mark 5:30,

> 30 And Jesus, immediately knowing in Himself that virtue had gone out of Him, turned Him about in the press, and said, who touched My clothes?

"And Jesus, <u>immediately knowing in Himself</u> that virtue had gone out of Him, turned Him about in the press, and said, 'Who touched My clothes?'" He knew someone had touched His clothes. Go back to the first part of the verse. First, "He knew in Himself," He had a knowing, "that virtue had gone out of Him."

Where did the power come from that healed the woman? It came out of Jesus. It did not fall from heaven.

Acts 2:17,

> 17 And it shall come to pass in the last days, saith God, I will pour out of My Spirit upon all flesh: and your sons and your daughters shall prophesy, and your young men shall see visions, and your old men shall dream dreams;

Last week I talked about how Spirit will pour out of you. "He poured out of His Spirit upon all flesh." It did not say He poured out His Spirit. He poured out of His Spirit. His Spirit is dwelling in men. His Spirit doesn't fall upon people in the sense of power to heal.

First of all, we do not find in the Bible that we are to pray for God to heal someone. When we minister to a person, the power to heal doesn't fall from heaven to them. It comes out of us. We are the conduit through which God works. However, our thought process definitely should not be, "We are not going to pray; let us just see what God does." No, we are going to fulfill the commission of God. We are going to do what He said to do. Then He will pour through us and accomplish what He said He would do. The key here is that it is not going to fall, but instead it is going to pour out of.

If you were in a room with 200 people and each of them were sick, then as you ministered, it would be harder for you to pray for 200 people one by one. We have done that; we have prayed for well over 1,500 people in one session. If you pray for the whole group, His Spirit will not fall like rain upon them. His Spirit pours out of you and disburses into 200 different directions. That is what you have to grasp.

What I am trying to get across to you today is the benefit of being Spirit filled. It is not the benefit of having knowledge of the Spirit. It is being Spirit filled and when you are, you can release the Spirit.

One of the things I love about John Lake is that he was very scientific minded, and he explained a lot of things scientifically in line with the

Spirit. He used scientific terms to talk about things of the Spirit. That is one of the reasons I am so excited about the current level of science discussions: we talk about quantum physics because, for the first time, we actually have a language in science that can describe the things of the Spirit and how they work. We've talked before about spiritual physics and we're going to talk about some more of these things in the next couple of weeks.

I want you to get ahold of this: you have something.

In Acts chapter 3, Peter and John were going to the temple to pray. They walked past the man who was lame from his mother's womb. He was begging for money. Peter and John stopped, and Peter said, "Look on us." He told him to look at them, and then he said, "Silver and gold I do not have, but what I have I give you." There was no hesitation. There was no, "Let us pray and see what God will do. Let us pray and see what God wants to do with you. Let us pray and see if God wants to do anything." There was none of that. Peter was speaking for God, as he always did, before he actually talked to God about it. Did you ever notice that? Peter was always shooting his mouth off and then expecting God to back him up.

Well, I have found that to be the secret to miracles. That is the key right there. It is just throwing yourself out there where God has to show up, or you look like an idiot. That is just the way it is. When you get out there, like that, is when miracles happen. If you stop and think about it too long, two things will happen: (1) You will talk yourself out of it, and you will not do it or (2) You will figure out a reason, mentally, why it won't work. The best thing to do, therefore, is to quit thinking about it, and do what you are supposed to do. You do what is right because it is right, and you do not try to figure it all out.

In 1 Corinthians 2:16 it says,

> 16 For who hath known the mind of the Lord, that He may instruct him? But we have the mind of Christ.

I do believe absolutely that we have the mind of Christ. I believe we can actually draw on that mind. I believe that we can walk in the fullness of the mind of Christ. I believe it is a growth process. It has to do with renewing our minds, and I do know it is possible, but I want you to understand this: at this point in time, most people are not walking in the fullness of the mind of Christ that they have within them (in the person of the Spirit of God). I am not putting anybody down for that. I am just saying that it seems to be a fact.

Because the mind of Christ is in you (the mind of Christ is the mind of God), you have access to it. Just because you have access to it does not mean that you are walking in it. It is what we used to call "positional" and "experiential." If it is positional, you have it all. If it is experiential, there are some things you need to experience.

If this is God we are talking about, and if the Spirit of God is God Himself that we are actually talking about here, then there are probably some things that you are not going to be able to figure out just because you are not God.

It is like this: I have grandchildren from ages two through ten. I can talk to each one on a different level, but regardless of which level they are, I have to get to their level to explain things to them. I do not expect them to understand everything the way I understand it. Why? They are not mature, yet so I have to talk to each one a little differently to get it across to them at their level. Even if I get the point across, it doesn't mean they fully understand everything I am talking about.

That is the same way it is between God and us. Sometimes when He says to do something, we don't need to know why or how. We couldn't even figure it out if we tried with our normal brain, especially with the un-renewed part of our brain.

You are not going to always figure those things out. Sometimes you just need to do them. I hope you all understand the Texas term of "figuring things out." Sometimes, when you are figuring those things out, they happen because you do them. Some things you will never understand until you do them. You have to do them first and then you understand. You don't understand it first and then do it, because if you understood it first, you might not do it. That is just the way it is.

Back in verse 30, Jesus noticed: "Virtue had gone out of Him." That is the main point of today: the Spirit of God dwells in you; therefore, any activity of the Spirit of God in your praying or your believing is the Spirit of God going out of you, not coming down from somewhere else.

Jesus turned about in the press, and said, "Who touched My clothes?" Notice, He did not know who it was. Isn't that something? He knew something had happened. He knew something had left Him, but He didn't know who caused it.

I love this verse about the woman. This verse and the pool of Bethesda are two of my favorite Bible stories. Why? Both of them prove that it can be "whosoever," and they can be healed of "whatsoever." Here is where I lose the religious people. When I say religious people, I am talking about dead religion. I am not talking about the pure and undefiled. Religious people have a problem with this because basically it says, "You don't have to get God's permission to get healed." I will say it again, "You do not have to get God's permission to get healed."

Understand what I mean by that. What I am saying to you is that you don't have to get His permission right now to be healed. Why? He has already given His permission. He gave it 2,000 years ago at the whipping post. His permission has already been granted. It has already been done. If you ask Him, "Well, God do You want to heal me?" it is a redundant question to God. He said, "I have already shown you. I showed you My Son. I showed My perfect will through everything My Son did including what He did at the whipping post. Therefore, by His stripes, you were healed." It is not a matter of asking God, "Will you heal me?" No, the question is, "Will you receive it? Will you take it?"

The Greek word for "*receive*" has the implication of *taking, grasping, and holding on to*. Generally what I say is this: You hold out your hand; you get something from God. He places it in your hand and then the devil comes along to see if he can take it out. The idea is that whenever you get something from God, you have to grab it, hold it, and say, "Devil, you are not taking this from me. You can't take it; it is mine." That is the fight of faith. There comes a point where you have to set yourself to say, "This is the way it is going to be."

Let's read Mark 5:30 again,

> 30 And Jesus, immediately knowing in Himself that virtue had gone out of Him, turned Him about in the press, and said, who touched My clothes?

Notice here that virtue had gone out of Him. He turned about in the press, and said, "Who touched My clothes?" It did not say who touched Him. Nobody touched Him. She touched His clothes. This is the benefit of being Spirit filled.

Mark 5:31 says,

> 31 And His disciples said unto Him, Thou seest the multitude thronging Thee, and sayest Thou, Who touched Me?

You get this picture of the press and His disciples forming a little circle around Him, trying to protect Him, getting Him to move through the crowd, and you can see the people trying to reach through, but this one little woman sneaks up behind Him and just grabs the hem of His garment. She gets healed, and Jesus says, "Whoa! Stop! Stop!

Something happened. I felt it. Hang on. Who touched My clothes?" They were saying, "Look. Look at that crowd." He was saying that somebody had touched the hem of His garment.

Mark 5:32-34,

> 32 And He looked round about to see her that had done this thing.

> 33 But the woman fearing and trembling, knowing what was done in her, came and fell down before Him, and told Him all the truth.

> 34 And He said unto her, Daughter, thy faith hath made thee whole; go in peace, and be whole of thy plague.

"And He said unto her, 'Daughter, your faith has made you whole.'" Your faith! Did you hear that? "Your faith has made you whole; go in peace, and be whole of thy plague."

This is the first case. I want you to go to Luke chapter 8. We are going to look at the same story again.

You think, "Why would they waste this space to put the same story in several of the Gospels when they could have used the space to do other stories?" The Bible is very clear. It says in 2 Corinthians, 13:1,

> 1 ...In the mouth of two or three witnesses shall every word be established.

Therefore, we are going to look at several different examples of witnesses. What I like about them is that each one is a little different.

Look at Mark. Mark was a young man when he traveled with Jesus. The one thing about Mark's Gospel is that he was always saying, "...immediately," and "...straightway." Young men are always in a hurry. "Let us do it. Yes. You want to go? Let us go now." There is always this immediacy.

© 2012 Curry R. Blake – John G. Lake Ministries

Now, look at Luke. Luke, before he was saved, was a physician. There is no evidence of his being a physician afterward or his continuing his medical career after joining up with Paul. The amazing thing about Luke was that he was so detailed. He had a physician's eye. He was the one who actually gave some medical terminology (if we could call it that) in his Gospel. Then, of course, he wrote the Book of Acts, also. Thank God he was so meticulous with details. That is why we have all of the material we have from the Book of Acts.

This is Luke's account of the same woman in Luke chapter 8, verse 43:

> 43 And a woman having an issue of blood twelve years, which had spent all her living upon physicians, neither could be healed of any,

It says, "And a woman having an issue of blood twelve years, which had spent all her living upon physicians..." You know that irked him. This was Luke the physician writing this, and he was writing that she had spent all of her money on physicians. For all we know, he might have been one of those physicians. There is nothing that says he couldn't have been. It says, "...neither could be healed of any."

> 44 Came behind *Him*, and touched the border of His garment: and immediately her issue of blood stanched.

> 45 And Jesus said, Who touched Me? When all denied, Peter and they that were with Him said, Master, the multitude throng Thee and press *Thee*, and sayest Thou, Who touched Me?

> 46 And Jesus said, Somebody hath touched Me: for I perceive that virtue is gone out of Me.

"And Jesus said, 'Somebody has touched Me: for I perceive that virtue [power] is gone out of Me.'" Do you get that? "I perceive." A while ago it said "knowing." He knew within Himself. *To perceive*, therefore, is *to know within yourself.*

47 And when the woman saw that she was not hid, she came trembling, and falling down before Him, she declared unto Him before all the people for what cause she had touched Him, and how she was healed immediately.

48 And He said unto her, Daughter, be of good comfort: thy faith hath made thee whole; go in peace.

Let us go to one more in Matthew chapter 9. There are two witnesses so far: Mark and Luke. We are going to get to the third witness, so this is something to be firmly established in our doctrine.

If we took the words that said, "In the mouth of two or three witnesses shall every word be established," as a rule for doctrine, that is all we would be able to preach as established doctrine.

Just a note: you can go to a Christian bookstore and find these fold-out pamphlets which have all the miracles and healings of Jesus. It is a harmony on one sheet of paper, like a little brochure. It is really handy. They also have harmonies of the Gospels, where they put together the stories that are matched, and you can go through and read all of them.

I took a brochure that had all of the healings, miracles, parables, and everything about Jesus' life. It showed where each one is in each Gospel. I went through each one of those.

If you were to take out anything that is not in at least two Gospels, it would be amazing how much would get eliminated and how little you would actually have to preach as doctrine. Every one of those instances that was in two or three cases has to do with the power of God ministering to people and setting them free.

All of the other little things that people build pet doctrines on are only preached once. People make pet doctrines out of them that lead to other things that deny the things that are established by two or three witnesses. It is a good study to do some time.

Matthew 9:19-22,

> 19 And Jesus arose, and followed him, and *so did* His disciples.

> 20 And, behold, a woman, which was diseased with an issue of blood twelve years, came behind *Him*, and touched the hem of His garment:

> 21 For she said within herself, If I may but touch His garment, I shall be whole.

> 22 But Jesus turned Him about, and when He saw her, He said, Daughter, be of good comfort; thy faith hath made thee whole. And the woman was made whole from that hour.

This time it has a little more detail because it has to do with, "…she said within herself." I know several different ministries make a major point out of her saying, "…within herself." I would, too. I would say if you are going to receive something on your own, then yes, you do have to get that built into you. Yes, we would say she was confessing; she believed, and she was saying within herself, "If I may but touch His garment, I shall be whole."

Notice again what it says. "She touched the hem of His garment; for she said within herself, 'If I may touch His garment I shall be whole.'" This, again, was the third time.

> 22 But Jesus turned Him about, and when He saw her, He said, Daughter, be of good comfort; thy faith hath made thee whole. And the woman was made whole from that hour.

Look at Matthew 14:35:

> 35 And when the men of that place had knowledge of Him, they sent out into all that country round about, and brought unto Him all that were diseased;

Who did they bring? They brought "all" of those who were diseased. It did not matter who they were. They heard about Him and said, "Hey, Jesus has come here. We have heard about the other stories. Go grab all your sick, grab anybody you know. Bring them in."

They brought "all" the sick and "all" who were diseased. That word "all" is the biggest word in the Bible. It includes everybody.

> 36 And besought Him that they might only touch the hem of His garment: and as many as touched were made perfectly whole.

"And besought Him that they might only touch the hem of His garment…" They went out into all of the areas around there, gathered all the diseased, and brought them to Him. All of these sick people were sitting and looking at Jesus, and they said, "We just want to touch the hem of Your garment." They didn't say, "We want You to lay hands on us." They didn't say, "We want You to heal us." They didn't say, "We want You to pray for us." They didn't say anything except, "We want to touch the hem of Your garment." Why in the world would they say that? It is because Matthew 14 happened after Matthew 9, and they had heard the story of the woman with the issue of blood.

These people were smarter than we sometimes give them credit for. If we didn't know Jesus the way we know Him, we might think along the lines of the man who brought his lunatic son to the disciples. They couldn't set him free. He said, "Lord, if thou wilt."

In Matthew 8, He talks about the leper. The leper said, "Lord, if thou wilt. If it is Your desire, You can make me clean. You can heal me." That man didn't have an understanding. He had no knowledge, no understanding of the nature of Jesus. He said, "If it is Your desire." If he had known Jesus' nature, he would have known it was always Jesus' desire to heal. Jesus healed everybody everywhere He went. The leper didn't know that, so he said, "Lord, if You will; if it is Your desire, You can do this." Even that is more faith than some Christians have today. If you had the level of that man's knowledge of Jesus, you might think, "If it's Your desire," which means that if it is not, then I will understand, "because You know best." Do you see the train of thought?

These people were smart. They didn't even put that to Jesus. They did not give Him the opportunity to say, "No, I do not want to heal you." They said, "We are not even asking You if You will heal us. We just want to touch the hem of Your garment because we know that if we touch it, we are going to get healed whether You like it or not."

This is where I lose some of the religious people because they want to be really reverent, and they think being reverent is humility, but it is not. *Humility* is *submitting yourself unto the mighty hand of God*, which means to do what He said to do and to believe what He said. That is humility.

It is not saying, "Oh, whatever You want. If You want to kill me, that is fine." No, that is not humility. That is an open door for the devil to try to come in and kill you, making you think it was God doing it because you prayed to God, and the devil heard you pray it.

Every answer to prayer is not always from God. The devil sometimes hears you pray, too, and sometimes he will give you an answer. If you don't know how to pray the right way, he will give you the answer that God wouldn't give you. You might have to think that one out.

Notice here that they did not ask Jesus, "Will You heal us?" No, they just wanted to touch the hem of His garment. "And as many as touched were made perfectly whole." All they did was touch His garment. He just had to stand there. Wasn't that an easy service?

I am fairly short, and many times the people I lay hands on are taller than I am. In the beginning, I would realize the morning after I had laid hands on them that my shoulders would be sore. I thought, "There has to be a better way."

I was reading the Bible, and it said, "They took them by the hand." I thought, "Oh. That is much better." I don't get tired when I take them by the hands, and my shoulders don't get sore. I figured that one out. What is easier than that, though, is to just stand there and let people touch your clothes. That is easy. Anybody can do that.

I was in Africa on my first trip in '97. When I walked out the door with a pastor, we walked past this elderly man who was blind. He and his grandson were standing there, and his grandson said something in Swahili. I didn't understand what he said, but I heard him speak. As we were walking by this man, his grandson spoke, and he just reached out. I walked into his hand, and he grabbed hold of my sleeve.

They had tried to pickpocket me in Nairobi, so I was a little cautious of people reaching for me. When he reached out and grabbed me, I immediately turned and spun toward him and kind of knocked his hand off as if to say, "Okay, what are you doing?" This old man stood there and raised his hands, and we stood there and watched him. His eyes were milky white. While we were standing there watching him, his eyes turned from milky white to brown. He started blinking, started crying, started looking, turned, and started walking off, praising God.

God opened his eyes. Honestly, I can say that I didn't feel anything. I can't say I knew within myself that virtue had gone out; I didn't. I was just as amazed as he was or as anybody else standing there.

They started walking off, and the pastor grabbed the little boy and asked him, "What is going on?" Apparently, someone had read a flier that had been passed out that said, "The White Healer is coming." They called me the "White Healer." He said that when he heard that, God had spoken to him and said, "Go and stand outside where the man is staying, and when he walks by, grab him," and he did. He was being obedient. Again, I didn't feel anything; regardless, that is what ended up happening. It was by a touch, and it wasn't even much of a touch. As soon as he grabbed me, it was done, and he was off, praising God.

These are the benefits of being Spirit filled. When you are Spirit filled, you can say what Peter said, "What I have, I give you." Peter didn't ask, "Can I give it?"

This is what John Lake's sermons did to me. When I read his sermons and when I started talking to people who knew him, this is what got ahold of me. I am working with God. I'm not constantly asking God to do this and to do that, trying to get Him to do something or to find out what He would do.

I found out that God lived within me and that I was working with Him. As His representative, I have certain things that I am allowed to do and to say without contacting headquarters. Why? Headquarters is with me. They will back me up.

A police officer knows that whenever he answers or responds to a call that if he needs backup, headquarters will send him backup. When a policeman needs backup, he doesn't jump on the radio and call another unit. He calls headquarters; he calls the dispatcher. The dispatcher dispatches the other units.

With us, the Spirit of God lives within us. That is what I wanted you to get ahold of. God is not distant; He is not far off. He dwells within you; that is what being Spirit filled is. You are filled with God, Himself. That means that you don't have to go somewhere to get help. You have help with you. Jesus said, "I will send you another Helper, another Comforter, One called alongside to help." The Helper dwells within you.

I have shown you several cases here. The woman got healed without asking Jesus.

What I love about John chapter 5 is that at the pool of Bethesda Jesus just showed up and healed the man. Jesus said, "Do you want to be healed?" The man said, "I don't have anybody who can help me get into the pool. Every time I head that way, somebody else gets in before I do."

Jesus didn't ask the question, "Why aren't you already healed?" He asked, "Do you want to be healed?" The man immediately started complaining. Sometimes Christians do that.

You ought to stand in a prayer line. This is what you get: "What do you want me to do?" "Well, you know it started when…" "That was not my question. What do you want?"

Do you realize that before Jesus ever showed up at the pool of Bethesda, people were getting healed? That is the part we miss sometimes. At the pool of Bethesda, people were getting healed before Jesus ever went there. An angel would come during a certain season, the Passover season, and people would get healed physically, tying physical healing with the Passover. It was tied, later on, to the crucifixion and resurrection of Jesus.

It said that at a certain season, an angel would come down and trouble the water. At the troubling of the water, whoever got in first got healed of whatever they had. What does that mean? That means that God doesn't care who you are. He doesn't care what you have. That is the good news.

God wasn't saying, "Today is your day." He wasn't saying, "No, you hold on to yours; this is their day; they are going to get healed today." No, that is not what He was saying.

He was saying, "I don't care who you are. All I care about is what My Son did. My Son made provision for you to get healed of whatever you have. Whoever you are is not an exception to what He did. Whatever you have is not an exception to what He did." We have the provisions that we have because Jesus did what He did.

In 1 Corinthians 14:18 Paul said,

> 18 I thank my God, I speak with tongues more than ye all:

I would say that Paul was a Spirit-filled person. He said,

> 19 Yet in the church I had rather speak five words with my understanding, that *by my voice* I might teach others also, than ten thousand words in an *unknown* tongue.

Some people think it sounds like he was putting down tongues in some way, but he wasn't. He had just said, "I thank my God, I speak with tongues more than you all." He was not putting it down; he was just saying, "There is a time and a place and there is a reason." The main thing to notice here is this: obviously, the speaking in tongues that Paul was talking about (that he did more than anybody else) was in his private life, not in his public ministry. He said, "Yet in the church I had rather speak five words with my understanding, than ten thousand words in an *unknown* tongue." He just said, "I thank my God, I speak with tongues more than you all."

All of the speaking in tongues that Paul did was in his private life, which goes back to his Baptism of the Spirit, his being filled with the Spirit. I'm showing you the importance of two things: (1) being filled with the Spirit, and (2) the result of speaking in other tongues.

In 1 Corinthians 14:2 it says,

> 2 For he that speaketh in an *unknown* tongue speaketh not unto men, but unto God: for no man understandeth *him*; howbeit in the spirit he speaketh mysteries.

Paul is also the person who wrote two-thirds of the New Testament. He is also the person who said, "I speak with tongues more than you all." Do you think there could be some correlation there? He also wrote Romans and 1 Corinthians, where he said that he spoke mysteries in the Spirit. That speaking mysteries in the Spirit is talking about speaking in other tongues. That is what he is talking about. He would speak in other tongues; then he would interpret his tongues; and then he would teach the church what he interpreted.

That is how Dr. Lake preached most of his sermons—the sermons that people read and say, "There is something different about this." Dr. Lake's sermons have something about them that are different from the other sermons of the average preachers during that day. Dr. Lake said, "This is how I developed my sermons. I would go and pray in tongues; I would interpret that; and then I would write out my sermon outlines." All of his sermon outlines, therefore, came from his praying in other tongues and then interpreting them.

That is why interpretation of tongues is so important. It is not just for public service. It is for your private language, also.

Paul said that when you pray in other tongues, your mind is unfruitful; your understanding is unfruitful. That doesn't mean it has to be. As you interpret, your mind and your understanding will become fruitful.

In 1 Corinthians 14:2 it said,

> 2 …howbeit in the spirit he speaketh mysteries.

Paul taught those mysteries to the Church. It was after he interpreted his tongues. Paul, being a Spirit-filled person, said, "I thank my God, I speak with tongues more than you all." He wrote two-thirds of the New Testament, and what he wrote was what he got mainly through tongues.

He had visions of Jesus. He talked with Jesus. He had interviews with Jesus, you might say. The revelations that he understood, that he spoke by the Spirit, the mysteries that he spoke in the Spirit, were a direct reference to speaking in other tongues, interpreting them, and bringing those mysteries into the church.

Look at Ephesians 5:18. This is Paul writing. Here Paul tells us how to stay filled with the Spirit.

> 18 And be not drunk with wine, wherein is excess; but be filled with the Spirit;

I am reading from King James, where it says "But be filled with the Spirit." The tense of the word "filled" is a word we would now write, "And be being constantly filled."

Paul then tells you how to "be being constantly filled with the Spirit."

> 19 Speaking to yourselves in psalms and hymns and spiritual songs, singing and making melody in your heart to the Lord;

He says, "Speaking to yourselves…" Do you hear that? "Speaking to yourselves in psalms and hymns and spiritual songs." Go right back to that beginning: "For she said within herself." Do you get that? "For she said within herself," and here he said, "Speaking to yourselves."

You have to realize that the way the world thinks is absolutely contrary and opposite to the way God thinks and of what God says to do.

Think about this: if the devil wanted to stop certain things, all he would have to do is think ahead. He has been here for a while, and he might not win that certain generation, but if he can plant some seeds that might grow up, he might be able to misdirect future generations.

When I was a child growing up, I remember hearing different people say, "Well, you know if someone talks to himself, it is a sign he is crazy, so don't talk to yourself. You don't want people to think you are crazy." Do you think that might have been the devil trying to get people not to talk to themselves? Why? The Bible is full of people who "said within themselves."

People will always be talking to themselves. That is the very meaning of the word to *meditate*: it means *to mutter, to think upon, and to say to oneself*. Then the devil comes along and says, "Oh, don't talk to yourself; people will think you're crazy." Why does he say that? It is to keep you from "saying within yourself." He does that in the secular world and then tries to bring it into the church, also, because secular people become church people. They bring those things with them.

Paul says, "Speaking to yourselves in psalms and hymns and spiritual songs, singing and making melody in your heart to the Lord." He tied this to being filled with the Spirit. Do you want to be filled with the Spirit? Do you want to stay filled with the Spirit? Do you want to "be being constantly filled with the Spirit?" It is very simple. All you have to do is talk to yourself, sing to yourself, and speak to yourself in spiritual songs and hymns. These songs and hymns are Scripture because when Paul was writing, the songs and hymns they had were in the Book of Psalms.

I am currently going through all of the Psalms and putting together the ones that we can sing. There are some Psalms we can't sing because they are contrary to New Testament revelation, but there are a lot of Psalms that we can actually sing. I believe we should be singing them, and I think we should be singing them everyday. You could get up in the morning and actually go through some Psalms. Start reading them to yourself, speaking them to yourself, and singing them out loud. Eventually, I will have them ready for a book.

I promise you this is not a social club. It will not be that. This is a training center. My job is to develop you, to train you, to grow you up, and to equip you so that you will mature to look like Jesus. That means we are going to have to do things differently because most churches I have been around didn't train people to look like Jesus.

We are not going to do things the way other churches have done them. We are going to do things according to the Bible. We are going to teach you things that will help grow you up to look like Jesus.

Look at Jude verse 20. We are talking about being a Spirit-filled person.

> 20 But ye, beloved, building up yourselves on your most holy faith, praying in the Holy Ghost,

"But you, beloved..." The Bible says we are accepted in the beloved because of Jesus, so when he says, "You beloved," he is talking about you. "But you, beloved, building up yourselves..."

Notice, he didn't say, "Wait until the Lord builds you up." Paul didn't tell Timothy, "Timothy wait until the Lord stirs you." He didn't say that. He said, "Timothy, you stir up the gift that is in you. You do it."

In Jude verse 20, he said here, "But you, beloved, building up yourselves." Notice "yourselves." It doesn't say "wait for someone else to build you up." "Well, you know I am just not built up." Well, that's your fault. It is nobody's fault but your own. If you have access to a Bible, it is your fault.

You have to remember what Paul said in Philippians 4:19:

> 19 But my God shall supply all your need according to His riches in glory by Christ Jesus.

God supplies your needs. He supplies everything you need. He supplies the answer to that need. You have been blessed with every spiritual blessing in heavenly places: that is past tense; that is the way it is; therefore, you are supplied. Your problem is not that you don't have what you need. Your problem is that you don't know how to use what you have.

The purpose of the Five-Fold Ministry is not to give you something. You aren't supposed to come here to get an impartation from me and to have me put an anointing on you. That is not the purpose of the Five-Fold Ministry. The purpose of the Five-Fold Ministry is to equip you. God supplies you; I equip you. God gives you the tools; I teach you how to use them. God supplies; I equip. *To be equipped* means *you have the tools*, but now you have to know how to use them.

It is not enough to bring a person in off the street as a soldier, throw him a rifle, and say, "Here, go and be a soldier." No, there has to be a drill sergeant somewhere who says, "Get up. Get down. Do a pushup. Do this thing." There has to be a drill sergeant somewhere to get you into shape with what you have and to teach you how to use the weapons you have been given.

It is up to the Kingdom of God, the government, to supply the weapons you need, and He has done that. It is up to the Five-Fold Ministry, the training core, to teach you how to use the weapons which He has given you. I am not here to give you something. I am here to reveal to you what you have and to teach you how to use it.

Jude verse 20 said, "Building up yourselves, beloved, on your most holy faith…" Then he told you how to build yourself up: "Praying in the Holy Ghost." That is a direct reference to praying in tongues, praying in the Holy Ghost.

He said in 1 Corinthians 14:15:

> 15 What is it then? I will pray with the spirit, and I will pray with the understanding also: I will sing with the spirit, and I will sing with the understanding also.

"What is it then? I will pray with the spirit, and I will pray with the understanding." It is the Spirit of God, praying through your spirit. You pray in other tongues and that builds you up in your most holy faith.

That builds up your faith, but you can be like a battery with faith stored. Kenneth Hagin used to say, "You may have all of the faith in the world. That may be your problem." At some point, having all the faith in the world doesn't do you any good. At some point, you have to release it.

There comes a point where you can build yourself up in your most holy faith, praying in other tongues, which charges you up, but you're going to have to release it. Usually when you release it, it's not released in tongues. It's brought in, built up, charged up like a dynamo in tongues that you can use anytime, anywhere, at your will.

Paul said, "I will pray with my spirit." That is up to you to do that part. He said, "I thank my God, I speak with tongues more than you all." He says, "I do that." It is up to you, therefore, to do that.

Now as you build up in the Spirit by praying in other tongues, at some point you are going to have to release it. Usually, when you release it, it is not released in tongues. You release it in your known language, and you release that power out through words that you understand: usually they are in terms of "be healed," or "be free." It would be something along those lines.

We looked at Jesus. We saw the results of Jesus' being Spirit filled. He walked around and anybody that touched Him got healed or got whatever else they needed from Him. It was because He had it within Him, and people could draw it out of Him even without His permission.

Then we looked at the Apostle Paul. He was Spirit filled. He talked about how to be Spirit filled and how to remain Spirit filled. He gave credit to praying in other tongues. We saw it also in Jude.

In Acts 19:11, we are going to look at the effects of being Spirit filled.

> 11 And God wrought special miracles by the hands of Paul:

Why would they call it "special miracles?" Well, because it was unusual. Why did He do that through Paul? Paul said, "I thank my God, I speak with tongues more than you all." Do you think there might be some correlation? In other words, it is not that God said, "Paul, you are special; do this." Paul said, "I am doing this," and because of that, he rose to where God said, "Oh, I see you." Do you see the difference there? It was not a matter of God dumping something on Paul. Paul spoke in tongues, charged up, and worked, and God worked miracles through him.

"God wrought special miracles by the hands of Paul."

Acts 19:12 tells us about some of them:

> 12 So that from his body were brought unto the sick handkerchiefs or aprons, and the diseases departed from them, and the evil spirits went out of them.

Paul had aprons; he had handkerchiefs. People would come and say, "I have a sick loved one. I have a person who is demon possessed who is a loved one. Can you help?" Notice what Paul did. He said, "Yes. Here, take this handkerchief," or "Here, take this apron." He passed these things out, and they took them back to the sick. The handkerchief or apron was placed on or near the person and it caused the sickness to leave. It caused demons to leave.

If someone says, "I do not know how to cast out a demon." Don't worry about it. Just take a handkerchief, and give it to them. Give it to a loved one. These are handkerchiefs, not prayer cloths. There is no mention of prayer, so they are not prayer cloths. They are spiritual batteries. Get this: they were taken off of Paul's body.

I am trying to stretch you. I am trying to break you out of religious mindsets. What if Jesus went into a department store and saw a robe and said, "Oh, I like this robe. I think I will try that one on." In a dressing room, He would take His robe off, and hang it on the hook. He would take the new robe, put it on, and say, "Yes, I like this." He would walk out and ask, "Can I wear this out? I will pay for it, but can I wear it out? I don't want the old robe anymore. I want the new one."

What would happen to a sick person if he or she walked into that dressing room and picked up that robe? He or she would be healed. Why? It would be the same thing that happened with Paul. All Paul did was take a handkerchief, or an apron, or a shirt off, give it to them, and say, "Here, take this." They took it, and they put it near the sick person, and the Spirit of God, the Spirit of life dwelling in Paul repelled sickness and disease. Why? Life and death are opposite.

Have you ever tried to put two magnets together? On one side they stick. You go to the other side and you can't make them touch. That is exactly the way it is between life and death. Life and death can't touch. Because of the Spirit of life in you, emanating from you, coming forth out of you, people ought to be able to touch your clothes and get healed.

I have several examples I want to give to you:

Number 1: In South Africa, John G. Lake and a preaching partner of his were really tired; they were looking for a place to rest. They were going over this mountaintop and saw this little village and said, "Let us go down and get something to eat and drink, and we will relax a little while."

They went down, and the people heard and said, "John G. Lake and his partner are here. Quickly, get everybody who is sick together!" Within a matter of minutes, hundreds of people started pouring in.

While they were there, they said, "We are not going to get any rest here." They were trying to take a break, but they said, "We can't leave these people sick." They couldn't say no, so they went out to the middle of the village to this post that was used to make sacrifices. (It was the thing they used to tie the animal to when they were preparing to have a feast.)

John Lake said, "Here is what we will do." He went out and put his hand on this post. He purposely, consciously, released the Spirit of God. He stepped back and said, "All right, we are going to leave because we need rest, but anybody who comes and touches this post will get healed." Then they left. Reports went out about that and for the next several weeks, people were lined up from all over the area. They said there were reports that as many as 70,000 people walked by and touched that post and were healed.

People say, "I just don't believe you can leave something like that." Really? Have any of you heard of a team called CSI? You put your hand on something, and they can tell if you were there or not. Why? You leave DNA. Well, you have the divine nature of God in you. You have "Divine Nature Attributes." The DNA of God is in you, and wherever you lay your hand, the Spirit stays on whatever you touch.

There is a chemical called "luminol" that is used to spray an area to detect the presence of blood. They can tell if there is blood when a black light is shined onto that spot, and it lights up a certain color. Well, I can tell you, "If the Spirit of God lives in you, wherever you put your hand and then remove it, the Spirit of God and the DNA of God in you has been placed upon that thing." I want you to understand what you have in you. You have the Spirit of the living God in you. You are a Spirit filled person, and because of that, you have something that emanates from you.

Number 2: Years ago we were helping to start an Assembly of God church up in Sherman, Texas. It was a little storefront church, and we went in to put up the chairs. That night we were going to institute the board of elders. I got there a little early and went around and started laying hands on the chairs and praying. The elders were going to be there, but I didn't know who was going to be sitting in which chair. I just knew that they were the chairs for the elders

There were seven chairs across the front. I started laying hands and praying, "God the person that sits in this chair, by Your Spirit, release Your Spirit into them. Let them be fully, faithful men of God that are going to lead this congregation." I did that with every chair.

That night we went into the service, and when we called the elders up, they came and sat down. I wasn't one of the elders in that church; I was just one of the guys who went there and was helping out. We had these seven people sitting down in those chairs. Within five minutes of their sitting, one by one, they fell out of their chairs onto the floor and started praying. We did not even get to have a service the way we had planned, but it went the way God had planned.

These men started praying, repenting, and confessing sins. This was the most unusual induction service I had ever seen at a church service. While they were confessing, we were wondering if they should really be elders or not. We weren't sure until they were done, but by that time, they were clean. It was just the laying on of hands.

I can give you other stories of situations like that.

Number 3: We took a cloth to a woman who was up in Springfield, Missouri. She had been diagnosed with cancer. We gave her the cloth; she wore it; and she was totally healed of cancer. Then she started passing it to her friends. It was not meant for them. I did not pray for them. I did not even pray for her, technically. I just laid my hands on the cloth and commanded, "Life," into this cloth and said, "Wherever this cloth goes, sickness will depart and demons will leave." Then we gave it to her. She was healed; she started passing it to her friends. She had a cancer support group. One by one, all of her friends who wore the cloth got healed.

The last time I saw her, we were sitting at a restaurant in Springfield, Missouri across the street from the Assemblies of God Theological Seminary. She said, "I have this; here is the cloth. I do not know if you want it back or not." I said, "Well, no, I don't need it." She said, "Do I need to send this in and get it recharged?" I said, "I don't know. I'll tell you what: if you ever find out that it quits working, send it back in, and we will send you another one." She was giving it to people we didn't pray for, and it was working. Why? It is the "life."

God is so much bigger than we give Him credit for. He is so much more powerful. He has so much more love. He is so much more willing to do, but it is usually our theological barriers that we put up that keep Him from being who He wants to be.

Number 4: We were in Toms River, New Jersey. I was doing a service there and at the end, a man came to me with a bandana-type handkerchief. He said, "I am going to go and visit my father. He has Alzheimer's. He is in a nursing home. Would you pray over this?" We took it and said, "In the name of Jesus, we command 'life' into this cloth. We command sickness and disease to go, in the name of Jesus."

He, his wife, and their kids went and visited this man's father every Sunday. They put the handkerchief around his neck. This man had total dementia from Alzheimer's. They said that he had never responded at all. While he was sitting there he suddenly started shaking to the point where he was scared. He was in a wheelchair, and he started sliding around in this wheelchair. All of a sudden, he looked up and said, "Jesus! What do You want?" He was looking and saw Jesus, and they were looking trying to see Jesus, too. They said, "We didn't see anything."

He said, "Alright," and he leaned his head forward and then apparently, Jesus touched him. The next thing this man did was look at them, and then he started talking to them. The Alzheimer's was completely gone in less than 30 seconds. Why? Life had gone into him and had driven that out.

Number 5: Years ago I was on the road, and my wife was at home. A lady from Florida called and wanted a cloth for her father who was in a nursing home. My wife was looking for prayer cloths because we had prayed over a bunch of them at one time and left them for people, but she could not find one.

She called me and said, "Where are they?" I said, "I don't know; if you don't find them, then we don't have any." She said, "Okay," so she went to my closet and took out a perfectly good shirt, cut the sleeve off, and sent it in the mail.

When we got the request, it just said, "I need a prayer cloth for my father." That is all that was said; we didn't know any other details. My wife cut off the left sleeve of my shirt and sent it down there. What we did not know at the time was that the reason she wanted a cloth was because her father in the nursing home had a withered left arm. It just happened to be the left arm sleeve of my shirt that my wife had sent to them.

She didn't know she was being led by the Spirit, but the Spirit of God knew and said, "Here. Send that." This woman took this sleeve and put it up on her father's arm. He had on a T-shirt, and she pinned it to his T-shirt and left it on him. She told the nurses that day, "Leave that on him. Do not take it off." They thought she was crazy. (They will think you're crazy if you do things according to the Bible.) She left that day, and the next morning when she walked in, they said, "Your father is waiting for you." When she walked into his room, he looked at her and started waving at her with his left arm.

Again, my wife didn't know it. I didn't pray over my shirt. It had been cleaned since I had worn it, so obviously the anointing can't be washed out. That is something even Tide can't take out.

If you know me, you know I am not super spiritual, wispy, or living off in some weird world. I live in another world, but I am able to talk with you and be normal. I am not different. I am not special. The only thing that makes anybody special is the special One Who lives in them. That is the only part of anybody that is special—it is Jesus. He is the only One Who is special. Amen? That is Who lives in you.

Number 6: A couple of years ago we got some stuffed animals, gathered them up, prayed over them, and then took them down to the Children's Medical Center. Generally, you cannot just walk in, but if you walk down the halls, the doors are open, the kids are in there, and if you show them the stuffed animal, they are like, "Yeah, bring it in." It is kind of our doorway in, and many times we don't get to pray for them. We had prayed over the animals, and by holding these stuffed animals, the children started getting healings because once you give them a stuffed animal, they don't let go of it. They keep it close.

I am telling you that you have to get God out of the box. He is so much bigger, and He wants to live through you by His Spirit.

I am going to read something to you, which was written by John Lake in 1910. You have to remember that this was while he was in South Africa. It was while he was still developing in his understanding of healing. He had developed quite a bit, but he was still in the stages of understanding.

In 1910 he wrote,

> *"Divine healing for the physical body is a ministry of the Spirit of God in healing virtue. The Spirit of God is governed by divine spiritual law. The healing ministry of Jesus was an impartation of the Holy Spirit through Him to the sick. He laid His hands upon the sick, and the Holy Spirit flowed from Him, entered into them, and they were healed. Jesus instructed believing Christians everywhere forever to practice this law of healing, not in their own strength, but relying on Christ to supply to their souls the needed measure of the Holy Spirit for the healing of the sick one.*

> *"Paul not only laid his hands on the sick, and they were healed, but they brought to him handkerchiefs and aprons that they might touch his body. We ask, "What for?" The answer is plain, that having touched his Holy Spirit-filled person, the same law operated. The handkerchiefs or aprons became filled with the Spirit of God. They were then carried to the sick and laid upon them, and the Spirit of God flowed into the sick and healed them. Demons, likewise, were cast out through this method.*

> *"The Holy Spirit is a tangible substance. He is the nature of God. He is the quality of God's being. He is the effervescence of God's mind. He is the life quality of His nature. It is God taking possession of the body, the soul, and the spirit of man that heals. Greater is He that is in you."*

In 1 John 4:4 it says,

> 4 …greater is He that is in you, than he that is in the world.

John Lake's letter continues:

"Greater is He that is in you than he that is in the world. (1 John 4:4) Greater than any situation. Greater than any condition. Greater than any disease. Greater than any sickness. Greater than any devil. Greater than any demon. Keep your eyes single to His greatness and power, and these things will become strangely weak before you."

Finally, Jesus said in Luke 10:19,

> 19 Behold, I give unto you power to tread on serpents and scorpions, and over all the power of the enemy: and nothing shall by any means hurt you.

"Behold," look, see, take notice, "I give unto you power to tread upon serpents and scorpions, and over all the power of the enemy, and nothing shall by any means hurt you." He said, "I give unto you power."

Peter said, "What I have, I give." A man can only give what he has received. What Peter received he gave out.

Jesus said, "I give you power. It is yours to use for the glory of God."

The great accomplishment of the cross is that it enables and guarantees that man can be a habitation of God through the Spirit. The purpose of the cross was to get the Spirit of God back into you. It wasn't just to save you. By getting the Spirit in you, it got you saved.

John Lake's writing ends with this:

> *"The great danger of Christianity is that we would lose the sense of reverence and awe that was present in the early church concerning the living presence of the Spirit of God within us."*

That is the benefit of being Spirit filled. You have something that you can give. You have something that people can take. That is what is in you. That is who you are.

Being filled with the Spirit of God is so much greater and so much deeper than any of us have probably ever really realized. We have seen glimpses. We get little bursts where we say, "Oh, yeah," but we seldom walk in it. Most of that is due to the cares of the world, the deceitfulness of riches, and getting entangled in the affairs of life. We should trade normal life with this life in the Spirit. This life in the Spirit is so much greater; it is so much deeper.

I am telling you that the way to be built up in the Spirit is by praying in other tongues. It is key. It is essential. Jesus said to do it. He said, "Those that are My disciples, those that believe, will do this. They will speak in new tongues."

It's not something you have to struggle for or strain for. You don't see that in the Book of Acts. What you see in the Book of Acts is, as they were preaching, "He fell upon them." Why? He has to fall upon to get within, but once He gets within, He comes out.

He said that if you ask, He will give you the Holy Spirit. I am not one for pushing and keeping it going and going. No, I believe the times I have experienced different things happening and have seen this, it has been something simple. Usually, what I tell people is this: "Go home. Go somewhere. Turn on some worship music. Begin worshiping, praising God, and thanking Him for it. Ask Him for the Holy Spirit. Ask Him to fill you with the Holy Spirit."

When you ask Him, continue to worship in your known language, and in a little while, just decide: "Okay, I'm not going to sing, and I'm not going to worship in my own language anymore. Father, put words in me that go beyond my understanding." Then open your mouth, and watch what comes out, and go from there because it is God.

It has to be real. It's either God, or it's not. Too many people try to fit in rather than try to get filled in. We do not want you just fitting in. We want the Spirit of God to fill you up, and then once you are filled, it is up to you to stay filled.

Let us pray:

"In the name of Jesus, Father, I thank You first and foremost for absolutely providing through Jesus the salvation of our souls, of our spirit. Father, I thank You that right now in the name of Jesus that those who are hearing, who are not born again will decide to be born again, will decide to make Jesus their Lord, to receive the Spirit of God, to be Spirit filled, to receive that infilling and that flooding over of the Spirit of God.

"In the name of Jesus, Father, I thank You right now that they were healed 2,000 years ago at that whipping post. We say in the name of Jesus right now, be healed! Be whole! Now! We break the power of the enemy that has tried to come against you. We say, no longer! It stops right now, in the name of Jesus. Sickness and disease will go! Demons go! Right now mental ailments go in the name of Jesus. I set you free by the name of Jesus Christ and at that Name, everything that has a name must bow its knees.

"In the name of Jesus, right now, Father, I thank You for the fullness and for the freedom of the Spirit of God Who comes within and creates within us the image and likeness of Jesus Christ. Father, I thank You for that. Even now, by Your Spirit, move throughout Your people. Fill them to overflowing and bring forth the things of the Spirit of God in order for them to draw on the counsel of God. In Jesus' name, right now, be blessed! Be healed! Be whole now, in Jesus' name. So be it. Amen."

DIVERSITIES OF TONGUES

Seminar given by Curry R. Blake

DIFFERENT TONGUES

"Father: We are gathered here together to hear Your word and to better understand Your Will. We thank You that the eyes of our understanding will be enlightened, that we will have a better grasp of Your will, and of how You desire to work through us. Father, we fully expect this to be a beginning of a new and greater level of cooperation even between us, and You, and Your Spirit. Father, we thank You for Your Spirit, that He always abides with us and that these things that we are going to delve into You have provided for us already; it is not something we have to attain but it is something that You have freely given. We thank You, and we bless You. Take pleasure in what takes place here. Father, we thank You, that by the Spirit of God, Your will shall be accomplished through these teachings. In the name of Jesus, Amen."

This seminar follows a series of sermons that I did previously. They are teachings on "Baptism in the Holy Spirit," "Speaking in Other Tongues," "Why Tongues," and "The Benefits of Being Spirit Filled."

I really believe that the Spirit of God directed us to study the "Diversities of Tongues." John Lake said, "Speaking in other tongues, or praying in other tongues, was the making of my ministry." When I read that 30 years ago, it struck me right away that his accomplishments, what he did, the miracles, and even his sermons were dependent on his speaking in other tongues.

People who have read Dr. Lake's sermons say, "You know, I've read lots of other people's messages and their books but there was something different about his sermons." Dr. Lake approached things from a scientific viewpoint. He brought out a lot of details and he explained things very well, but more than anything else, he said, "Truth has a certain ring to it. It has a certain feel. When you hear it, you know it." That is what rings out in Dr. Lake's material.

As many of you know, I've researched and studied Dr. Lake's life and I have talked to people who were around him and trained under him. This was as late as 30 to 35 years ago. I talked to everyone I could find that was still alive. One of the things they always mentioned was how he did his meetings. During his message, he would stop his preaching, speak in other tongues, do his interpretation of it, and then go back to preaching his sermon. In the sermons that were written out, I noticed how the speaking in other tongues and the interpretation flowed together.

It all just came together for me about ten years ago when I was in Grand Junction, Colorado, when I met Simeon Stewart who had been under A.A. Allen's ministry. He was an elderly gentleman and he could hardly walk at that point. He was almost deaf; his eyesight was starting to dim, and there were a lot of things that shouldn't have been there even at his age.

After our meeting was dismissed, we met in a small room. He had the reputation of praying for people as he would meet them. I have a habit and that is when I get around elderly saints, I want them to pray for me. I have had lots of them pray for me.

He sat down in a chair and we prayed for him. God restored his hearing and started restoring his eyesight at that point, and that continued on even after our meeting. During that meeting, I remember getting down on the floor. We actually have picture of that.

He prayed for me and spoke prophecies over me. If you have any of our manuals, you'll see the prophecies that he spoke over us. They all have been transcribed and written out. All of these prophecies are now coming to pass.

Brother Stewart put his hand on me, and he was shaking a little. He began to pray for me. When he prayed, he began speaking in English, then he would go into tongues, and then he would interpret. It just flowed back and forth. It was the most beautiful experience of tongues, interpretation, and prophecy all mixed together.

It was the way it's supposed to be. It wasn't a show; it wasn't in the middle of a meeting. It was just the Spirit of God speaking through a person to another person. As they said about Dr. Lake's material, there was just the ring of truth to it.

Dr. Lake loved to walk and pray. As he walked and prayed, he would pray in other tongues. When he got back home, he would sit down and start to interpret those tongues, and he would write everything down. Those written notes became his sermons that you've read. Tongues and interpretation preceded almost every sermon he ever preached.

I firmly believe that is one of the reasons they have the ring of truth and the impact that they have. Most of them were preached almost 100 years ago yet they still ring as true today as ever. As a matter of fact, just before this meeting, I was reading one of the sermons on the Baptism in the Spirit; it was amazing. It is really easy to be reading his sermons, especially the Baptism in the Spirit, and just get caught up in it. It is so easy to get lost in it. I had to remind myself that I had a meeting to go to.

That is what I expect to happen with this teaching. I expect for us to get caught up in it. There has to be teaching first and then the training. Discipline comes in when you discipline yourself to do what you've been trained to do. That is when the freedom will come. It looks spontaneous but it's not spontaneous; it is structured by the Spirit of God.

This is not supposed to be just me talking to you the whole time, although, I'll be doing a lot of that. At the same time, we'll be putting teaching into practical application. We're going to have sessions where we are actually going to operate in each aspect of the diversities of tongues.

These sessions are going to be more Holy Spirit focused. In most of our meetings, we bring forth what the Spirit of God wants brought out. This time we're focusing on Him, so it's going to be a little different.

The Bible says that we are to exercise ourselves unto godliness. That means that you can purposely choose to do things to build yourself up and take you in the path and the direction you're supposed to go. We're going to be doing exercises in the Spirit. That means that I'm going to have to give you some directions.

This is not going to be a free-for-all. At most Holy Ghost meetings, some people come in with their own purpose in order to stand out; that's where you get the parking lot prophets who catch people coming out and prophesy over them. There's no need for that. I'm not saying that it's always wrong because I've had some good prophecies in parking lots. One was just before I went to Africa in 1997, and that was definitely God, so I can't just tell you not to give prophecies in parking lots.

During these meetings, because of the direction we are going and because of where we want to take you during these meetings, I am going to be giving you certain directions. One of the main things that we have to understand is that the spirit of the prophets is subject to the prophets.

The Holy Spirit, being a gentleman, is not going to try to take over the meeting. I have spent time with Him; this is the direction that He wants to go. There will be times when we will stop, because we will know that the Holy Spirit wants to bring forth tongues and interpretation. We will recognize that, and we will do it.

This is a time of growth, understanding, and moving into things. We are going to take it step by step. I firmly believe, unless you have had a lot of experience in the Holy Spirit and tongues specifically, when we get finished, you are going to be in a new realm that you probably have never been in before. That's what I expect.

When we go into some of these exercises, I want you to follow my directions, which means you will have to watch. You can pray with your eyes open. It says, "Watch and pray," so you can watch and pray.

I will have you praying in other tongues and, as you do, you're going to have to watch me because there's going to be a lot of speaking, and it's going to be loud. I'm not going to be able to speak over your voices. You won't be able to hear me, so you're going to have to watch. I'm going to give you hand signals.

We will all be speaking in other tongues at the same time. I've been in other meetings where people say it's not right because Paul spoke against that. Before anybody tries to say that it is not right, this is not the service he was talking about. When I tell everybody to speak in tongues, it is a not for a sign to unbelievers. It is for you to be edified. There are certain purposes for different types of tongues. The word for that is "*diversities*," which means *differences*.

Because God has put me in charge of the meetings, from a human standpoint, then we are going to take it this way. If I say to do it a certain way, it is going to be the right way to do it. Even if I missed it, if you were obedient to that in faith toward God, God would get it right on your part, even if I missed it. Isn't God awesome?

When we start speaking in other tongues, there will be a point where I will raise my hand palm up, and that means for you to get louder. That means for you to get louder, to get more boisterous, and to get stronger. When I lower my hand, palm down, I will want you to quiet down because I want to say something and I want you to hear it.

If I put my hand up, palm facing you, stop. You say, "I can't stop because it's the Holy Spirit." No, that's not true. You can start it, and you can stop it.

If we are singing in the Spirit, take it into a kind of melody and let it flow out of you. What may happen is that you all start with your own melody, but within a matter of seconds, it will all blend into one melody. Why? That's because it's the same Spirit generating all of it, and He likes harmony.

Let us begin on the first page of the manual where there are some foundational Scriptures. The first Scripture is Isaiah 28:11, which says,

> 11 For with stammering lips and another tongue will he speak to this people.

We saw this fulfilled on the day of Pentecost. Just because it was fulfilled doesn't mean it stopped. It can be fulfilled and also carry on. Today, "stammering lips" usually refer to people who have never moved on past their initial experience of the Baptism of the Spirit with speaking in other tongues.

If you spoke with other tongues once when you were baptized in the Spirit, and you never did it again or you did it sporadically, then you probably still speak with stammering lips. Their word for "stammering" would be more like our word "stuttering." Stammering lips would be like stuttering lips, in the Spirit.

As you begin to speak in other tongues, you will be saying the same syllable, or the same sound, over and over again. Every now and then you get another syllable but it mostly stays in that area. The reason for that is that it is the babyhood state of your spiritual language. What we want for you is to become fluent. We want fluency in the Spirit.

We've taught on healing and spiritual warfare, but nothing comes as close to being the pure heart of God as what we are going to be doing during this seminar. For this to operate correctly, we are talking about an absolute union between you and the Spirit of the Living God. It doesn't get any closer than that.

Go to Acts, chapter 2, which says,

> 4 And they were all filled with the Holy Ghost, and began to speak with other tongues, as the Spirit gave them utterance.

Later, in verses 16-18, it says:

> 16 But this is that which was spoken by the prophet Joel;

You can go back to Joel and see what he said. In the book of Joel, there were a lot more than just tongues that he said were going to take place.

> 17 And it shall come to pass in the last days, saith God, I will pour out of my Spirit upon all flesh: and your sons and your daughters shall prophesy, and your young men shall see visions, and your old men shall dream dreams:
>
> 18 And on my servants and on my handmaidens I will pour out in those days of my Spirit; and they shall prophesy:

In 1 Corinthians, chapter 12, verse 28, it says,

> 28 And God hath set some in the church, first apostles, secondarily prophets, thirdly teachers, after that miracles, then gifts of healings, helps, governments, diversities of tongues.

The word *"diversities"* simply means *differences or different tongues.* There are two categories of tongues. There are differences of tongues and then there are different uses of tongues. On the Day of Pentecost, they were speaking in the tongues of different nations and nationalities. That was a sign to them and it was a fulfillment of Isaiah 28:11.

You also see that there were different purposes for tongues. That's where most people get confused and that's where a lot of the Cessationist teaching comes from. Cessationist teaching says that tongues have passed away, and healing has passed away, and so forth.

They say, "Well, what the Pentecostals, the Charismatics, or tongue-talkers do today is not what's in the Book of Acts. In the Book of Acts, chapter 2, they spoke in the language of people. They spoke in human languages, and they don't do that today." That is their basis for saying that what is done today is not true. They are saying that it's not done in the languages of humans.

In 1 Corinthians 13:1, Paul also said,

1 Though I speak with the tongues of men and of angels, and have not charity, I am become *as* sounding brass, or a tinkling cymbal.

This verse shows that there are also angelic tongues.

Just so we can put this to rest right from the beginning, there are current testimonies of those speaking in tongues that are recognized as a tongue of man. We recently received a message from a sister on a trip to Nicaragua. It reads,

"Hi everyone, I'm sorry it's taken me so long to send this. I'm back at home now from my trip to Nicaragua ... and glad to be a bit further from the equator. It was an awesome trip getting to minister God's Word to people as well as give them food and gifts and to pray for them.

"One thing that I'd like to tell you about is what our awesome God did through me on the very last day before we left to come home. We were at a small church ministering, and I went to pray for the 40 or 50 people who were outside waiting to see the doctor who was with us that day. It was noisy, so I decided to pray for them in my Spirit prayer language. When I was finished going down the line of people, I got onto the bus to get some water. There were two bilingual ladies sitting on the bus. One of them had a headache and agreed to let me pray for her. I said, "I'll pray for you like I did the people outside." When I'd finished, they said that they didn't know I spoke Spanish, to which I replied that I didn't, but had been praying in tongues. They answered that the tongue was beautiful Spanish! When I asked what I'd said, they said it was: "Jesus has healed you. No weapon formed against you shall prosper, and you are a blessed person." As you can imagine, I was extremely thrilled over that!!! I'm thinking the people outside may have heard me in Spanish, too, since they looked at me differently than other groups had when I was praying and most of them said, "Amen!" when I'd stopped talking. God is so good!"

Blessings,
Nancy

I have many other testimonies that I'll be sharing with you of people that did speak in tongues of men, from recent days all the way back to early Pentecostal days and all the way back to the book of Acts. We are going to be looking at these things so that you will know that what we are doing is biblical and the more you understand it, the more fluent you will actually become.

There are several uses for speaking in other tongues and we're going to get into some details. I am trying to give you an introduction or an overview at this point. Our primary focus is to teach you the various ways that you can speak in tongues and the various uses for tongues.

We are not only going to teach it to you, but we will get you to practice it. You will move into the various areas of different types of tongues. At the same time, we are going to come back to the number one, primary reason for tongues for the Christian today which is for personal edification. That is the primary reason we have been given tongues; it is for personal edification.

Jude 20:

> 20 But ye, beloved, building up yourselves on your most holy faith, praying in the Holy Ghost,

Jude 20 tells us that we are to be built up in our most holy faith by praying in the Holy Spirit. That is a reference to tongues. I will show you other Scriptures that are direct references to speaking in tongues, yet many times, they have not been tied together.

One of the byproducts you will get from speaking in other tongues is that it will bring an increase in spiritual dreams, visions, and awareness. I am just telling you this right from the beginning. I'll give you the actual teaching from the Scriptures a little later on.

You can pray in tongues anytime you desire. You can start when you want and you finish when you want. Now, I will admit that once you get started, when you really get going, it's harder to stop, even if you want to.

I know of several stories that illustrate this experience. One involves Dr. Lake. When he was first baptized in the Spirit, he was in the insurance business. As he was trying to deal with men's insurance needs, he would catch himself speaking in other tongues and then interpreting it, telling them the secrets of their lives. They would break down under the conviction of hearing their sins exposed, and they would get right with God. After a period of time, he got to where he couldn't do business any longer because of that. That was in the early 1900s.

I have a picture of myself with Pauline Parham that will be going up on the wall, shortly. She was the daughter in law of Charles Parham who was the founder of the Pentecostal movement in the 1900s. It was at his Bethel Bible School where that outpouring started, about six years before Azusa Street.

The first person who began speaking in other tongues was Agnes Ozman. She was 38 years old and had been a missionary on the field but came back in to go to Parham's Bible School. As she began speaking in other tongues and it started spreading to others, the government sent some people in to investigate her tongues.

Not only did she speak in tongues, she wrote messages. I actually have copies of some things she wrote down. The languages that she was speaking were actually several different dialects of Chinese. Government people that came to investigate were linguists, and said, "Yes, we understand this dialect." Then she would switch to another dialect.

She had no idea about the languages or anything else. The linguists were convinced. For three days she could not speak in anything but her prayer language. She couldn't come out of it and couldn't stop speaking in it.

The same thing happened to a Bible scholar named Finis Dake. When he was baptized in the Spirit, he couldn't stop speaking in other tongues for three days.

A lot of this I'm teaching came out of Dr. Lake's material. Dr. Lake had a woman with him that was his secretary named Emma Louise Wick. In a letter Dr. Lake wrote that his secretary had a knack for getting people to speak in other tongues without being baptized in the Spirit. That is totally contrary to a lot of teaching in the church today. However, there have been many people throughout history that spoke in other tongues and had no other evidence of the Spirit in their lives. In every century, history records outbursts of speaking in other tongues, but it wasn't until 1901 that speaking in tongues was connected with the Baptism of the Spirit.

Charles Finney had the exact same experience. He was already saved, and God was dealing with him. At one point, Finny, a lawyer by profession, walked out of his office, went into the woods and spent some time there with God. Through these groanings that were coming out of him, he said a language started coming out that he could not understand. He was afraid someone was going to hear him, so he stopped it and returned to his law practice. After that, he started having phenomenal success as an evangelist, getting people converted, and saved.

When we talk about the Baptism of the Spirit, I want to make sure that we understand what we're talking about. I am not going to relate the Baptism of the Spirit just to speaking in other tongues. Something that has been lost in the last 75 years or so is that more and more the church is losing a reverence for the Holy Spirit. They're in for the party. They want to have all kinds of manifestations, but usually those manifestations are not accompanied with a reverence for the Holy Spirit.

One of the things we see is people very flippantly saying, "Oh, have you received your Baptism? Do you speak in tongues? Oh, you haven't received your Baptism? Well, okay, you'll get it and then we can move on." It's like we want to move through these things so fast. We have to realize that what we're talking about is an infilling, an overflowing, an immersion, and being saturated with the Spirit of God.

I want to make sure that you realize we're not talking about a doctrine. We're not talking about an experience. We are talking about a union between God and man that takes man to an entirely new level of experience and being.

I'm not saying we have to be quiet. I am saying that we need to reverence the Holy Spirit for who He is and not take Him for granted.

One of the prophecies spoken over us before we started this ministry was that we would be called a "Restorer of the paths to dwell in" and a "Repairer of the breach." Early on, we started emphasizing praying in other tongues, speaking in other tongues, and how that works together with healing the sick.

You don't have to speak in other tongues to heal the sick, but it was meant to be that way. Speaking in tongues and healing the sick are meant to be together. It's not a matter of, "Well, what do I have to have?" It's more like, "What do I get to have?" We should have the fullness of God in our lives.

Looking at these old teachings, seeing what the early Pentecostals did, how they acted, and how they reverenced the Spirit, I began looking around at the church as a whole. I actually found a survey that was done by George Barna around 2002. George Barna was the founder of a market research firm specializing in studying the religious beliefs and behavior of Americans, and the intersection of faith and culture.

Based on Barna's studies and his surveys, he predicted that if things didn't change in the church, by the year 2025, Spirit-filled, Charismatic/tongue-talking Christianity as we know it would cease to exist. He said that even in churches that considered themselves Charismatic or Spirit-filled, roughly 20 percent of the people ever spoke in tongues and that 20 percent included people who had spoken in tongues one time only and that was when they received what they understood to be the Baptism of the Spirit. The other 80 percent had never experienced speaking in other tongues. Essentially, speaking in other tongues was almost dead.

In the early days of our ministry, we preached speaking in tongues, emphasized it, and God brought it out more and more. We've emphasized healing the sick by faith, by trusting God, and by the Word. We've not emphasized gifts. We've not emphasized anointings or any of the typical things that you hear about in Christianity.

I was a firm believer that you should go as far as faith could take you and once you exhausted faith, then you could get whatever help you needed. That was my understanding at the beginning. It worked because it kept us focused purely by faith and didn't lead us off into tangents that some of the groups got into.

Nevertheless, we want to realize the role of the Holy Spirit. I know that Jesus came to save the lost. There's no doubt about that. Yet, part of that saving the lost was a byproduct of Him getting His Spirit back into man. His assignment was to come, make things right, and leave so that He could send His Spirit back to dwell in us.

The Spirit of God in Jesus was limited to the locale where Jesus was. That was never God's intention. John 16:7 says,

> 7 Nevertheless I tell you the truth; It is expedient for you that I go away: for if I go not away, the Comforter will not come unto you; but if I depart, I will send him unto you.

Jesus said, "It is expedient for you that I go away, because if I don't go, I cannot send the Spirit back." It had to be important, because we know how important the saving of the lost of the world was to Him.

He told them, "You stay in Jerusalem and do not go anywhere until you receive the promise of the Father." Obviously, He knew that they would know when they received it. We see that it happened on the Day of Pentecost.

He told them, "Stay. Don't go out. Don't go off preaching. Don't go off healing the sick. Don't go into all the world until you receive power from on high."

In Acts 1:8, He said,

> 8 But ye shall receive power, after that the Holy Ghost is come upon you: and ye shall be witnesses unto me both in Jerusalem, and in all Judaea, and in Samaria, and unto the uttermost part of the earth.

He said, "You shall receive power, after that the Holy Ghost is come upon you." The only reason that Jesus gave for us receiving the Spirit was to be a witness "unto the uttermost part of the earth," meaning to all of the world.

That witness should come out of our lives. There has to be that union, that joining together of God and man.

That witness should come out of your life. There has to be the union; there has to be that joining together. The idea is that it's not just a gift for you to have. It was never meant for you to have and keep it for yourself. The gift was to empower you so that you could win the world.

Turn to page 4 of your manual. I am going to give you some basics, because I want you to get a solid foundation. It's not how much ground we cover; it's how well it gets into you. We want you to get ahold of this. It is better that you know a few things well, rather than to know a whole lot of things halfway. If I can get a few things into you very well, then it will grow from there.

If you look at the ingredients on the back of a soft drink can, the first thing it says is carbonated water. The first thing on there is the most of what's in there. Then, it goes down in decreasing amounts. The most that's in this bottle of all the ingredients is carbonated water. The second ingredient is fructose corn syrup. The third is caramel coloring. Then, there's phosphoric acid. It then says there are natural flavors, and then it tells you how much caffeine is in it.

When you look at the liquid, the first thing that comes to your mind is not water, even though that is the number one ingredient in there. There's more water than there is any other ingredient, but it doesn't look like it. Why? That's because the lesser ingredient, the caramel color, so overwhelms the other that you see more of the caramel color than you do the water. Because of that, you think soft drink instead of water.

The outside of the can is what you can feel, just as you can put your hands on your body and feel body parts. You are a spirit, but you have a body and you live in a soul. The part that is on the outside is the least important in eternity and in spiritual matters. You do need one in order to stay here, but when the body quits working, you leave.

What's really important is what's inside. What you can touch is your body; inside you is your spirit. Your spirit is you.

When the Spirit of God comes into you, He is supposed to permeate and saturate you so much that it's no longer you that live. It is God who is seen in you. He should overwhelm your spirit with His Spirit. It doesn't take a whole lot of Him; just a little bit of Him will overwhelm all of you. Amen?

The soft drink is like it is because it is mixed together. If I had two glasses, I couldn't just pour the part that is water into one glass and pour the rest into the other. When you pour it out, you get whatever is mixed together in the can.

In 1 Corinthians 6:17 it says,

> 17 But he that is joined unto the Lord is one spirit.

That's how united you are with the Spirit of God. "He that is joined to the Spirit is one Spirit with the Lord." Because of that, you are permeated together. That is what John Lake was trying to get across. I'll refer to him a lot during these sessions because, of all the people I've read about and studied their material, he is the most exact in his language concerning the union of the Spirit of God with man.

When the Spirit of God joins with yours, He overwhelms you, but that doesn't make you God. You are in union with Him. That means that He is in union with your spirit. It's not like you have lungs and one lung is you and one lung is the Holy Spirit. It is you who are in union with Him. It is no longer divisible.

Now, can the soft drink be divided? Yes, there's actually a process where you could extract the water out of the mixed liquids and leave just the other liquids. I don't know why you'd want to do that, but there is that process. It would be possible, but the idea is He gave us His Spirit to work in union with us. We should never be in a state where we are separate from the Spirit of God, even in our thoughts.

When John Lake referred to the Baptism of the Spirit, he was referring to sanctification. He agreed with John Wesley's definition of *sanctification*, which means *to have the mind of Christ, all of the mind of Christ.* In other words, the Holy Spirit is so joined with you that you are supposed to be functioning together on this earth. He is the helper that is there to constantly guide you, even when you don't know you're being guided.

It is like the lady whose father was in the nursing home and had the withered left arm. It just so happened that my wife sent the left sleeve. The point of that is that my wife didn't feel led to take the left sleeve. She just did it. Was she led by the Spirit of God? Yes, obviously, so it's not whether you know you're being led or whether you feel led.

So many times we miss God by trying not to miss God. We're so focused on getting it right, that we walk right past people that need our help because we're so focused on, "Oh, I don't want to mess up. Oh, I don't want to do this." Don't get so focused on other things so that you miss God. In reality, you just need to relax.

I can tell you, I am generally a pretty relaxed person. Do I mess up? Yes. You can ask my wife, or you can ask my kids. I mess up. Do I worry about it? No. What does that mean? Does that mean that I live loose, and say, "Hey, if you sin don't worry?" No, I'm not saying that at all. I'm saying that I'm busy after the things of God.

If I make a mistake, I recognize it. I don't go back and say, "God, I probably messed up so much today. I'm so sorry." I don't say, "I messed up here, and I messed up there." I don't go through a list. I don't keep account. Why? Love doesn't keep account of wrongs. Amen? Instead, I walk with God, and if I mess up, and I know it, then I recognize it, and I say, "I'm sorry. Yes, I see that. I'm sorry."

Sometimes you say you're sorry, and you say, "Well, I didn't mean to do that." You know you meant to do it, you just didn't really think it through before you did it. You know that God is there.

I am not one that is so legalistic that I'm always trying to go through every sin and everything that I have done, because with my life, it's more sin by omission rather than by commission. It is more about things I should've done that I didn't do rather than doing things I shouldn't do. I walk through life, and I'm very relaxed.

Now, I'm on a mission, and I'm focused on that mission. I'm always busy. My mind is constantly going. That is the hardest thing. That's why it's hard for me to sleep at night. My mind is going, and it's easier to sit up, take notes, write out sermons, and just study.

I'm so focused on what I'm doing, but at the same time, I'm very relaxed in that I'm not afraid of messing up. Why? I expect God to walk with me, and if I start to mess up, I expect Him to say, "Whoa. Don't do that." It's more like I'm going until He tells me not to, rather than waiting for Him to tell me to go.

I want you to get the understanding of that. Please understand, too, that I have by no means attained. I'm not super spiritual in the sense of the way most people think of super spiritual, where you have to walk around all the time and act a certain way. I am not out into the mystical somewhere. I'm not that way.

I'm practical, and I believe in getting things done. I believe in making plans. Like the Scripture in Proverbs says, "I make my plans, and God directs my steps," so I make my plans.

As I move forward, I expect Him to walk with me. I also know that even if I make a mistake or even if I mess up, He can fix it because He is God. He is bigger than me, and I cannot make a mistake so big that He can't fix it. I had rather make a mistake trying to do the right thing than to be so afraid of making a mistake that I don't do anything, which is the biggest mistake you can ever make. Amen? Our basic motto is: "It's easier to get forgiveness than it is to get permission." That's the way we operate. I don't mean that to be disrespectful, but we move forward with things.

Above everything else we're going to be doing here, I want you to get the part about the Spirit of God, Himself, living in you. With Him living in you, He's going to be talking with you. The primary purpose of you being able to speak in other tongues is for that *edification*, which means *to build up and to strengthen*. We're going to look at these specific Scriptures that talk about it.

The amazing thing about speaking in other tongues is that they magnify or glorify God. Go back and read all of the accounts, around 21 different accounts in the New Testament, and every time they spoke in other tongues it always said that they magnified or glorified God.

Even on the Day of Pentecost, it says, "We hear them speaking in our own language, magnifying God." When you're speaking in other tongues, you are magnifying God. You have to realize it is the Spirit of God coming into your spirit and uniting with your spirit. It is like the example we were using with the soft drink ingredients; it is a merging together until you can't tell one from the other. That is God's plan.

In 1 Corinthians 14:2, Paul said,

> 2 For he that speaketh in an unknown tongue speaketh not unto men, but unto God: for no man understandeth him; howbeit in the spirit he speaketh mysteries.

From that verse we learn that as you speak in other tongues, you are speaking, not to men, but to God. Now, here's the amazing thing: when you speak to God, it is the Spirit of God praying through you. It is your spirit praying.

In 1 Corinthians 14:15, Paul said,

> 15 What is it then? I will pray with the spirit, and I will pray with the understanding also: I will sing with the spirit, and I will sing with the understanding also.

He was saying, "I will pray with my spirit, and I will pray with the understanding." When he said, "...pray with the Spirit," he was referring to speaking in other tongues, but when he said, "...pray with the understanding," he was making the distinction that he was praying in his normal language.

Then he said, "I will pray with the understanding, and I will sing with my spirit." Notice he said, "I will pray with my spirit," so he was doing that.

It is not for you to just open your mouth, and say, "Okay God, do something." No. You begin with the very basic understanding of how you work with God. If you don't lay your hands on the sick, He can't help you by healing them. He's the helper. You're not the helper. You are the doer, and He's the helper. When you lay hands on the sick, He can help and do His part.

It is the same way when speaking in other tongues. When you speak in other tongues, He joins with you, and makes the tongues that you speak out. He forms them into a language. You may be the only person on the earth that speaks that language. It may be a direct language just to Him.

Every good commander has a good system of communication with their forces on the ground. That communication is encrypted so that those around, the enemy, can't understand it. That's the purpose for encrypting it.

I am not saying the devil can or can't understand. I've always heard it said that he doesn't. I don't see anything in the Bible that actually says he doesn't understand it, but he is carnal. I would assume that since the carnal mind can't understand the things of the Spirit of God, I figure he can't either.

As you speak in other tongues, it is the Spirit of God. While you're speaking, the Spirit of God helps you. He joins with you, and He speaks to God. As He is speaking to God, He is magnifying God and He's edifying you. Isn't that amazing? As you give out worship, and praise, and magnify, and glorify God, you actually get stronger. Why? That is because your spirit is being recreated and is made of the same material that His Spirit is made of. When He speaks, then it strengthens you. As we are all different parts of the Body, as one speaks, we all get stronger.

Again, we're going to look at all of these things. The essence of what we're going to be talking about is Him praying through you. As you speak to Him, you're going to get stronger.

Until we had fiber optics, we really didn't have a way of talking about this. With fiber optics, you can have information going both ways at the same time. As you pray to God, strength is coming to you at the same time.

Let me give you another one. If you have your Bible, go with me to Romans chapter 8, verse 26. It says,

> 26 Likewise the Spirit also helpeth our infirmities: for we know not what we should pray for as we ought: but the Spirit itself maketh intercession for us with groanings which cannot be uttered.

"Likewise the Spirit also helpeth our infirmities." The word *"infirmities"* does not necessarily mean sickness or disease. It means *any frailty, any lacking, or anything that is not right*. How does the Spirit help our infirmities? When it says, "For we know not what we should pray for as we ought," He is talking about helping our infirmities in relation to prayer. "Likewise the Spirit also helps our infirmities." In other words, the Spirit also helps our weaknesses, our frailties, and our shortcomings. "For we know not what we should pray for as we ought." We don't know how to pray the way we always should, "but the Spirit itself [Himself] makes intercession for us with groanings which cannot be uttered."

Notice, it is saying that the Spirit makes intercession for us, helping our infirmities, because we don't know how to pray.

Verse 27 says,

> 27 And he that searcheth the hearts knoweth what *is* the mind of the Spirit, because he maketh intercession for the saints according to *the will of* God.

I'm going to give you an answer to a lot of questions that most Christians have asked. They have asked, "God, don't You care? Where are You? Why aren't You helping me? You said You gave me a Helper, why isn't He helping?" When a person goes through problems and situations, the reason they lack the help that they need at times is because they don't pray in tongues. The Helper is there to help a person by praying through them when they are praying in other tongues. If they are not praying in other tongues it limits His ability to help pray the will of God through them and to intercede for them.

When you go through problems and situations you say, "I need help. Why don't my brothers and sisters help me? Why doesn't God just help me?" God is saying, "If you will just open your mouth, I can help you. If you will pray in other tongues, I can help you." How? The Spirit can make intersession for you, and He will pray the right prayer the right way so that God can answer according to His will.

People say, "Well, I just don't know what to do." All they do is talk about what they don't know. The Bible says that when you don't know how to pray for some specific thing or situation, pray in tongues. When you don't know what to do, stop talking about the fact that you don't know what to do and start praying in other tongues, and let the Spirit pray the perfect will of God through you.

By the time we finish these sessions, I will have taught you how to interpret what you've prayed and what the Spirit of God has prayed through you. Then you will know what the perfect will of God is for you as you pray it out. Amen? Then you'll know what's coming.

What we're talking about is a walk in the Spirit, with the Spirit, that should take you to a higher level. If you do what I teach you to do, it will absolutely take control of your life. What I mean by that is that the Holy Spirit is going to come into you.

The Spirit won't come in and manhandle you to make you do something. I'm not saying that at all. I'm saying that the Spirit will consume you. It will get to a point where when people talk to you, whether you like it or not, it will interrupt your communication with God. You are going to stay in communication.

It is like when you are talking to someone on the phone and a person walks up and starts talking to you. You say, "Hang on just a second." You don't hang up the phone. You just deal with the person in front of you and then hurry back to the phone call. That's what is going on in the Spirit when you're praying in other tongues.

That does not mean walking around praying out loud in tongues where people can hear it. You can pray under your breath. You can pray quietly. There are all kinds of ways to pray. If you get this, like I said, it will consume your life, and it will change your life.

Romans 12:2-3 says,

> 2 And be not conformed to this world: but be ye transformed by the renewing of your mind, that ye may prove what *is* that good, and acceptable, and perfect, will of God.

> 3 For I say, through the grace given unto me, to every man that is among you, not to think *of himself* more highly than he ought to think; but to think soberly, according as God hath dealt to every man the measure of faith.

This is amazing, because we know that by the renewing of the mind, your life is transformed according to Romans chapter 12 verses 2 and 3. We're talking about renewing the mind. This is part of the key that we've not walked in. Part of that renewal is praying in the will of God and drawing out the counsel of God by the Spirit. That is done by speaking in other tongues.

It's not the speaking that draws the counsel of God by the Spirit out, because when you pray in tongues, your mind is unfruitful. Your understanding doesn't have to be unfruitful if you interpret it. When you interpret it, then your mind is fruitful as well as your spirit, and as your mind is fruitful, you will start to renew your mind to the Word and to the will of God, by the Spirit of God. You will start to look on the outside the way you look on the inside. Amen? That's where we're going to go.

WHAT YOU NEED TO KNOW ABOUT TONGUES

We are on page 4 of the manual. Let's look at what you need to know about tongues. These are some of the basics.

A. God Prophesied Tongues Through The Prophet Isaiah

Isaiah 28:11,

> 11 For with stammering lips and another tongue will he speak to this people.

We have already read Isaiah 28 verse 11, but notice that God prophesied this through Isaiah and this was approximately 800 years before it happened. This was not just something that somebody came up with. This was God-ordained. He decided it. He prophesied it, and then He brought it to pass.

B. Jesus Stated/Prophesied That His Disciples Would Speak in Tongues

Mark 16:15-17,

> 15 And he said unto them, Go ye into all the world, and preach the gospel to every creature.

> 16 He that believeth and is baptized shall be saved; but he that believeth not shall be damned.

> 17 And these signs shall follow them that believe; In my name shall they cast out devils; they shall speak with new tongues;

Jesus said that His disciples "shall," not get to, not maybe, not if, not some, but "They shall speak with new tongues." This goes much deeper than just this statement. Again, in combating some of the wrong doctrines that have been taught concerning tongues, some would try to quote Paul in 1 Corinthians 12:27-31 to say, "Do all speak with tongues?" In reference to the church, the inference there is, "No, they don't."

Not everyone speaks in tongues. However, in Mark 16:17, Jesus is not talking about giving a message in tongues to the church. He's talking about believers receiving tongues and speaking in other tongues. He's referring specifically to the gift of the Holy Ghost which those who believe on Him should receive, as the Bible says.

This is something every believer is supposed to do. There are denominations that say, "Tongues are for everybody." The other end of the spectrum says, "Tongues are not for today at all." Some groups even go beyond that and say, "If you speak in tongues, it's of the devil." Other denominations say, "Speaking in tongues may be for today, but not for everybody. It's for some people, but not for others. It's a gift and it depends on God's will." That is not what Jesus said. Remember: the words of Jesus are the words of the Supreme Court of the universe. His words are what you're going to be held accountable to. He said that if you believe in Him, you will speak with new tongues.

C. Jesus Commanded His Disciples To Wait Until They Received The Promise of The Father, Which Would Bring Tongues With It

Go back to Acts chapter 1:

> 4 And, being assembled together with *them,* commanded them that they should not depart from Jerusalem, but wait for the promise of the Father, which, *saith he,* ye have heard of me.

> 5 For John truly baptized with water; but ye shall be baptized with the Holy Ghost not many days hence.

By this Scripture we know that what happened on the day of Pentecost was the promise of the Father. We know it was the Baptism of the Holy Spirit, and we do know that it was accompanied with tongues.

> 6 When they therefore were come together, they asked of him, saying, Lord, wilt thou at this time restore again the kingdom to Israel?

> 7 And he said unto them, It is not for you to know the times or the seasons, which the Father hath put in his own power.

You will notice that Jesus was actually speaking and told them, "You're going to be baptized with the Holy Ghost," and then one of the disciples, I'm guessing it was Peter, because he was always quick to speak up. The first thing he said was, "Are you going to restore the Kingdom at this time?"

It could have been James or John; they were really concerned about sitting on His right and left hand. If the Kingdom was going to be restored, that meant that those guys were going to be just sitting pretty good at that point. It could have been any one of those three: Peter, James, or John.

Jesus was talking about the Baptism in the Holy Spirit. He was saying, "All of this is done. I'm getting ready to leave. You're going to get the Baptism in the Holy Spirit." Then one of them asks, "Are You going to restore the Kingdom?" He answered, "No, it's not for you to know the times that the Father has set by His own hand."

It was as if they interrupted Him. He answered the question, and then went right back to what He was talking about. Do you see that? He said, "You're going to be baptized with the Holy Ghost, not many days hence." Then they asked, "Is this the time?" and He said, "No, don't worry about that. Let Me get back to what I was talking about before you interrupted Me." He said, "We're not talking about you being over this land and you getting a physical kingdom." He said, "What you're going to get is miraculous power when the Holy Ghost comes upon you."

In verse 8 He said,

> 8 But ye shall receive power, after that the Holy Ghost is come upon you: and ye shall be witnesses unto me both in Jerusalem, and in all Judaea, and in Samaria, and unto the uttermost part of the earth.

He was saying, "What you are going to get is power when the Holy Ghost comes upon you." When Jesus said, "You will receive *power*," He used the Greek word *dunamis*. It means *miraculous ability;* specifically *miraculous power*.

In Acts 3:16, Peter used the name of Jesus and faith in that Name. Do you realize that this happened after they had received the Baptism of the Spirit?

> 16 And his name through faith in his name hath made this man strong, whom ye see and know: yea, the faith which is by him hath given him this perfect soundness in the presence of you all.

I am currently working on a project of organizing the Bible chronologically, in the order it was written. I am using the definitions for key words. For example, since there are so many different words in the Greek for "*power*," I am taking each word and putting the definition in there instead of the word "*power*." Where it says "You shall receive *power*," I am substituting the definition for "*power*." Then it will read, "You shall receive *miraculous ability* (which is the definition for the word *dunamis*) after that the Holy Ghost has come upon you."

We should focus on the idea of already having received *miraculous ability*. If you have received the promise of the Father, the Baptism of the Spirit with speaking in other tongues then, at the same time that you received that, you also received *miraculous ability*. Since we use the word *"power,"* the *"miraculous ability"* concept gets lost. He says, "You shall be witnesses," and so we think, "Oh, the miraculous ability must be me being able to witness to the man at the bus stop," as opposed to you receiving *miraculous ability*, which means you will be able to produce irrefutable evidence (which is what a witness does) toward Jesus in every nation. Do you see the difference?

By the time we're through with this teaching, you'll actually see the progression. Right now, we're giving you the definitions so you will get the whole meaning behind the words.

Probably the worst hindrance to people really understanding the Bible is familiarity with Scripture. When you're familiar with a Scripture, I can start reading it and your mind will finish it before I finish reading it. Then your mind moves on to something else. Your mind wanders while I am still reading because your mind works faster than I can talk.

What I'm trying to do is give you words that you're not used to so that you actually have to slow down and read every word. When you slow down and read every word, the Scripture has its full impact, as opposed to you being religiously trained to just quote the Scripture and move on to the next thing. I really think this will help. Even in my own studies, it has helped me.

Jesus says in Acts 1:8, "But you shall receive power." It doesn't say, "Maybe." "You shall receive *power*," or *miraculous ability*, "after that the Holy Ghost is come upon you: and you shall be witnesses unto Me both in Jerusalem, and in all Judaea, and in Samaria, and unto the uttermost part of the earth."

D. When The Promise of The Father Came, THEY ALL Spoke With Other Tongues

No exceptions. We need to not resist the Holy Spirit. These 120 believers that were sitting there didn't know what they were going to get. They had no clue what "the promise of the Father" was going to look like. It wasn't like they were sitting there saying, "I can't wait until we get those new tongues. I can't wait until the fire comes down and we see tongues of fire upon each other." They weren't thinking that at all.

All they were thinking is, "We're waiting here until we get something. We're waiting. He said, 'Wait,' so we're waiting." The difference was that they didn't resist Him. The number one way you resist the Holy Ghost is with wrong teaching and wrong doctrine.

In 2 Corinthians 10:4, we are told:

> 4 For the weapons of our warfare *are* not carnal, but mighty through God to the pulling down of strong holds.

Those strongholds are not demons. They're not principalities; they're not spiritual forces in heaven.

> 5 Casting down imaginations, and every high thing that exalteth itself against the knowledge of God, and bringing into captivity every thought to the obedience of Christ;

Notice that it tells us, "Bring into captivity every thought to the obedience of Christ." These strongholds are nothing more than wrong teachings and wrong doctrines that have been built into you.

Actually, if you go back to see what a stronghold is you will see that it is like an old castle. If you look at the old castles or old fortresses, especially in Jesus' day, you will notice that they were built in rings. Every wall was meant to slow down the enemy so that the defenders inside had more time to repel the attackers. As the enemy overran one wall, those inside would retreat behind the next wall, shut the doors, and fight from there. The enemy had to take the castle one wall at a time. There would be a series of walls to take before they ever got to the heart of the city.

That's what Paul was referring to when he said we are to pull down these strongholds. The strongholds are layer upon layer upon layer of wrong teaching and wrong doctrine. Wrong doctrine is not only what we hear in church.

These strongholds are built up by commercials. The biggest stronghold against healing is not devils, but it's every commercial that seems to come on every seven and a half minutes. "The flu season's here and it's going to get you. Get your medicine and get your shot, quickly. Yes, the shot will make you a little sick, but it's better than being a lot sick." Who said I was going to get sick at all? I had rather live in divine health. Amen?

I heard this one commercial the other day that was ridiculous. "Are you having a hard time moving? Are your joints a little sore? If so, then you need this medicine. This medicine can cause bleeding ulcers. It can cause headaches. It can cause sudden death. It can cause heart attacks and strokes—but your joints will move easily." Not if you have sudden death!

When we talk about strongholds, those are some of the things we're talking about. Strongholds resist the Holy Ghost. We build up the layers of strongholds by what we listen to and what we watch. We resist Him, not on purpose, but because we've already built up a resistance to Him.

The first step in submitting to the Holy Ghost is to turn that TV off. Spend that time with Him. Take a walk. Go out, walk around, and pray. Pray in tongues. Walk 30 minutes out and 30 minutes back.

During the 30 minutes out, pray for every person you can think of. Believe me, you'll probably run out of people to pray for before you walk the entire 30 minutes. On the way back, just pray in tongues the whole way. It will charge you up. You'll walk right past your house. You'll be walking so fast that you won't even realize it! The faster you pray in tongues, the faster you walk. That's the way it works.

Notice in Acts chapter 2, verse 4,

> 4 And they were all filled with the Holy Ghost, and began to speak with other tongues, as the Spirit gave them utterance.

They were *all* filled with the Holy Ghost and they *all* began to speak with other tongues. No exceptions.

Look at Acts 2:16-17. We read this earlier.

> 16 But this is that which was spoken by the prophet Joel;

> 17 And it shall come to pass in the last days, saith God, I will pour out of my Spirit upon all flesh: and your sons and your daughters shall prophesy, and your young men shall see visions, and your old men shall dream dreams.

"And it shall come to pass in the last days, saith God, I will pour out of my Spirit upon all flesh: and your sons and your daughters shall prophesy." Notice that prophesying is connected with the pouring out of the Spirit. This is seen many times in the Book of Acts. Acts 21:8-9 tells about Phillip and his daughters. When they were filled with the Spirit they began to prophesy.

That's why I say that when you get filled with the Spirit, speaking in other tongues may not always be the first thing that happens—but it will happen. Remember: tongues with interpretation equal prophecy. It could be that when they prophesied, they really spoke in tongues and interpreted those tongues. They didn't call them tongues and interpretation; instead, they used the word prophesy because the two together equal prophecy. There are a lot of things that we automatically assume but we don't know because we weren't there.

He says in the rest of verse 17, "…and your young men shall see visions, and your old men shall dream dreams." Then the next verse says,

> 18 And on my servants and on my handmaidens I will pour out in those days of my Spirit; and they shall prophesy:

Notice that the Apostle Peter connected the disciples' speaking in tongues with the "prophesying" spoken of by the Prophet Joel. Do you see that? He relates them speaking in tongues with a fulfillment of a Scripture that does not even talk about speaking in tongues, but talks about prophesying. The fact that he connected tongues and prophesying says that these two are, in fact, united.

E. The Promise Is To You And To As Many As God Shall Call

Acts 2:38 says,

> 38 Then Peter said unto them, Repent, and be baptized every one of you in the name of Jesus Christ for the remission of sins, and ye shall receive the gift of the Holy Ghost.

"Then Peter said unto them, 'Repent, and be baptized every one of you in the Name of Jesus Christ for the remission of sins, and you shall…'" In both the English and the Greek, that word, "*shall*," is the strongest word available to indicate that something *will* take place. There is no stronger word that can be used than the word "*shall*." Peter says, "You *shall* receive the gift of the Holy Ghost." Notice that the gift of the Holy Ghost is related to speaking in other tongues and to the Baptism of the Spirit.

Acts 2:39,

39 For the promise is unto you, and to your children, and to all that are afar off, *even* as many as the Lord our God shall call.

"For the promise is unto you." What promise? The promise spoken of here is the promise of the Father that Jesus referred to earlier. "The promise is unto you and to your children, and to all that are afar off, even as many as the Lord our God shall call." Peter is connecting the Baptism of the Spirit, the promise of the Father, and speaking in other tongues to any person that God calls.

Therefore, if somebody says, "Well, it's for some, but not for all," you can reply, "No, if you're called, you shall get the promise, you shall get the fulfillment, you shall get the Baptism of the Spirit, and you shall get to speak in other tongues."

I don't want to scare anyone, but Mark chapter 16 is really strong, especially verses 17 and 18.

17 And these signs shall follow them that believe; In my name shall they cast out devils; they shall speak with new tongues;

18 They shall take up serpents; and if they drink any deadly thing, it shall not hurt them; they shall lay hands on the sick, and they shall recover.

Jesus talked about what His disciples would do. They would cast out devils, take up serpents, drink any deadly thing, speak with new tongues, and lay hands on the sick. He was saying, "Those that believe shall do these things, and these signs shall follow them."

I want to share what I thought when I studied these verses. I'm not putting this on you, so don't get under condemnation. When I read these verses, I thought, "If I'm not doing these things, how do I know I'm saved?" Jesus said that if I was His disciple, if I believed in Him, I would do these things.

Jesus said in John chapter 14 verse 12,

> 12 Verily, verily, I say unto you, He that believeth on me, the works that I do shall he do also; and greater *works* than these shall he do; because I go unto my Father.

Did Jesus do these things? Yes. People say, "Well, Jesus didn't speak in tongues." He also said you would do greater works. Speaking in tongues is one of the greater works you get to do.

Most people don't even think of tongues as one of the greater works. They say, "Well, speaking in tongues is the least gift." The Bible never says that. That's religious teaching. That's just an example of that wrong teaching that has been in the church to the point that it has been said so much that people think it is Scripture rather than actually looking it up and finding out that it doesn't actually say that.

The promise is to you and to as many as the Lord our God has called.

F. GOD HATH SET... Diversities of Tongues in the Church

In 1 Corinthians chapter 12, verse 28 says,

> 28 And God hath set some in the church, first apostles, secondarily prophets, thirdly teachers, after that miracles, then gifts of healings, helps, governments, diversities of tongues.

Let's read that very first section. "And God hath set some in the church." Who has set some in the church? God has set some in the church. Then He gives a list. In the church, He has put apostles, He has put prophets, He has put teachers, He has put miracles, He has put gifts of healings, He has put helps and governments, and He, Himself, has put diversities (differences) of tongues. Where did He put these things? He put them in the church.

Number 1: Is there a God? Yes. Is He still around? Yes.

Number 2: Is there a church? Yes. Is it still around? Yes.

You've got God on one end and the church on the other end. It says, "God has put in the church these things." If God is still here and the church is still here, then apostles, prophets, teachers, miracles, gifts of healings, helps, governments, and *diversities of tongues* are still in the church.

If you go to a church where they don't have apostles, prophets, helps, gifts of healings, and diversities of tongues then leave that dumb, dead thing. This is a word from the Lord, "Leave it." It's not a church. It may be a man-made organization, but it is not a church unless it has what God has put in "the Church."

"I don't like what you are saying," somebody might complain. "I like my cold, dead church." That's why you're cold and dead. Don't be dead. Be alive. Get around live people.

You would be amazed at how many people sneak over here and then they sneak back to their mausoleum on Sunday. One time a man came to Dr. Sumrall and said, "You are stealing my sheep." Dr. Sumrall said, "I've never stolen a sheep in my life, but I have been known to not send them back if they wandered into my fold."

That is the way we look at things. If you want to be around the living, get around the living. If you want to be acceptable to men, you can find that. Lots of churches are acceptable to men. There is only one Church that is acceptable to God, however, and that's the Church that has apostles, prophets, gifts of healings, and diversities of tongues.

One of the things you are going to have to realize is that what you are ashamed of will not work for you. You've got to get bold, you've got to be able to speak out, and you can't do this thing in a corner. "Well, we believe in speaking in tongues, but we don't do it at the Sunday morning service because the mayor comes to our church." He probably needs to hear a message in tongues. He probably needs to hear an interpretation in tongues. You might even reveal the secrets of his heart and his governing might change. Amen?

G. The Apostle Paul Said That His Writings Were the Commandments of God, and He Said NOT TO FORBID Speaking With Tongues

We will go through chapter 14 of 1 Corinthians and comment on it in detail.

> 37 If any man think himself to be a prophet, or spiritual, let him acknowledge that the things that I write unto you are the commandments of the Lord.

> 38 But if any man be ignorant, let him be ignorant.

Paul was blunt. I like Paul. He said, "If you agree with me, you're spiritual. If you don't, you're just stupid. If you're stupid, just stay stupid." I'm just saying what Paul said. I'm just reading what Paul said.

> 39 Wherefore, brethren, covet to prophesy, and forbid not to speak with tongues.

"Wherefore, brethren, covet," or desire earnestly, "to prophesy, and forbid not to speak with tongues." That is pretty clear.

To summarize:

7 Things You Need To Know About Tongues:

1. God prophesied tongues through the Prophet Isaiah.
2. Jesus stated/prophesied that His disciples WOULD speak in tongues.

3. Jesus commanded His disciples to wait until they received the Promise of the Father, which would bring with it – tongues.
4. When the Promise of the Father came, THEY ALL spoke with other tongues.
5. The Promise is to you and to "As many as God shall call."
6. GOD HATH SET... Diversities of tongues in the Church.
7. The Apostle Paul said that his writings were the commandments of God, and he said NOT TO FORBID speaking with tongues.

If you know these seven things you are farther along in real spirituality than most churches are in this country and around the world. To see real spirituality, you almost have to get out of the United States because usually people follow the money. If you follow the money, you can usually find out why they're preaching what they're preaching.

Keep in mind that the two things the devil has fought most in the church are healing and tongues. These are two things that have been promised to us. I think one of the reasons he fights healing is because he wants you to die before you realize the value of tongues. Once you get the value of tongues, he wants you out of here quickly, because once you understand the value of tongues, everything changes.

God has a way to speak vocally, audibly, into any situation where there is a believer who speaks in tongues. Where there is a believer that speaks in tongues, God has the ability to interact with that group and bring out a message. He can then interpret that message and bring it to everybody's understanding. The devil does not want you to speak in tongues.

Speaking in tongues is a gateway gift. Imagine an hourglass. Even though there is an abundance of supply available at the top, it can only be delivered by way of the narrow connecting channel in the middle.

That channel is the gateway. It controls the flow. In spiritual matters, speaking in tongues is that gateway in the middle.

Go to 1 Corinthians, chapter 12.

> 7 But the manifestation of the Spirit is given to every man to profit withal.
>
> 8 For to one is given by the Spirit the word of wisdom; to another the word of knowledge by the same Spirit;

"For to one is given by the Spirit the word of wisdom." *"Word of Wisdom"* is the top one. The next one is the *"Word of knowledge."*

> 9 To another faith by the same Spirit; to another the gifts of healing by the same Spirit;
>
> 10 To another the working of miracles; to another prophecy; to another discerning of spirits; to another divers kinds of tongues; to another the interpretation of tongues.

After *"Word of Knowledge"* we'll put *"Faith."* Then we will put *"Gifts of Healings"* and then *"The Working of Miracles."* After that we'll put *"Prophecy."* Then we'll put *"Discerning of Spirits,"* then *"Divers Kinds of Tongues."* "Divers" actually means "different," as in "different kinds of tongues." The last one is *"The Interpretation if Tongues."*

These are the nine gifts in 1 Corinthians 12, placed in order in an hourglass from top to bottom. Hold on to that image while we look at Ephesians chapter 4.

> 11 And he gave some, apostles; and some, prophets; and some, evangelists; and some, pastors and teachers;

Ephesians chapter 4 says that God has given to the Church what we call the Five-Fold Ministry, which is the ministry of apostles, prophets, evangelists, and pastors, who are also called teachers.

> 12 For the perfecting of the saints, for the work of the ministry, for the edifying of the body of Christ:

> 13 Till we all come in the unity of the faith, and of the knowledge of the Son of God, unto a perfect man, unto the measure of the stature of the fullness of Christ:

Why does the body of Christ need the Five-Fold Ministry? They are to equip the body. For how long are they supposed to equip the body?

They are supposed to equip the body of Christ until it attains the stature of the fullness of Jesus Christ. When the Five-Fold Ministry gets finished with us, we're supposed to look like Jesus.

Let's look back at the hourglass, and let's say it is Jesus. Remember, I said that speaking in tongues is a gateway gift.

Notice how the hourglass is shaped. It's wide at the bottom and then gets narrower, and then it gets wide again. There are more people that operate in tongues and interpretations (at the bottom) than there are that operate in the word of wisdom, or in word of knowledge, or in faith (toward the top). Speaking in tongues is more prevalent, hence the wideness at the bottom.

The center is a gateway. The further up the hourglass it goes up, the narrower it becomes. Thus, speaking in tongues is a gateway gift. The narrowing represents fewer people operating in each gift. Now, I'm not saying that's the way it's supposed to be. I'm saying that's just the way it works; that's the reality of it.

When you get up past the center, it starts to widen again. A Christian would be made up of all of these. Each one of these is a manifestation of the Spirit of God. Does the Spirit of God only want to manifest through a person only one way? No.

Did Jesus operate in all of these? Yes. He operated in all of these. Consequently, if we are going to grow up into the fullness of His stature, then that means we are going to operate in all of these.

If you never needed a word of wisdom, then there would never need to be a manifestation of the Spirit for that, but I don't know anybody that doesn't need a word of wisdom at some time.

This is not a spiritual gifts seminar. However, notice that as you get to word of knowledge, and word of wisdom, fewer believers operate in those gifts.

Usually, what we think of as prophecy is not what we think it is. Prophecy is to comfort, to edify, and to exhort. It is not to tell the future. To tell the future is actually a word of wisdom; it is God's wisdom about something that's going to happen in the future, and how you're supposed to handle it. You have wisdom as an adult that you didn't have as a child. A child will do things not knowing the consequences, but a parent will say, "Don't do that. If you do that, then this is what's going to happen." Children will do it anyway and it ends up exactly the way you predicted it would. Why? That's because you have wisdom. Wisdom is the ability to foresee potential future problems and to take the necessary actions to ensure that they don't happen.

The word of wisdom is not a wise thing that God says. It is the future. It's whenever He predicts the future. He says what's going to happen and why, and then He starts to work it out. That is the word of wisdom.

Do you remember when Samuel anointed Saul? He said, "Today you're going to go by this way and you're going to meet these two men. They're going to have oil and bread, and they're going to have these animals in their arms. Then they're going to give you the loaves of bread. You're going to take the loaves and you're going to go on from there." All of that was a word of wisdom. That was not prophecy.

We may call it prophecy because it is a general term and it does exhort and edify. After all, when Saul got there and it happened as Samuel had predicted, Saul knew it was of God, and it did exhort.

The word of wisdom is a predictive future. You see very few people operating in that.

You start with tongues and interpretation of tongues. As you grow in these, the other gifts will start to manifest more easily because you're already functioning and flowing fluently in the Spirit. These are all of the Spirit manifesting in different ways.

When you get to the middle of the hourglass, it gets narrow because so few people are operating in this, but as we come back up in the hourglass, you see the fruit of the Spirit.

Galatians chapter 5, starting in verse 22 says,

> 22 But the fruit of the Spirit is love, joy, peace, longsuffering, gentleness, goodness, faith,
>
> 23 Meekness, temperance: against such there is no law.

We have the gifts of the Spirit, and we have the fruit of the Spirit.

When I did the Apostolic Alignment teaching, I showed from the Bible how an apostle teaches you. You don't become an apostle because you sit under an apostle but you can acquire an Apostolic DNA, so to speak, which usually has strong governmental qualities and is very mission orientated. I don't mean missions like in foreign countries, although that often happens, but more goal oriented missions in order to take ground for the Kingdom.

It is the strong spirit of being able to govern and say, "This is right. That's not right. Do this. Don't do that. We don't allow this to happen in our city. We decree this to happen in our city." Then you start governing behind the scenes in the spirit. What goes on in the spirit you will see in the natural. If you don't like the way things are going in the natural, it's because the church hasn't formed them in the spirit.

If you want things to change, change them in the spirit, and then you will see them in the physical. If we want things to change, that means we've got to spend time forming them in the spirit.

Paul said, in Galatians 4:19,

> 19 My little children, of whom I travail in birth again until Christ be formed in you,

"I travail in birth again for you, until Christ be formed in you." The reason we don't see things happening in the world the way we want is because the church is not travailing like it used to. We are not seeing that travailing. I'm going to prove to you that men are supposed to travail, too. Amen? It's not just for women. Men are supposed to do it. It's even in the Old Testament. The prophet says, "I saw the men with their hands upon their loins and travailing like women giving birth."

Whenever the Church gets back to functioning in the Spirit of God, in the "groanings that can't be uttered," in the travailings and weepings, and they're not ashamed of it, and they start to function in the flow of God, then we're going to see things happen in a day. First, we have to move into these things and start praying.

Here's the big thing. You can't just listen to this teaching and say, "I'm glad I know that now." You've got to start doing it. You've got to move into this thing. That is one of the reasons we are going to start practicing. I'm going to take you through these things and you're going to be doing all of them.

You are not going to be working it up, and I am not going to be working it up. I refuse; I do not believe in it. We are emotional beings and God blesses that and God can use that. However, this is not a working up—it's a settling down, like Dr. Lake said. That settling down is that you have to dig into the Spirit and bring out the counsel of

God. The way you do this, oftentimes, is through travailing and weeping, and you cannot be ashamed of it.

There was a time when I couldn't cry. It wasn't manly and I wouldn't do it. Yet, I reached a point where I said, "I will do whatever I have to do to get this person free."

If you look on the wall of the hallway coming into the sanctuary, there are four pictures hanging there. They show a man that was brought to one of our meetings in Africa. He was dying of AIDS and everyone thought he would die before they could get him to the meeting. When I got to him, there was no sign of life. I'm not saying he was dead; I'm just saying you couldn't tell either way. I knelt down by him. I was going to pray. I had every intention of praying but, when I put my hands on him, I started crying.

After crying for a few seconds, I got up, nudged him with my foot, and said, "Get up! Take up your bed and walk!" His mother was standing there and she pulled the blanket off of him. Then we saw the first sign of life. He turned over, sat up, got up, turned around, and walked off.

He was skin and bones when he arrived. You can see the pictures. Before he left the meeting that night, he had gained 20 pounds. You might ask, "How did he do that?" I do not know. I guess that would be one of those signs and wonders. I simply don't know. Gaining weight is not something most people ask me to pray for. For most people, it's the other way around.

Do you grasp this now? Do you see what I'm saying? As you move up the hourglass of gifts, it gets narrower and narrower because fewer and fewer people function in those gifts. Why? The answer is because so few people really function fluently in tongues. People speak in tongues once, seeing it as a requirement of the Baptism of Holy Spirit, rather than functioning in it fluently.

Know this: the language of heaven is "knowing."

Every testimony you hear of somebody going to heaven, every time they communicated with somebody, they didn't talk to them. They just "knew." Immediately, they "knew" back and forth with each other, like they could read each other's minds.

Jesus said He perceived in Himself what they were thinking. Why? He "knew." He was functioning in the fullness of the Spirit. Why? He was a full-grown Son of God. He knew what they thought. Jesus didn't have to communicate through words, but He did, primarily so we could have them written down.

The language of heaven is "knowing," but the communication of the Spirit is tongues. Whenever you want to communicate in the Spirit, you speak in tongues, but in Heaven, you automatically know, so there's no need to have a method of communication.

Did you know that it has been scientifically proven that when you pray in tongues, the part of your brain that has to do with speech and language doesn't work? People say, "Oh you're just making up gibberish when you speak in tongues." That is impossible. Do you know why? Dr. Lake spoke about how scientists put electrodes on people that were praying in tongues and it showed that the part of the brain that functions when people pray or speak was NOT operating.

If a person was making up gibberish, the part of the brain that has to do with words would function because they would have to think to make the sound.

When scientists test Spirit filled people praying in tongues, the part of the brain that has to do with forming words actually shuts down, and another part of the brain that is totally separate begins to function. This other part of the brain is what is called the Limbic system. The Limbic system is a part of the brain that controls our emotions, behavior, and motivations. It is connected to the very nature of who we are, and it has nothing to do with words or the action of communicating.

Science can prove the existence of tongues. Studies have proven that when recordings were made of people speaking in tongues it showed that what was spoken had all of the elements of a language. It had syntax; it had sentence structure, words, and sentences.

When someone speaks in tongues it flows like a language flows. Scientists don't know what the language is saying, but they can see the patterns of structure in it. They admit what's going on, but they cannot understand it. They can't explain where it's coming from.

When they did this research, the scientists proved that when a person is speaking in other tongues, or is praying in other tongues, that the normal brain section that handles language is not functioning in such a way as to make it happen. Rather, it is responding to being acted upon by an outside source. It's the same thing that happens when someone comes up behind you and pushes you and it takes you by surprise. Your brain registers an outside source acting upon you, causing you to be surprised. The part of your brain that registers this action is the same part that registers when you speak in other tongues. Your brain recognizes that there is an outside force working upon you. The scientists don't know what it is, but we do. This is scientific fact.

Some people say, "You believe in tongues? Well, that's just foolishness. You ought to move into the 21st Century." God is way past the 21st Century. Science is just now starting to catch up and is finally using language to explain some things about the Bible. That language is called Quantum Physics.

In 1 Corinthians 1:27, it says,

> 27 But God hath chosen the foolish things of the world to confound the wise; and God hath chosen the weak things of the world to confound the things which are mighty;

God has always chosen the foolish things to confound the wise. He always started something among the Pentecostals, on the other side of the tracks, in the worst buildings, in the worst part of town, where there was no money, where the socially accepted people wouldn't dare go. That's where God always seems to show up first. Isn't that amazing? It is just like Azusa Street. He's still doing the same thing today.

I firmly believe that the number one reason why God chose tongues is because it just confounds the wise. It seems that the more educated you are, the harder it is for you to receive. I think God does that on purpose. I believe He says, "I'm going to totally confound you and just when you finally understand that it's me confounding you, you will have to become like a little child and realize that all that you've learned doesn't mean a thing."

You can take one word by the Spirit, and you can far out-stretch what medical science or any other science group can come up with.

We have had prophetic words spoken over us that are starting to come true. We've even had some that have said that in the near future, those in the medical profession will come to us and ask, "How are you getting people with this disease healed?" God will answer them by His Spirit, and He will give us the medical terminology to explain it to the doctors. They will then wonder, "Why didn't we think of that?" Then they'll be able to go back and reproduce it in the science field.

People say, "Why would God do that?" Why *wouldn't* He? If there's not a Spirit-filled Christian in the medical profession doing it, He'll give it to science so that they can do it naturally, because God wants to help people.

Most religious Christians would rather that people stay sick, and say, "They didn't come to God," than to show them the goodness of God, which should draw them to repentance. God wants to help people.

If you have all of the fruit of the Spirit operating, then you have the DNA of the Five-Fold Ministry. DNA is the scientific term for what you are made up of.

In 2 Peter 1:4 it says,

> 4 Whereby are given unto us exceeding great and precious promises: that by these ye might be partakers of the divine nature, having escaped the corruption that is in the world through lust.

It says, "We are partakers of His divine nature." When you become partakers of His divine nature, you take on His attributes. In our terminology, the Five-Fold Ministry's DNA is Divine Nature Attributes. The attributes of God's Divine Nature are brought about through the Five-Fold Ministry. Then, you have the work of the Spirit and the fruit of the Spirit.

People tend to want the gifts, but they don't want the fruit. You have to remember that gifts are given instantly, but fruit is grown and takes time. All the time you're working on acquiring gifts, be working on developing fruits, too. In that way, you'll have the fruit to carry the gift.

Every failure in ministry is because somebody had more gifts than they had fruit. They ended up suffering because of it.

Usually what happens is that somebody will come into the church, get born again, Spirit-filled, and excited about God. They will start operating in a gift. As he begins operating in this gift, all of a sudden, the church says, "Oh, you've got a gift. Come up and speak." What he says could be totally wrong, but because he has a gift, people think he must be right. They say, "Well, look at the healings," yet there's no fruit.

If you're going to go by one or the other, go by fruit, not by the gifts. If you go by fruit, then you will see the character of God in that person. The gifts will have something to be built upon.

You have the gifts, you have the fruit, and you have the Five-Fold DNA. Would you say that Jesus had the fruit of the Spirit? Would you say He had the DNA of the Five-Fold Ministry? Was He a good teacher? They called Him "Teacher," or "Rabbi" all the time. Was He a good pastor? Was He a good shepherd? He said He was the "Good Shepherd." Was He an evangelist? Yes. He went about preaching the Gospel.

Deuteronomy 18:15 foretold the following:

18 The LORD thy God will raise up unto thee a Prophet from the midst of thee, of thy brethren, like unto me; unto him ye shall hearken;

Acts 3:22 refers back to Deuteronomy saying,

22 For Moses truly said unto the fathers, A prophet shall the Lord your God raise up unto you of your brethren, like unto me; him shall ye hear in all things whatsoever he shall say unto you.

Was Jesus a prophet? Moses said, "God will raise up a prophet, like unto myself, but greater." Jesus was that prophet. Was He an apostle? He was the first Apostle.

Jesus had all of the Five-Fold Ministry within Himself. He had the fruit and He had the gifts of the Spirit, and He functioned in all aspects of the Five-Fold Ministry.

Ephesians 4:13 says,

13 Till we all come in the unity of the faith, and of the knowledge of the Son of God, unto a perfect man, unto the measure of the stature of the fulness of Christ:

Romans 8:19 says,

19 For the earnest expectation of the creature waiteth for the manifestation of the sons of God.

When you have all of these operating together, you are an Ephesians chapter 4, full-grown and Romans chapter 8, fully-manifested son of God walking on the earth. At that point, you will take command of things on the earth because the earth is groaning, waiting for the manifestation of the sons of God to step up and say, "No, you don't.

I heard a report recently about the West Nile virus. They said that out of the 131 deaths in the United States, the majority took place in Texas. They're saying that Dallas is ground zero. First of all, they don't know what they're talking about. That's a lie from the devil, and they're just repeating it.

We are going to place a board on the wall that says, "Knees That Must Bow," at the top. Then, we're going to write the name of each disease on a piece of paper affixed with double-sided sticky tape. We're using tape so we can take the paper off the board once the disease has bowed its knee. We're not going to paint the names on there because then they would be permanent and they're not going to be permanent; they've got to bow their knee.

We are going to put up diseases like cancer and the West Nile virus. We're going to put up hurricanes and various other disasters going on in the world. Then we're going to start going after these things, whether they are weather related or disease related.

We've had tremendous success with Amber Alerts. When Amber Alerts go out and we hear about them, we immediately start saying, "This child will be found. This child will be found unharmed. This child will be found. The person who took this child will be found." We go after each alert we hear about and, so far, every time, the child has been found unharmed.

We're going to create a kind of hotline. When people hear about something, they can call and have it put on the board. Then, we'll assemble a team of Prayer Warriors to go after it.

We're going to start fulfilling the governmental aspect of the Kingdom of God, on this earth so that we can start seeing the fulfillment of the Five-Fold Ministry throughout the earth. We're going to raise up sons and daughters of the most High God so that they will accomplish Romans chapter 8, verse 21,

> 21 Because the creature itself also shall be delivered from the bondage of corruption into the glorious liberty of the children of God.

Therefore, the whole earth that is groaning, waiting for the manifestation of the sons, can quit groaning because it will be delivered into "the glorious liberty of the children of God." That's where we're going.

To get there, we have to pray in tongues. It is not as if you are running down a check list. It's not like you are going to say, "Okay, I've interpreted. Check! Now, I've spoken with tongues. Check! I've done some discerning. Check! Prophecy? Well, I haven't done that. No check for that box."

It's not checking one off and thinking, "Okay, I'm done with that." No, it's this one plus the next one, so that you function in each one. When you function in one, you will continue to function in it as you move to the next one and then function in that.

Have any of you heard of a guy named Bill Hamon? We have ministered with him before. He is one of the first people I've come across to actually function correctly in the gift of prophecy within the Body. His functioning is real, not weird, wispy, or hyped up.

He invited me to teach the Divine Healing Technician Training at his school, and they liked it because the way we teach healing is the way they teach prophecy. How we activate people in healing, they activate people in prophecy. I noticed that the same principles are used for both.

In January, February, and March of next year, we're going to be doing the Dominion Bible Institute here at our sanctuary. One of the courses is going to be "Spiritual Gifts."

I am absolutely convinced that the same principles that operate in healing and prophecy also operate in tongues and in the working of miracles. Therefore, in this course, we're going to activate each one of these gifts in your life. By the time you finish the course, you will be functioning in each of these gifts fluently and not haphazardly. You will function in each gift, normally.

The beauty of this is that you're going to be like Jesus. You're going to be normal. Kids are going to love you; they're going to run to you. They're not going to be afraid of you. They're not going to run from you in fear because you're acting weird.

You're going to be able to function in these things and move in them. We are going to take you through them so that you will be fluent.

You will be able to talk about it and not get puffed up. First the devil says, "You can't do it. Who do you think you are?" Then, as soon as you do it, he gets behind you and says, "Ooh, you're somebody." We are going to take care of that right in the beginning. We're going to make sure you know who you are and who you are not.

We're going to grow people up to have the gifts, the fruit, and the DNA so that they can be like Jesus.

I have told you what you need to know about tongues. Let me show you what the Bible says specifically about tongues.

WHAT THE BIBLE SAYS ABOUT TONGUES

A. It's A Sign for the Unbeliever

Mark 16:15-18,

> 15 And he said unto them, Go ye into all the world, and preach the gospel to every creature.
>
> 16 He that believeth and is baptized shall be saved; but he that believeth not shall be damned.
>
> 17 And these signs shall follow them that believe; In my name shall they cast out devils; they shall speak with new tongues;
>
> 18 They shall take up serpents; and if they drink any deadly thing, it shall not hurt them; they shall lay hands on the sick, and they shall recover.

First, the Bible says that speaking in tongues is a sign. Mark 16 says, "In my name these signs shall follow them that believe. In my name they'll cast out devils; they shall speak with new tongues."

Speaking in tongues is a sign. Signs are for unbelievers, not for believers. The Bible is very clear that speaking in tongues is not a sign for believers, but a sign for unbelievers.

My biggest problem with the statement, "The Baptism of the Holy Spirit, with the evidence of speaking in tongues," is that the implication is directed toward Christians being able to have evidence. Thus, tongues become a sign for Christians, and I don't believe that. I'm not saying that you don't get tongues with the Baptism. I just don't like the terminology that tongues are the evidence.

Hebrews 11:1-3,

> 1 Now faith is the substance of things hoped for, the evidence of things not seen.

> 2 For by it the elders obtained a good report.

> 3 Through faith we understand that the worlds were framed by the word of God, so that things which are seen were not made of things which do appear.

Faith doesn't require evidence. Faith *is* the evidence of what the Bible says. Correcting terminology is the first step toward seeing the real picture.

B. It is Direct Communication Between You and God

In 1 Corinthians 14:2 it says,

> 2 For he that speaketh in an *unknown* tongue speaketh not unto men, but unto God: for no man understandeth *him;* howbeit in the spirit he speaketh mysteries.

C. It Confounds the Wise

In 1 Corinthians 14:23 it says,

> 23 If therefore the whole church be come together into one place, and all speak with tongues, and there come in *those that are* unlearned, or unbelievers, will they not say that ye are mad?

That is how speaking in tongues confounds the wise. As I have said before, "I think that's one of the reasons God chose it. I think it gives Him a good laugh."

D. It Requires Faith

Mark 16:17 says,

> 17 And these signs shall follow them that believe; In my name shall they cast out devils; they shall speak with new tongues;

Speaking in tongues requires faith. Do you realize that every time you speak in tongues, you are stepping out in faith? Stepping out in faith is stepping into the unknown. If you don't exercise faith when speaking in tongues, it would be a sin, because what is not of faith is a sin.

You exercise faith when you speak in tongues if you've been raised in a denomination that says that speaking in tongues is not for today. Every time you speak in other tongues, you are stepping out in faith that you believe the Word of God over what some man told you.

The following is one of the core things that you will learn during this seminar.

E. It is a Rest and a Refreshing

Isaiah 28:9-12 says,

> 9 Whom shall he teach knowledge? and whom shall he make to understand doctrine? *them that are* weaned from the milk, and drawn from the breasts.

10 For precept *must be* upon precept, precept upon precept; line upon line, line upon line; here a little, *and* there a little:

11 For with stammering lips and another tongue will he speak to this people.

12 To whom he said, This *is* the rest *wherewith* ye may cause the weary to rest; and this *is* the refreshing: yet they would not hear.

"Whom shall He teach knowledge? and whom shall He make to understand doctrine?" Notice that He is talking about understanding doctrine. *"Them that are* weaned from the milk, and drawn from the breasts" are the ones that understand doctrine.

That word *precept* in verse 10 is the Hebrew word which means *commandment or injunction.* "For precept *must be* upon precept, precept upon precept; line upon line, line upon line; here a little, *and* there a little. For with stammering lips and another tongue will he speak to this people." We have already read this part, but I am trying to put it into context for you.

If you go back and read Isaiah 28, this is almost a rebuke. It's as if he says, "Who is going to understand this? Who is he going to teach it to?"

"For with stammering lips and another tongue will he speak to this people." Now, listen carefully: "To whom he said, 'This *is* the rest *wherewith* you may cause the weary to rest; and this *is* the refreshing,' yet they would not hear." In other words, he was saying, "I'm trying to teach you. I'm trying to give you this precept upon precept, line upon line. I'm trying to give it to you 'with stammering lips' and 'other tongues,' and you won't get it, but 'this is the rest by which the weary can be made to rest.'" Speaking in other tongues gives you a rest. It gives you a strength. It is "the refreshing."

The word religion is not a bad term and the word religious is not a bad term. It means to worship. We have made it bad because we think of it in bad terms. We think of religion in terms of a cold, dead, formal religion.

James 1:27 says,

> 27 Pure religion and undefiled before God and the Father is this, To visit the fatherless and widows in their affliction, *and* to keep himself unspotted from the world.

The term religion, as God uses it, is good. However, cold, dead religion has emphasized that tongues are not important and has emphasized this understanding over the Spirit to the point where no one wants to even get involved with it, at least in many cases.

The church does this despite the fact that Isaiah was saying, "I want you to understand doctrine. The way you're going to understand doctrine is by stammering lips and by other tongues. You're going to pray in tongues."

Your head won't get it at first, but your heart will draw out the counsel of God. As you interpret it, you will understand it. By understanding the interpretation, you will understand doctrine." This is basic.

Galatians 6:9 says,

> 9 And let us not be weary in well doing: for in due season we shall reap, if we faint not.

Here it says that if we don't get weary in well doing, if we continue on, if we don't quit ahead of time, we will eventually get what we believe for. I want to emphasize the part that talks about "not getting weary in well doing."

"This is the rest wherewith you may cause the weary to rest." If you don't get weary and give up, then you'll get the reward. If you get weary and quit, you won't get the reward you are seeking. Therefore, what can you do if you are getting weary? How can you get rest and keep going on? Pray in tongues. It gives you a rest. It gives you strength.

Religion, in itself, is always trying to make its own way to God, rather than accepting the way God has prepared. That's the part of religion we don't like. That is the part that is formal and dead, and it's actually anti-Christ.

Because they have formalized it, we come to church thinking we're coming to God, and we want to cry out for a revival. *Revival* is another word for *refreshing*. We say, "God, we need a refreshing. Oh, this is a time of refreshing."

The Bible says, "Be watchful in the times of refreshings." Hence, people say, "Oh, we're waiting for another time of refreshing." In essence, Isaiah was saying, "You want a time of refreshing? You can have it anytime you want."

You ask, "How do I get the refreshing?" Isaiah said, "This is the refreshing and you would not hear it." They said, "We're waiting for a refreshing." He said, "No, don't wait; pray in tongues. When you pray in tongues, you get the rest, you don't become weary, and you get the refreshing."

We say, "We want to come and wait until we get the refreshing." Isaiah said, "Pray in tongues, then you'll get refreshed." What are we doing? We want to form our own way rather than do what he said. Most of the people in church that are down at the front, crying out for a refreshing, don't want to speak in tongues. They say, "That doesn't make sense. It's just gibberish. I've never received it, and I don't want anything to do with that." There is a whole movement against it.

The big danger right now is Christianity without the Spirit of God. It is Christianity without the Spirit of Holiness. We've moved so far from the Spirit, that we have let our liberty in Christ move us into a "license to sin." We have moved to a point where we think, "Well, grace covers it." Grace covers, but it also gives you the ability to change. Grace does not leave you the way it found you.

If you're still the same way you were, you've not been changed. You can fit into Church and say you're a Christian and not be changed. When you reach that point, you start changing your definitions. Instead of rising to what the Bible says, you bring the Bible down to the level of your experience. That's the danger the church is in right now.

The Bible talks about a falling away and I can easily see it happening just by a mere change of definition. We say, "Well, but we're all under grace." Grace is not a license to sin. Grace changes you.

I tell everybody, "I sin all I want to. I just don't want to." That's the part that people don't understand. God changes your "want to." That's the hardest part for unbelievers to understand. They say, "I don't want to come to God if I have to quit doing this and quit doing that." They don't understand that when they come to God, He changes their desires. If those desires don't change, they haven't come to God.

God puts His Spirit within you, and the Spirit that is within you is the Spirit of Holiness. You are changed. You are a new creation. You have new desires, new ambitions, and new goals. Everything has changed.

One of our biggest problems is that we have a lot of people that are convicted sinners and not converted saints. We've got to get back to what the Bible says and live the way God says for us to. I'm not talking about legalism. I'm not talking about following rules and regulations.

Hebrews 10:16,

> 16 This *is* the covenant that I will make with them after those days, saith the Lord, I will put my laws into their hearts, and in their minds will I write them;

He said, "I will put My laws in their hearts." People say, "We're not under the law anymore." No, I'm not under law, the law is in me. I'm not under law. I'm not trying to live right. Law is in me and now, the righteousness of the law is fulfilled by me, because my nature has been changed. Now, I love God with all my heart, mind, soul, and strength, and my neighbor as myself. I do to them what I would want done to me. I no longer try to always fit into a box or try to make sure I don't make mistakes.

If any man sins, then he can confess it to the Father and it's gone. It's that simple. It's not a drawn out thing. The problem is when they sin, most people don't run to God; they run from Him. Then condemnation just builds up. The farther they get from God, the more condemnation comes in, and the more they hide from God. Soon, God is walking in the garden saying, "Where are you?"

The Prodigal Son said, "I didn't deserve to be your son." God wanted to put a robe on him and say, "What are you talking about? I've got My son back. I'm happy." "Yes, but you don't know what I've done." "I don't want to know. I don't care. Whatever it was, it's gone." "Why?" "Because you're with Me now." Amen? That's who we are. That's the glory of the Gospel.

The glory of the Gospel is not that God says, "I know you can't help it, just keep on sinning and I'll turn My head the other way." The glory of the Gospel is that God can change a man. God can take a person and change him. Can a leopard change his spots? No, but God can change a man's heart.

Speaking in tongues is the rest you are seeking. When you get tired, when you get worn out, when you just don't feel like doing anything, pray in tongues. Why? You get rest. You get built up. You get charged up. "This is the rest that you may cause the weary to rest."

F. God Chose It

Finally, the biggest reason, as far as I'm concerned, is that God chose to use tongues. You say, "I don't understand?" Who says you have to understand? We do not always understand every reason God has for doing something.

I have five grandchildren. They range in age from 2 to 10 years of age. I have to talk with each one differently, because each one is at a different level of maturity. I do not expect any one of them to understand theology. Yet, I can still talk to each one about God.

One of my favorite quotes is by Albert Einstein: "If you can't explain it simply, you don't understand it well enough." It's not how many big words you can use that is important. It is how many people can understand what you are saying. If you really understand what you are talking about, a six year old should be able to understand you.

I understand the theological terms *regeneration* and *justification*, but I don't talk to my grandchildren using those terms. I say, "Do you know that Jesus loves you? Do you know that Jesus died for you?"

My grandson, Levi, came home from school one day carrying a picture of a hand with a nail hole in it. That's what he was thinking about that day. He used to like pictures of Angry Birds. Angry Bird was on the cross with the little Angry Bird guards standing nearby. Now, instead of Angry Birds on the cross, he has people. Pointing to the picture, he explains, "This is Jesus, and this is what's going on." It's amazing to watch the development of these concepts as he matures.

I didn't say, "Now, you understand you were justified when you received salvation, and now you're in the process of sanctification." He wouldn't understand that, so I don't say that at this point. As he develops, I'll talk differently.

I want you to realize that God chose tongues. I don't have to understand why God chose tongues. Why did He choose tongues? I don't know and I don't care. The fact is that He chose it.

I can tell my grandson, "Go pick up that pencil and bring it over here." Then, when he puts it down, I can say, "Okay, now, pick it up and take it over there." He might ask, "Why do you make me do this?" I don't have to have a reason. I'm his elder. He will do it. Maybe I have a reason, maybe it's just discipline training. Whatever it is, it's the way that I've chosen.

In the same way that I wouldn't expect him to understand everything, I don't understand everything, in detail, right now. However, I do know that whenever I do what God says to do, I begin to understand it. The more I obey the more I understand, and the more I understand the more revelation comes to me. Why? That's because of obedience. If for no reason other than because God chose it, I should do it. It is just that simple.

People say, "Well, it doesn't make sense." God was the One that decided to use tongues. Like I said, we do not always understand every reason God has for doing something. If we have faith in God, then we know that He is our Heavenly Father. If He has commanded us to do something, we know it is for our benefit, as well as for the outcome of the thing commanded.

The more you understand, the less faith is required. Sometimes it's better not to understand so much. Then, you will move to a new problem that's going to require faith. Do you see? You never get to the end. We're not trying to get to the end of faith. We're trying to get to where we can use our faith more often and in more places.

I am going to quote from page 9 in the manual. I touched on it a little before, but I want to include it in this session.

The Language of Heaven is Knowing.

Communication in the Spirit is through tongues.

"In a recent scientific research project, electrodes were attached to the brain of many subjects. Each prayed in a way peculiar to their spiritual discipline, which included Buddism, TM, Catholic reciting of the Rosary and Pentecostals, praying in tongues. All forms of prayer/meditation showed some slight calming benefit, BUT, the persons praying in tongues showed that the part of the brain that functions when people pray or speak was NOT operating, yet high activity was operational in a part of the brain that is associated with the Limbic system. The Limbic system is the physical part of the human body/brain that is most closely attached to the spirit. When a person dies, the Limbic system shuts down first.

"This proved to scientists that the persons speaking in tongues were getting their "input" from a source not located within the human body systems. Scientists did ascertain that what those speaking in tongues were saying had all the components of a highly sophisticated language system, including words, sentence structure, syntax, and dialect change.

"John G. Lake once underwent scientific testing with electrodes being attached to his brain. He went through a series of various vocal recitations. He quoted poetry, and prayed with his understanding (in English). The machine recorded a higher than average range of activity. Then, he began speaking in other tongues (praying in the Spirit), and the instrument readings went off the chart. Those *conducting the tests said they had never tested anyone that had charted such a response.*

"He explained to them that he had simply "let God do the talking" and that no instrument other than the human spirit was able to register such activity, let alone understand it."

If you have not received the Baptism of the Spirit, I'm going to pray. I'm not going to force it. We're not going to stand and yell at you for an hour. You speaking in other tongues is either God or it isn't. We want it to be God. We don't want to work somebody up to just make sounds. We want it to be God.

Luke 11:13,

> 13 If ye then, being evil, know how to give good gifts unto your children: how much more shall your heavenly Father give the Holy Spirit to them that ask him?

Your Heavenly Father said He will give the Holy Spirit to any of His children that ask Him. First, you have to be born again, because the world can't receive the Spirit of God. Because you are His son, He can send the Spirit of His Son into your heart, and it can cry, "Abba Father."

The second step, after becoming a son, is to ask for the Spirit. When you ask Him for the Spirit, He will not give you a stone, He will not give you a serpent, but He will give you His Spirit. It's His desire. He desires it for you more than you desire it.

After you tell Him you want it, and then say, "I accept it. You said You wanted to give it to me. I believe that I receive it, and I thank You for it." Then just begin to worship Him. You ask, "Worship Him in tongues or in English?" Just let the Spirit come out. Let it be God.

I'm expecting this to happen. I'm expecting this to come out of you. I will pray that you receive the Holy Spirit in fullness so that you can be fluent in a Spirit language.

"Father, I thank You for these people. I thank You right now, Father, that by Your Spirit, You are filling many of them for the first time, to overflowing. Lord, as You said, we will be baptized with the Spirit, not many days hence. Father, we thank You that Your Spirit has already been poured out, so we receive Your Spirit now. Father, I thank You that even now Your Spirit is filling to overflowing Your children who are asking for it. Father, we thank You. We bless You for it, in the name of Jesus. Amen. Amen."

REMAINING IN PEACE

"Father, we thank You that we are able to gather again today and to fellowship with your Spirit and to fellowship with one another. Father, in the name of Jesus, we ask You today to continue to flow forth, to speak, to lead, to guide, as You promised. We thank You for it, in Jesus' name. Amen."

There are several Scriptures that you're going to be hearing over and over again. We're just going to keep drilling them in until they become a part of you.

Isaiah 28:11 and 12 says:

> 11 For with stammering lips and another tongue will he speak to this people.
>
> 12 To whom he said, This *is* the rest *wherewith* ye may cause the weary to rest; and this *is* the refreshing: yet they would not hear.

In verse 12, he said, "This is the rest wherewith you may cause the weary to rest; and this is the refreshing." He talks about these two things. He says, "This is the rest and this is the refreshing."

I was going to bed last night, and things were still going on in my head, because they don't stop. When I woke up this morning, I was going through the same thing. I kept going back to this subject and I don't know why. Of course, that's why we follow the Holy Spirit, sometimes without question, because we don't always know why. We do it anyway because He's pushing. I would say that the majority of Christians need this, but I do think that somebody here needs this.

In the last session we read Isaiah 28:12 where He said, "This *is* the rest *wherewith* ye may cause the weary to rest." In Galatians, chapter 6, verse 9, it says,

9 And let us not be weary in well doing: for in due season we shall reap, if we faint not.

I really believe that's one of the reasons why most Christians fail to receive. They get weary just before their due season and they give up. Sometimes, the battle gets very hot and heavy. It will be very strong right at the end, and that is when people quit. They are weary. The enemy knows that.

What we want to do is make sure that you understand that you don't have to get weary. You can remain strong. You can remain rested. You can remain refreshed.

Most people get weary for two reasons. One reason is due to long, drawn-out battles. When battles go longer, especially about sickness or disease or when you're praying for somebody or yourself, you get can weary because it is a constant battle. It keeps dragging out, obviously not on purpose, but it just continues to go on. You get tired and weary and eventually just give up. The minute you give up, the enemy wins and then you don't receive in due season.

Another reason people get weary is due to no peace. People are weary because they don't have a peace. Those that are on the frontline in the military for too long get weary because they are always on guard; they are always tense and it wears them out.

Human bodies are made to only go through that for so long before they start to break down. The idea is that they have to have "times of rest and times of refreshing" as the Bible says. They have to take them off the frontline, and put them back in R&R so that they can get rest and recuperation.

With Christians, that is a big problem. It is the one problem that should never be. Go to John 14:27. Jesus says,

> 27 Peace I leave with you, my peace I give unto you: not as the world giveth, give I unto you. Let not your heart be troubled, neither let it be afraid.

He is telling you right there, "I'm leaving you My peace." It is not just any peace. It is not the peace you can get from the world. Jesus says, "My peace I'm giving to you." We should never be weary due to lack of peace. In other words, we should never be always on edge. We are to have that peace.

Peace and love are the two things that Jesus said for us to have. This is how the world is going to know you. Yet, the two things that the world doesn't usually see from the Body of Christ are peace and love.

Here is something that I want to point out. One of the reasons why so many Christians do not have peace is because of where peace comes from. Let's look at the context here. Go back to verse 26, and let's see the source of the peace.

> 26 But the Comforter, *which is* the Holy Ghost, whom the Father will send in my name, he shall teach you all things, and bring all things to your remembrance, whatsoever I have said unto you.

Then He says, "Peace I leave with you." The peace He's leaving is in conjunction with the Holy Spirit reminding you of everything He's said. It's not just, "I'm going to give you blanket peace." No, the peace is within what He said. That comes from the presence of the Holy Spirit in the middle of the problem reminding you, "Don't worry about that. Remember what He said. You're taken care of. You have a Heavenly Father."

He even says, "In the world you're going to have tribulation," but He said, "Don't worry. I've overcome the world." The whole idea is that this peace comes through the presence of the Holy Spirit.

Jesus said, "This Comforter, the Holy Spirit Himself, is with you, and He shall be in you." That's the key. He was with them and He would be in them. With us, He is in us, not just with us.

One thing that I loved about Dr. Lake was that he constantly emphasized our union in the Spirit with the Holy Spirit and that the Holy Spirit dwells within us. He's not some far-off God. When we have a problem we don't have to go and find Him and hopefully bring Him into the situation. He is with us the whole way.

Jesus is speaking in chapter 14 of John. He starts out in the very beginning saying, "Let not your heart be troubled."

> 1 Let not your heart be troubled: ye believe in God, believe also in me.

A little over halfway through the chapter, He starts talking about the Comforter which will be present. Verse 23 says,

> 23 … If a man love me, he will keep my words: and my Father will love him, and we will come unto him, and make our abode with him.

It also tells us that we are to be made habitations of God through the Spirit, so God dwells in us by His Spirit. In other words, His Spirit comes in and He can dwell in us by His Spirit. The Father and the Son dwell within the Spirit within us, which makes us habitations of God. Watch what He said: "We will come unto him."

I don't normally work backward, but we're going to keep working backward. Verse 18 says,

> 18 I will not leave you comfortless: I will come to you.

We know that He will not leave us comfortless, because in verse 26 it said, "The Comforter, *which is* the Holy Ghost, whom the Father will send in my name." The Comforter is one that doesn't leave you comfortless. The way He's not going to leave you comfortless, is by Him coming into you as the Comforter.

The word "*Comforter*," here in the Greek, is "*paraklētos*" which means *one called alongside to help*. It literally means *to take up together against*. What He does is work with you, takes up your problems, and works against those problems as you are against them.

I am absolutely convinced, according to how Jesus operated and what we've seen in the Scriptures, that the Holy Spirit works through you and for you against your problems to the degree that you put forth the effort and apply Him to the situation. You don't just stand there and say, "Okay, I need help," and then He comes in like a whirlwind to do everything.

In other words, you lay hands on the sick, He helps by healing them, but you've got to lay hands, and speak to them. You've got to minister to them before He can actually help. If you're doing nothing, He can't help. He helps someone who's doing something. If you're doing nothing, He can't help you.

This whole chapter here is about the Spirit. In verse16, He said,

> 16 And I will pray the Father, and he shall give you another Comforter, that he may abide with you for ever;

In other words, He says, "I'm leaving, but I'm going to send you another Comforter who is not going to leave. He's going to stay with you; He's always going to be with you. He's not going to come and go." That is also an aspect of the anointing that we talk about to show that the anointing does not come and go. If you're ever anointed, you're always anointed but that is another teaching.

What I teach, I teach because I know you need it. That's why we teach it. We're not trying to come up with something new. I'd much rather not have anything new but have you do what I've already taught and to get that to working in your life, rather than come up with something new every week and have you not walking in any of it.

> 17 *Even* the Spirit of truth; whom the world cannot receive, because it seeth him not, neither knoweth him: but ye know him; for he dwelleth with you, and shall be in you.

He said, "The Father shall give you another Comforter," and then He says, "Even the Spirit of truth." Now we know that the Holy Spirit is the Spirit of truth, "Whom the world cannot receive."

The world cannot receive Him, "Because it seeth him not, neither knows him: but you know him; for he dwells with you, and shall be in you." Notice: Jesus made a distinction between being with you and being in you.

I know there are some good Bible teachers that have said, "Well, He's not actually in you. When it says, 'in you,' it means in conjunction or in union with you, in agreement with you," but Jesus made a specific point here to say, "He is with you and shall be in you." He is talking about Him dwelling and abiding within. That's why we are temples of the Holy Spirit. A temple is where a god lives.

In verse 15 He says,

> 15 If ye love me, keep my commandments.

I'm still working backward. In going back, I want to make the main point. We started with the Holy Spirit being given. He's going to give you peace, because it is the Holy Spirit that brings the peace. He gives you that peace, and that peace comes by the Comforter, whom the Father will send in Jesus' name.

Watch what this is all in conjunction with. Go back to verse 14,

14 If ye shall ask any thing in my name, I will do *it*.

Verse 13,

13 And whatsoever ye shall ask in my name, that will I do, that the Father may be glorified in the Son.

Verse 12,

12 Verily, verily, I say unto you, He that believeth on me, the works that I do shall he do also; and greater *works* than these shall he do; because I go unto my Father.

This whole section of you getting peace has to do with the Comforter coming to abide in you, but it also has to do with this Comforter and the reason He is there. Jesus had to leave and when He left He sent this Comforter which is going to allow you to do the same works and greater.

If you're going to claim peace from God, you also have to be able to claim verse 12 which says that you can do the same works and greater. They are all connected. The One who does the greater works is the One He sent in His place to continue His ministry through you. Amen?

This all goes back to you having peace and remaining in peace.

A lot of people get really nervous when it comes to praying for the sick or anything where they need God's help. The nervousness comes from not being sure that God is going to show up. I want to put that to rest right now. How can God not show up when He abides in you and you're there? If He abides in you, He will show up. He has to show up. The key is not getting Him to do something. The key is Him getting you to do something.

What I don't see in most Christians is that peace. I see turmoil. I see worry. I see fear. I see all of these things. Half of the people are worried that they're not even born again. They say, "Well, I think I am. I'm not sure; I hope I am. I prayed and I'm not sure if it's going to happen." It seems like with everything a Christian does there is this "un-peace" connected to it.

It's like they're always saying, "Well, we're doing this, but I'm just not sure about God." God is the stable one. It's the believers who generally are not the stable ones. We have to get to a place where we know.

Jesus was constantly using a father as an example. He said, "If you being evil know how to give your children good gifts, how much more will your Heavenly Father give good gifts to His children?" He was using an earthly father as an example, and saying, "If you can depend on an earthly father, how much more can you depend on a Heavenly Father?"

We need to make sure that we have that peace, because He promised us that He would send the Comforter, and that the Comforter would abide in us. Do we have the Comforter? If you have the Comforter, then you know that Jesus has already kept His word, and if He kept His word, then whatever you ask, you will receive. He said, "If you ask the Father in my name, I will do it." At some point you just have to settle down.

There came a point in my life where we were praying for the sick, and we were praying for a lot. We were seeing a fluctuation. We would get results, and it would taper off and we wouldn't get as many results.

For a while we saw just great results. Then, I started travelling. The results dropped because I wasn't able to stay and work with them like I had before. We saw it climb back up and then we saw slight dips here and there. I noticed that the fluctuations and the dips in results were never on God's end. It was always on my end. That was usually because I would end up getting the cares of the world, as the Bible says. When you get caught up in things, it's really easy to get your attention distracted.

That's one of the reasons why living a simple life is so important because you'll be able to focus and be single minded about the Word. Some people say, "Well, you are too narrow minded." Narrow minded is single minded. It works.

Our problem is that we keep doing these other things, which is one of the reasons why the enemy wants to make sure that the Church is always about something else. In the Church right now, the biggest thing is all about you being blessed. First of all, you are blessed. The Bible says, "You have been blessed with every spiritual blessing in heavenly places." There is no question about you being blessed.

I am absolutely amazed how God, even under the Old Covenant, promised His people that if they would do what they were supposed to do, they would be blessed. Under the Old Testament it was hard; now it is not hard. Jesus said, "My burden is not hard. Take the burden off of you and put My yoke on you, because My yoke is light." It's not hard.

Under the Old Covenant, He said, "If you do what you're supposed to do, you won't even have to chase blessings; all of these blessings will overtake you." In other words, they could not have outrun them.

I am a living example of blessings preceding me. I have not prayed for my own self, my own things, my finances, or anything else in years. We're just doing what we're supposed to be doing. I trust God. I believe what He said. I accept it as fact. Blessings precede us. I'm a blessed man. Nobody knows how thankful I am for what God has done for us.

I want you to realize that we're in the New Covenant. He said in the Old Covenant that these blessings would overtake them. That meant that the blessings had to catch up to them and then overtake them. He said they would.

In the New Testament, they don't overtake you. You got them when you got born again. He said that if He gave us Jesus, would He not with Jesus, give us all these things? When did you get blessed? You got blessed when you got Jesus. Why? When Jesus moved in, He moved in with all of His blessings. They came with Him.

The hardest part is that many times we resist His blessings by doing things that squander His blessings. That's why people don't walk in the blessing because the life they live is squandering the blessings that God is trying to pour into them. If you've got holes in your life, all of the blessings are just going to pour out faster than you can contain them. That's the problem. It's one thing to have holes in your life so that it just pours out, but it's another thing to be able to give out those blessings. You ought to be able to just pass them right on.

The Comforter is supposed to bring peace to you. If you have the Comforter, if you have the Spirit, you should be able to live in peace.

The real point is that when I was praying for the sick, I had to get to a place where I believed the Bible more than I believed my eyes. I had to believe what He said, "Lay hands on the sick, and they will recover." Even if I didn't see them recover right then, I had to trust Him. I did my part, and if I can be faithful, how much more faithful is He to do His part?

We are all about results. We believe that if it's in the Bible and you do it, it should work. Results are important. At the same time, there has to come a time when you can rest knowing that even if you don't see it, it's done.

I'm not talking about somebody that has been standing ten years for healing, saying, "I believed, I received, and I'm just waiting for the manifestation." I understand that; I was taught that myself. The problem with that is, people hurt for a long time. God is against people hurting.

I'm not saying that you have to play make believe, saying, "I laid hands on ten people, so I got ten people healed today." The problem with that is that people start making claims.

There was a guy riding with me one time when we were going to a meeting. As we were going down the road, and he was pointing at people saying, "Be healed. Be saved. Be healed. Be saved." I asked him, "What are you doing?" He said, "I'm blessing these people." I said, "Okay, that's better than cursing them, I guess."

That night at the meeting I noticed that he was talking to people. As I walked past him, he said, "Yes, as a matter of fact, on the way up here, we had 45 people healed." I stopped, and I listened a little more. I had to go because I was getting ready to preach. Later that night, I asked him, "When did you pray for 45 people on the way up here?" He said, "Remember in the car when you asked me what I was doing?" I said, "Are you telling people that you're counting those people as healed? You are deceiving them."

I said, "Now, I understand what you're saying, but those people are not seeing it by faith as you are. They're thinking that you saw 45 people actually get up and walk off healed." I said, "You need to be a little more specific, unless you're trying to deceive them." He quit travelling with me shortly after that.

I believe, absolutely, that I do what I am supposed to do, and God does what He's supposed to do. You have to settle down in that, and not be nervous about it, and accept it as truth, no matter what.

I was talking about that peace; you have to have that peace. You have to be able to settle down and have a peace. It's a knowing. Peace comes from knowing.

Let's go to the third point on page 10 of your manual.

KINDS OF TONGUES – TONGUES OF MEN AND ANGELS

We are talking about different kinds of tongues. In 1 Corinthians 13:1 Paul mentioned that there were tongues of men and of angels. It says,

> 1 Though I speak with the tongues of men and of angels…

In 1 Corinthians 12:10 it says,

> 10 To another the working of miracles; to another prophecy; to another discerning of spirits; to another *divers* kinds of tongues; to another the interpretation of tongues:

You will notice that the word "divers" there is in italics which means that it was not in the original Greek. It was added to give clarity.

We just read Isaiah 28, verses 11 and 12 about tongues. We are going to start moving into tongues.

In the previous sessions, I said that there were diversities of tongues and different kinds of tongues. The main thing we're talking about now is what we would call public tongues and private tongues.

Public tongues are for meetings and they are usually a message for the group. It is usually not personal; it's not about you or to you.

As we said before, the number one reason for private tongues is for edification and for you to build yourself up.

Now, if people are looking for a reason to argue, they're always going to find one. Many times people will argue with tongues because they go into 1 Corinthians chapter 13. They think that chapter 13 does away with the need for tongues.

When you go into chapter 14, it talks about how to do this with one or two, at the most by three, and only if there's an interpreter. It has all of these requirements and regulations. Then, he starts talking about these things. We have to discern what he's talking about, whether it's private or public tongues and what the purpose of each kind is.

Acts 2, starting in verse 1, it says:

> 1 And when the day of Pentecost was fully come, they were all with one accord in one place.
>
> 2 And suddenly there came a sound from heaven as of a rushing mighty wind, and it filled all the house where they were sitting.

It does not say there was a rushing mighty wind. It says there was a sound as of a rushing mighty wind.

In looking at this, we know that this is when the Holy Spirit descended upon them and at this point they were all filled and began speaking in tongues.

I did think that it was great that they used the term "a rushing mighty wind." Luke was the one talking about this. If you go to the Book of Revelation, it says that the sound of God's voice is as the sound of many waters, which could sound like a rushing mighty wind.

There was a sound of God's voice that I believe they were hearing. It sounded like a wind rushing in, and I think it was just because they could not discern it at that point.

Verse 3 says,

> 3 And there appeared unto them cloven tongues like as of fire, and it sat upon each of them.

"And there appeared unto them," is the first time they saw something. They heard something. Then they saw something. Remember that. They heard it and then they saw it. "And there appeared unto them cloven tongues like as of fire, and it sat upon each of them."

> 4 And they were all filled with the Holy Ghost, and began to speak with other tongues, as the Spirit gave them utterance.

"And they were all..." "All." That's the biggest word in the Bible. "And they were all filled with the Holy Ghost, and began to speak with other tongues, as the Spirit gave them utterance."

It says they "began." It never says they stopped. I know they stopped at some point there, but they continued to speak in tongues the rest of their lives. It wasn't a one-time event.

Acts 2:5 says:

> 5 And there were dwelling at Jerusalem Jews, devout men, out of every nation under heaven.

He was pointing out, "Out of every nation under heaven, they all came together." They were all there in Jerusalem.

> 6 Now when this was noised abroad, the multitude came together, and were confounded, because that every man heard them speak in his own language.

"Now when this was noised abroad, the multitude came together." Who was the multitude? The multitude was made up of men from every nation under heaven. It says, "The multitude came together, and were confounded." Again, tongues confound people. It confounded them because, "...every man heard them speak in his own language."

In verse 7, they started to detail where the people speaking in tongues were from.

> 7 And they were all amazed and marveled, saying one to another, Behold, are not all these which speak Galilaeans?

That would be like us saying, "How in the world are these hillbillies speaking Latin?" I can say that; I'm a hillbilly. Seriously, my ancestors were Hatfield's so I come by it naturally. As a matter of fact, if you look in my office, you'll see an old oval picture on the wall. Those are Hatfield's in that picture. Actually, when my Mom came up this time, she brought me a gun that has been passed down through the family. It is one of the original Hatfield guns that was used during the Hatfield/McCoy feud, and it has been passed down to me.

They asked in verse 7, "Behold, are not all these which speak Galilaeans?" Verse 8 says:

> 8 And how hear we every man in our own tongue, wherein we were born?

He started mentioning where all of the other people were from in verse 9:

> 9 Parthians, and Medes, and Elamites, and the dwellers in Mesopotamia, and in Judaea, and Cappadocia, in Pontus, and Asia,

It says, "...dwellers in Mesopotamia." That is the area where the Tower of Babel was. At the Tower of Babel, God confounded the languages and scattered the nations, but here, all of these men, even people from Mesopotamia, were hearing these men speak in their own languages.   What was removed at the Tower of Babel had been restored.

Verse 10 says:

> 10 Phrygia, and Pamphylia, in Egypt, and in the parts of Libya about Cyrene, and strangers of Rome, Jews and proselytes,
>
> 11 Cretes and Arabians, we do hear them speak in our tongues the wonderful works of God.

When they were speaking in the tongues of men—tongues that men could understand—they were speaking the wonderful works of God. They were magnifying God. These men were listening in on them as they were glorifying God. They were speaking in tongues but they weren't being spoken to those men; they were being spoken to God. As they spoke to God, they were glorifying God and these men were hearing them glorify God in their own languages. They were listening in when these people were speaking to God.

> 12 And they were all amazed, and were in doubt, saying one to another, What meaneth this?
>
> 13 Others mocking said, These men are full of new wine.
>
> 14 But Peter, standing up with the eleven, lifted up his voice, and said unto them, Ye men of Judaea, and all *ye* that dwell at Jerusalem, be this known unto you, and hearken to my words:
>
> 15 For these are not drunken, as ye suppose, seeing it is *but* the third hour of the day.
>
> 16 But this is that which was spoken by the prophet Joel;

Underline "this is that."

Then he begins to quote Joel:

> 17 And it shall come to pass in the last days, saith God, I will pour out of my Spirit upon all flesh: and your sons and your daughters shall prophesy, and your young men shall see visions, and your old men shall dream dreams:

"And it shall come to pass in the last days, saith God, I <u>will</u> pour out of my Spirit." It doesn't say, "I might." It doesn't say, "If you live up to it and deserve it." You have to realize the Holy Spirit is given, not because you deserve it, but because you need it. You need the Helper.

"I will pour out of my Spirit upon all flesh: and your sons and your daughters shall prophesy." The prophesying is connected with the pouring out of the Spirit on all flesh. "And your young men shall see visions, and your old men shall dream dreams."

Verse 18 says,

> 18 And on my servants and on my handmaidens I will pour out in those days of my Spirit; and they shall prophesy:

He was repeating there. This was the first time that tongues were displayed and the tongues were the tongues of men.

In 1901, when Agnes Ozman went to Charles Parham's Bethel Bible School, she spoke in other tongues.

Back then, people didn't run down front to get the Baptism in the Holy Spirit. Back then when you spoke in other tongues, the first thing they did was try to find out where that language was spoken. If you received that language, it meant you had become a missionary. If you spoke in another tongue, they sent you to the place where that language was spoken.

It wasn't a matter of, "Oh, I just want to get filled with the Spirit," or "I just want to have a good charismatic church service." When you volunteered for the Baptism of the Holy Spirit, you were volunteering for missionary service.

In the early days they had many people who went out. They used to call them the "Missionaries of the One-Way Ticket," which meant a lot of them went out and never came back home. They didn't have mission boards supporting them. They did it all on their own, with God helping them and taking care of them.

As they went out, they didn't have the idea of tongues being the tongues of men and angels. It was understood that when a person received tongues, it would always be a language spoken somewhere on the earth. Later on they found out that that wasn't true, and that it wasn't always tongues of men. Unfortunately, many missionaries would go to a place and think that they could speak the language and they couldn't, but there were many other cases where they actually did. I'm going to give you a couple of examples.

Remember the testimony of the lady who spoke Spanish to the Spanish people and she didn't speak Spanish? As she was praying in tongues, the tongues were understood in Spanish. They understood her in their own language. That is exactly what happened in the Book of Acts.

The story about Agnes Ozman is on page 12 in the manual. In the first paragraph it says:

"1901 – Agnes Ozman – Charles Parham's Bethel Bible School student began to speak in other tongues shortly after midnight on January 1. For the next several days the news spread such that government language specialists were sent in to study and examine her 'tongues.' It was determined that she was speaking in a dialect of the Chinese language. She even claimed to have written in Chinese under the inspiration of the Spirit."

The next paragraph says:

"This began a missionary movement in which the missionaries that went to foreign lands became known as "Missionaries of the One-Way Ticket." They had neither missionary sending board nor any promise of support.

"When early Pentecostals received the Baptism of the Holy Spirit and began to speak in other tongues, it was automatically assumed they were speaking in foreign human languages. They would determine which language it was and where that language was spoken and then they went to that place as missionaries.

"All of this was based upon Acts chapter 2.

"After a short period of time, this seems to have died out. Then, the Scripture was found that stated that tongues might be of men or of angels.

"John Lake reported that he spoke Italian to a group of Italian workers in Logansport, Indiana, after his Baptism of the Holy Spirit. He preached to them for about an hour about Jesus' ability to save, heal, and deliver.

"The same thing happened to Smith Wigglesworth. He was reported to have spoken to various people of different nationalities in their own language and dialect.

"Many cases of speaking directly to various ethnic groups in their own languages have been reported.

"A Japanese Buddhist woman, married to an American, an American Christian, visited her husband's church and when a call was given to come to the altar to pray, she went forward intending to pray in her Buddhist manner for her ancestors.

"A woman kneeling next to her was speaking in tongues. When the Buddhist knelt near her, the tongues in which she was praying switched to classical or formal Japanese. The Buddhist heard the woman say, 'You've tried Buddha, now come to Me. I am Jesus, Lord and Savior.' The Buddhist woman tried to converse with the Pentecostal woman in Japanese, but could not because the Pentecostal could not speak ANY foreign language EXCEPT when she was praying in tongues."

This next case was my own mother.

My mother ministered at a Native American church in Oklahoma, and while she was preaching, she began to speak in other tongues. She had actually bowed her head and was just praying in tongues, and my Dad was standing next to her. While her eyes were closed and she was still speaking in tongues, the congregation began lining up in front of her.

When she opened her eyes, she was surprised that they were lining up. When she asked them what they were doing, an Indian woman answered that they were lining up like she told them to do in their language, because she was going to pray for them.

After they finished the service, they went to the back. They had food cooked and everybody would eat and they would stand there for a while.

My Mom has no Indian in her; my Dad did. He was actually Choctaw Indian. He was there with her and the funny thing was, she would preach and she was the one that spoke in the Native American tongue. When they went back to eat, they invited her to eat but didn't invite him.

I will give you other instances:

When I was in Africa in 1997, the first time I went over, I got picked up at the airport. My luggage and everything was put into a taxi. We left the airport and within about a couple of blocks, we pulled over and the driver let another guy in the front. We were driving along, and I thought, "Well, that's unusual." It was my first time to Africa, and I wasn't sure what had taken place."

As we were driving, they were speaking in Swahili, and I remember thinking, "That's neat; it sounded neat to hear them talk."

I was just sitting there and all of a sudden, I understood them. I completely knew what they were saying. They were talking about how they were going to take me to the trash dump, steal my things, do whatever was necessary to me in order to keep my things, leave me out there, and then take off with all of my things. When I heard that, I was looking at them, and I was thinking, "Don't they know I can understand them?"

They were still speaking Swahili, so I started talking to them. I started telling them, "Hey, my government knows where I am. You need to take me to my hotel, because if anything happens to me, they'll send a bomb and drop it right on top of this taxi."

Then, the guys started getting really nervous. They pulled over and they jumped out of the car, and started throwing my luggage out. I got out to gather up my luggage, they jumped back in and took off, so I had to catch another taxi.

It's fun going to a new country. I think it is really great because you go through all kinds of experiences and, if you live through them, you've got some great testimonies. If you don't, you're a martyr. That just means that you get to be with Jesus. It's a win-win either way.

When the Bible speaks of "diversities of tongues," it is a reference to not only different kinds of human and angelic languages, but also various kinds of tongues in reference to purpose and function.

As we've already said, there are public tongues and private tongues, but even within private tongues, there are distinctions for different reasons. I have some listed here:

- Maintenance Tongues
- Intercessory Tongues
- A Message in Tongues to a Congregation
- Warfare Tongues

Maintenance Tongues are just for edification on a daily basis. It's like eating every day to maintain energy and health. It's just something you do every day. There is that aspect of tongues which is just for maintenance. If your body needs life given to it every day, your spirit continues to need life to continue to flow at a natural level.

You can get weak in spirit or you can be strong in spirit. People ask, "If you died weak in spirit would you still go to be with God?" Yes, as long as you were connected to Him, but you can be weak in spirit and not be born again. You can be strong in spirit and not be born again, but the spirit you're strong in is not a good spirit. Do you get that? Whether you're born again or not, your spirit can be weak or strong; it just depends on to whom you are connected.

Witches are strong with the wrong spirit, but the strongest witch is weaker than the weakest Christian connected to the right Spirit. Always remember that.

Again, these are Maintenance Tongues, Intercessory Tongues, A Message in Tongues to a congregation, and what is called Warfare Tongues. We're going to talk about these.

Some things have been taken to extremes and have been done the wrong way; hopefully we can bring some balance to that. There are times to get loud, times to get strong, or times to be quiet. There are different purposes. Loudness does not necessarily mean strength. It's not volume. Again, we'll delineate some of these things in more detail.

In 1 Corinthians 14:15 it says,

> 15 What is it then? I will pray with the spirit, and I will pray with the understanding also: I will sing with the spirit, and I will sing with the understanding also.

We know that Paul was saying, "I will pray with the spirit (which is talking about praying in tongues) and I will pray with the understanding (praying normal prayers) also." Then he was talking about singing with the spirit (singing in tongues), and singing with understanding (normal language) also. We know these are all possible.

Ephesians 3:16 says,

> 16 That he would grant you, according to the riches of his glory, to be strengthened with might by his Spirit in the inner man;

"That he would grant you, (according to the riches of his glory)…" You can put a parenthesis around "according to the riches of his glory." What He's going to grant you is on the next line, where it says, "…to be strengthened with might by his Spirit in the inner man." It is saying, "That He would grant you to be strengthened with might by His Spirit in the inner man." That inner man is a spirit—that's you. He is granting that you be strengthened in your spirit by His Spirit.

When there's some error going on in the church, it may be derived from a wrong premise. When you start with a wrong premise, everything you develop after that is wrong. That is one of the things that causes a large portion of the Body of Christ to really go off in a wrong direction. It has to do with when people say, "Well, I'm born again," and then they claim to operate in the finished work of Christ. Christ's work is finished, but your work is not. You need to get that. His work is finished. Your work is not.

In the spirit, when you were recreated, you were recreated perfect and complete in Him. That is not enough. If that's all there was to it then as soon as you got born again, you could just go ahead and die and you wouldn't have to worry about the rest of it, because the rest of your life would be getting the rest of you to line up with the inside of you. Most people consider all of that already done, and it's obvious that it's not.

He says that He will grant you *to be strengthened* with might in the inner man. Literally, "*to be strengthened*," means *to be empowered, enabled; empowered with might.*

The word "*might*" there is a variation of the Greek word "*dunamis.*" "*Dunamis*" means "*miraculous ability.*" He was saying that He would grant you to be empowered with *miraculous ability* by His Spirit in your spirit, in your inner man. It is saying that even though you're born again complete in Him, you still have to exercise yourself unto godliness to grow up into Him so that the outside looks like the inside.

Your inner man can be weakened or strengthened, but if it's going to be strengthened, it's going to be strengthened by His Spirit.

How is it going to be strengthened by His Spirit? We know that the Ephesians believers were born again, Spirit filled, and spoke in other tongues because the Book of Acts records them speaking in other tongues. We know they did that but how was He telling them that they were going to be strengthened in the inner man by His Spirit?

Jude 20 tells us:

> 20 But ye, beloved, building up yourselves on your most holy faith, praying in the Holy Ghost,

We are to be built up on our most holy faith, praying in the Holy Ghost. Your inner man is strengthened by speaking in other tongues. Reading the Bible lines up your mind, and it should start to renew your mind with understanding, but speaking in other tongues gives you things that you don't understand.

Many times when I am driving, God will give me something that I want to remember. Because I'm driving, I can't make notes. As soon as I have that thought, I don't want to lose it, so I will immediately start to pray in tongues. When I pray in tongues like that, it's usually loud, strong, and very forceful. Then, when I get to where I am going, I will stop and say, "Okay, now what was that?" I try to remember and I can't remember, then I will just pray in tongues, loud and strong like I did before.

What I'm doing when I pray in tongues, in conjunction with that revelation I had at the same time that I got the nugget, is lock it or seal it together. Then, when I get to where I'm going, I pray in tongues again and that thought is released and it is brought back to my remembrance. That's the purpose of the Holy Spirit. It is to bring to my remembrance everything that Jesus speaks to me. That way I won't forget anything even though I don't get to write it down.

How do you think the New Testament was written? I guarantee it was written the same way John Lake wrote his sermons. It was by inspiration. They prayed it out in tongues, and then they interpreted it, and the Holy Spirit brought to their remembrance everything Jesus had spoken to them.

You have to remember that every church in the early days in the Book of Acts, was a Spirit-filled, charismatic church. When they found a church that wasn't, they fixed it. They didn't go in and say, "Oh, that's okay. Sorry, I didn't see your denominational sign. We'll just leave you alone and you can stay that way." There aren't different sects in the Body of Christ. There's one body and the one body flows from the head and the head always thinks the same way. The head doesn't think differently about its arm than it does about its foot. It wants it all, and it wants the same life in all.

The purpose of the Church or the plan of God for the Church, is that the Church, "all," the total Church, be Spirit-filled, speaking in other tongues, building themselves up in the most holy faith.

In 2 Timothy 1:6 it says:

> 6 Wherefore I put thee in remembrance that thou stir up the gift of God, which is in thee by the putting on of my hands.

Paul told Timothy, "Timothy, stir up the gift that is in you." Paul said, "You stir it up." You don't wait for God to stir it up; you don't wait until God moves on you; you stir it up. That means that you are the one to initiate the stirring up.

We've got to get specific here. He was not talking about a specific gift, like a gift of the word of knowledge or a gift of faith. Paul was telling him, "Stir up the gift of the Holy Ghost that was placed in you by the laying on of my hands."

You will not find one place in the Book of Acts or any other Scripture, where any specific gift was ever given to any person by the laying on of hands. What you will find throughout the Book of Acts is that many times, whenever an apostle would pray for someone, they would lay hands on them and the person would receive the Holy Spirit and begin speaking in other tongues.

The gift Paul gave him by the laying on of hands wasn't one of the nine gifts that we read about. It was the gift of the Holy Spirit. He was saying, "Stir up." He wasn't saying stir up a gift. He was saying stir up "the gift" in which all of the other gifts abide because all of these other gifts are just manifestations of "the gift."

Whenever he said, "You stir up this gift that is in you," he was telling them to fan the embers. In other words, "You've let this die down." He probably said, "Timothy, you need to focus. I put you there to do this; you've gotten very mental on this thing; you're trying to figure it all out. Just take a break and pray in tongues. Stir up the gift that is in you. As you pray in tongues, you'll get strengthened again, and you'll be encouraged again. You won't let it bother you that these people are saying you are too young to know this or too young to do this. You will rise up, you'll be who you're supposed to be, and you'll do what I put you there to do."

As you get weak in spirit, you start letting men push you around. You'll start going from one doctrine to the other to please men, but if you stay strong in spirit, no man can bully you, push you around, or try to make you do something. Actually, that's what you see in churches a lot. You see where someone bullies you into a position just because of his or her position. If you're strong in spirit, you will either speak to that or you will leave. You will do one of the two.

I don't get into arguments with people anymore. It's a waste of time. I'll present the truth of the Word of God. If they accept the Word, it is a wonderful act. If they don't, I'm gone. I do not waste my time with people who don't want to walk with God. There are too many people who need help and want help. I can help them. I do not spend time with somebody who wants to fight me over anything, whether it's healing or something else.

I live in peace. I refuse to fight over things because they're not going to change me. The things I've done, I see in the Bible, I've experienced it, and I'm solid in it. I'm not saying I can't grow; I'm not saying I'm not open to correction or teaching. I'm not saying that at all. I'm just saying that you're not going to badger me into a position and say, "Do it because I say so." That generally doesn't work for me. Show me chapter and verse in context, and we will go from there.

Ephesians 3:16-19 helps again to emphasize this.

16 That he would grant you, according to the riches of his glory, to be strengthened with might by his Spirit in the inner man;

17 That Christ may dwell in your hearts by faith; that ye, being rooted and grounded in love,

18 May be able to comprehend with all saints what *is* the breadth, and length, and depth, and height;

19 And to know the love of Christ, which passeth knowledge, that ye might be filled with all the fulness of God.

"And to know the love of Christ, which passes knowledge." Do you hear that? You're going to know something which passes knowledge. He's not talking about knowing it here. You're going to get the understanding of it here, but you're going to know it there. It says, "That you might be filled with all the fullness of God."

Here he has mentioned all three aspects. He has mentioned God, relating mainly to the Father. He's mentioned Christ, but he's also talking about the Spirit, because he says that's how you're going to be strengthened. You will be strengthened by the Spirit.

Remember, I told you before that the Spirit comes to dwell in you, and the Father and the Son dwell within the spirit within you. He is going to strengthen you because His Spirit is there. Then, the Father and the Son are going to come, and dwell, and share, and then the Holy Spirit's going to relate. They work together, and the Holy Spirit says what Jesus tells Him. Jesus tells Him what He has heard from the Father.

© 2012 Curry R. Blake – John G. Lake Ministries

TONGUES FOR PERSONAL EDIFICATION

We've been talking about various kinds of tongues, different reasons and purposes of tongues, and now we're going to talk about tongues specifically for personal edification. This is talking about building up and for maintenance.

The number one reason for speaking in other tongues is on page 14 of your manual. John Lake said: "Tongues are the making of my ministry." That is a good endorsement in and of itself. He said that by praying in other tongues and speaking in other tongues, it was the making of his ministry.

Let's go to Jude. There's only one chapter, but in verse 17, he says,

17 But, beloved, remember ye the words which were spoken before of the apostles of our Lord Jesus Christ;

18 How that they told you there should be mockers in the last time, who should walk after their own ungodly lusts.

19 These be they who separate themselves, sensual, having not the Spirit.

Notice, it says, "having not the Spirit." By not having the Spirit you're already labeled as sensual. In the Greek, that word, "*sensual*," is an amazing word. Look it up. It is literally the word *psuchikos*, which is the word for *soul.* In other words, they are *soulish*, they are naturally minded, and they think more in the senses. They think more with their feelings, so they're more earthly minded.

He was saying that they were sensual, and they were soulish. The Bible tells us that even witchcraft comes out of the soul. It's not spiritual in that sense. Now, spirits attach to it, but it is soulishly energized.

20 But ye, beloved, building up yourselves on your most holy faith, praying in the Holy Ghost,

In other words, "These people have not the Spirit, but you beloved, who have the Spirit, are building yourselves up on your most holy faith, praying in the Holy Ghost."

21 Keep yourselves in the love of God, looking for the mercy of our Lord Jesus Christ unto eternal life.

You'll notice it says that by building yourselves up, by praying in the Holy Ghost, you also keep yourself in the love of God. This is an aspect of keeping those embers fanned into fire, as we might say, like Paul told Timothy. This is one of the main important points of speaking in other tongues in your private life. It keeps you on fire, so to speak.

The Apostle Paul said in 1 Corinthians 14:18,

18 I thank my God, I speak with tongues more than ye all:

That in itself is a good recommendation. I want you to think about this: the Apostle Paul wrote at least one-third of the New Testament. Most of the time, however, when you mention revelation, usually you're referring to Paul. The body of Paul's work was all about revelations, because none of it was spoken about before time.

Of all the people in the New Testament, you don't usually hear people refer to revelation in regard to the Apostle Peter, even though we know he was the first person who had revelation because Jesus asked him, "Who do you say I am?" and Peter said, "You are Christ, Son of the living God." Jesus said, "Flesh and blood has not revealed this unto you. It has been revealed to you by my Heavenly Father." By this, we know that Peter was the first person to have a personal revelation from God.

I've always said that after somebody gets saved, they should start out in the Book of James. James was the first book written in the New Testament. Why? That's because they needed a primer on how to live the life. That's why it was written. It's a fairly small book.

After that, the next book written was Galatians. There Paul was telling about how they were not to go back under the Law.

Paul's entire work was revelatory, and you can't find anything in reference to what Paul was talking about in any of the Gospels. Those men had been with Jesus and walked with Him for almost four years, and yet there's not one hint of it in any of their gospels. Paul was the first one to start bringing that out.

It is not a coincidence that the man who said, "I thank my God, I pray in tongues (or speak in tongues), more than you all," was also the man who had the most revelation of any person in the New Testament.

On a personal level, praying in other tongues builds you up, but it also brings revelation. That is what really builds you up.

John Lake called praying in tongues, "The dynamo of the Spirit."

In John Lake's day, the idea of electricity was just starting to be really common. Back then they had these dynamos that you could go and watch. As they turned these things, they would generate electricity and then the electricity would be transferred through wires into a battery to store it. He would watch those things.

Have any of you seen the end of the old Frankenstein movie? Remember when they would start to reanimate Frankenstein? They would turn these things, and you could see the electricity sparks flying off of them. That was the way it was in Lake's day.

When he saw that he said, "That's what speaking in tongues is in the Spirit." He said, "What the dynamo is for electricity in the natural is what praying and speaking in other tongues is in the spirit realm, in that it develops and becomes a way of charging up, and that charge is then stored in the battery."

Most people want to wait until they have a problem, and then they want to run to God and say, "God help me." They expect Him to drop power on them at that point. God has put Himself in you and given you the ability to charge your batteries and have them charged so that when the need is at hand, you can release it at will, rather than having to hope that God is going to show up so you can release Him.

That is why this teaching, like all of our teachings on healing and things like that, is different from what you hear in the Church as a whole.

I've studied Dr. Lake's material. By far he was the most advanced in the Church in the last hundred years concerning the things of the Spirit, even to the point where he called it "The Science of the Spirit." He broke it down into pieces and analyzed it. Using the Bible and his experience, he was able to define it in a way that I've not heard from anybody else.

In going with what Dr. Lake taught, now we should be able to take this even farther. That is why I'm bringing it out like I am, because for the most part, it has been lost to the Church. It's time for the Church to bring it back in, because it is THE power of God dwelling in us. God has put it in us so that we can do what He has called us to do, but in order to do that, we have to know how to use it.

The purpose of the Spirit dwelling in you is to charge you up so that you can draw this charge and you can release it at will.

John Lake said, "Any person who claims to be a minister of God should be able to manifest the Spirit of God, at will, to the point of need." That's what you see in the Book of Acts.

That's what we're trying to do here. We are trying to get this into the Church as a whole, to where we can begin to build ourselves up. Rather than just hoping and praying whenever we're in a bad situation, we can actually stand there in faith and boldly say what our God will do through us.

Turn to page 15. We've already talked about this, but I'm going to keep bringing it back in and reiterating it. In Isaiah 28:12, it says,

> 12 …This *is* the rest *wherewith* ye may cause the weary to rest; and this *is* the refreshing: yet they would not hear.

Anytime you just get worn out going through your daily life, and anytime things get too hectic, just take a few minutes to pray in tongues. Take a walk, pray in tongues under your breath or out loud. Do it however you want to do it. When you come back in, you will be refreshed.

Speaking in other tongues provides a rest and a refreshing!

Smith Wigglesworth was once asked why he did not take vacations (or "holidays," as the English would say). He replied, "I do. I take a holiday every day. I pray in other tongues, and I am refreshed, rested, and ready to continue working in the Father's vineyard." I am absolutely convinced one of the main reasons many ministers get burned out is because they don't pray in tongues enough.

The Apostle Paul made some very blunt statements. He said, "I thank my God, I speak with tongues more than you all." Then later on he even says, "I have labored more abundantly than all of the other apostles." Do you think there may be some correlation there?

If what we do is the ministry of the Spirit and by the Spirit, then by us building ourselves up in the Spirit it should make us more efficient, more proficient and more effective in the ministry of the Spirit. There is a reason to pray in tongues.

We've already read Galatians 6:9, but again, it says,

> 9 And let us not be weary in well doing: for in due season we shall reap, if we faint not.

In 2 Thessalonians 3:13 it says,

> 13 But ye, brethren, be not weary in well doing.

What is he telling them? Pray in tongues. That's not all he's saying, obviously. He is saying, "Just don't be weary." How is it that you are not weary? You pray in tongues. We have actually talked about this, and we're going to go into it more.

After long battles, we may become tired and tempted to let up or relax. Praying in other tongues will bring the need of renewal and refreshing that is able to carry you through. Praying in other tongues causes the rivers of living water to flow through you, bringing the rest and the refreshing.

Take your Bible and go with me to John 7, and look at verses 37 and 38. It says,

> 37 In the last day, that great *day* of the feast, Jesus stood and cried, saying, If any man thirst, let him come unto me, and drink.

> 38 He that believeth on me, as the scripture hath said, out of his belly shall flow rivers of living water.

Now, let's just look at this, and take it apart piece by piece.

Number one: "If any man thirst let him come unto me and drink." Who's responsible for getting filled? We are. We come to Him and then we drink.

We already know that He said, "If you come to Him and you drink, you will no longer thirst." That does away with the things that people always say about being thirsty. I'll prove it on this next point.

Verse 38 says, "He that believeth on me, as the Scripture has said…" Then it said, "…out of his belly shall flow rivers of living water." It doesn't say it is going to fall out of heaven. Your refreshing doesn't come from heaven.

People say, "Well, we're just waiting for times of refreshing, and God will rain refreshing on us." It doesn't say that at all. It doesn't have to fall on you; it has to come out of you.

If it was up to God, it would already be done, but it's not up to God. It's up to you. It's out of your belly, where it has to flow rivers of living water. If you're not walking in these rivers of living water, and if it's not flowing out, it's not God's fault. It is your fault.

People say, "Well, I don't understand. I've just grown cold toward God." I can understand it. You are not letting the rivers that are in you out.

He says, "Out of his belly (he that believeth on me) shall flow rivers of living water." Where is it coming from? It is coming out of your belly. Why? That's where He came into.

Your body is a temple, and He dwells within you. He is with you and He is in you. The key is not getting Him to come down upon you. The key is getting Him to come out of you.

Let's go back to Isaiah 28:11. It says,

11 For with stammering lips and another tongue will he speak to this people.

The word *"lips"* there is the Hebrew word, *śâphâh; śepheth*. The second form is in dual and plural. Sâphâh is pronounced saw-faw', and śepheth is pronounced sef-eth'.

It can literally mean one of two things, depending on how you intend it. One way it can mean *a spout out of which something flows*. Your lips are a spout out of which flow rivers of living water.

The other definition of that word is *a dam*. With stammering lips He's going to speak to another nation. These lips are going to become a spout, and if they're not a spout, they are a dam.

What stops the rivers of living water? Your lips stop the river. They are the dam of the living waters that want to flow out of your belly. It flows up and out through your lips.

When it talks about lips, it even gives the idea of a shoreline. In other words, as far as your lips pour out this water, that's the shoreline of these rivers of living water.

That's why I love studying the Bible. When you get down to it, it's neat how it all fits together.

In John 7:38, it said, "The rivers (plural) of living water shall flow out of the belly of he that believeth on Me." The living water is there, and that is the Spirit. Let's read the next part, just to make sure you know it. Verse 39 says,

> 39 (But this spake he of the Spirit, which they that believe on him should receive: for the Holy Ghost was not yet *given;* because that Jesus was not yet glorified.)

"But this spoke He of the Spirit…" He was talking about the Spirit, so the Spirit has to come out of your lips as living water.

How does the Spirit come out of your lips? Obviously, it can come out in Scripture, because He said, "My words are Spirit and they are life," so you can speak His words and they will come out as Spirit and life.

He said, "Out of your belly will flow rivers." It is plural. It doesn't say, will flow a "river." It says rivers. That means there are several ways for the Spirit to come out of your mouth in different forms. It can come out in your normal language or in tongues.

In tongues, there are several rivers of tongues—maintenance of tongues, intercessory tongues, a message in tongues to a congregation, warfare in tongues—and they come out in all of these different ways. What I'm trying to emphasize is that the Spirit of God in you wants to come out in various rivers. It does not say river, as in singular. It says rivers, as in plural. The Spirit will come out of your belly in various ways.

Obviously, your normal language is one river, but there are rivers. If you are only letting the Spirit out through your normal language, you are operating in a river and not rivers, so you are not fulfilling Scripture.

He says,

> 39 ...for the Holy Ghost was not yet *given;* because that Jesus was not yet glorified.)

He was pointing to a future time, when Jesus would be glorified. The Spirit could then come and then men could receive Him. He was talking about the day of Pentecost.

Another way that rivers could have come out was that each of those people who heard them speak, heard them speak in their own language. Each language was a river.

I'm just trying to lay this whole thing out to let you see that there is a depth to it that the Church, as a whole, does not walk in. There is much more to living and walking in the Spirit than just coming to church on Sunday, singing a few songs, maybe even praying in tongues a little bit, and then going home. It's deeper than that. This has to do with your entire life.

The reason Jesus came was so that the Spirit could abide in us. The reason the Spirit came to abide in us is so that He could get out of us and infect the world.

TONGUES AND INTERPRETATION

We're going to talk about tongues and interpretation. This is one aspect of it. In 1 Corinthians 12, we have the description. There are diversities of tongues and then there are interpretations of tongues.

If you go through John Lake's material, almost every sermon has tongues and interpretation in it. It was the same with Smith Wigglesworth. As a matter of fact, that was the way it usually was in the early days.

A lot of that has ceased now because of television and because people don't want to be seen in their ideas as backward. They let people watch them so they have to clean up their program, rather than just keeping it real before God.

We have had a shift away from the on-line Sunday sermons. When we first started, we didn't have a congregation in front of us. We just broadcasted over the Internet. Obviously, it was very Internet driven in the sense that we were speaking to a camera and there were just a couple of other people in the room who were actually running the cameras.

I didn't want to keep it that way. We wanted a live congregation. When we first started with the live congregation, it was as if they were sitting in on a TV broadcast. I didn't like that because it was too sterile. It was like, "Here we are doing broadcast. Time's up, so quit."

What we want is for the congregation to be here and then we just turn on the camera, let it roll and whatever we get, you get, rather than gearing it toward a particular broadcast. We want the Spirit of God.

We never know who's watching by Internet, but it shouldn't matter. We preach what God gives us to preach, we do what God leads us to do, and we just walk in that. If somebody watches the broadcast and they like it, that is great, but if they don't, it is too bad. Why? That's because we're responsible before God for what we do. We shouldn't do anything here that we would be ashamed to do anywhere else. That's why we shifted the way we're doing the Sunday services. It is now a time of fellowship and more. It is not sterile like it was before.

Let's go back to tongues and interpretation being one aspect of this.

In 1 Corinthians 14:13 it says,

> 13 Wherefore let him that speaketh in an unknown tongue pray that he may interpret.

When most people pray in other tongues, they don't interpret it; they just pray. It says that if you do speak in other tongues, pray that you can interpret. That is talking, in that case specifically, about a congregational type meeting. If you can interpret that, you can interpret any of it.

One of the things you'll have to realize is that when you receive gifts, these gifts are manifestations of the Spirit. The only thing that hinders His manifestation, usually, is your not knowing the will of God concerning that. Your faith cannot go beyond your knowledge of the will of God. Once you know what the will of God is, then you can step out in faith in that area.

Once you are aware of how the Spirit of God can manifest Himself and once you experience that, from then on you can step out in faith and experience that at any time. That's why gifts of healing can operate anywhere, and the working of miracles can operate anywhere.

Usually, when people start out, it's hit or miss. The longer they do it, the better they get at it. Why? In a way, their faith builds to where they start to expect God to be there whenever they get ready. Then, they step out into it. It's the same thing with prophecies, and the same thing with healing; they operate the same way.

We don't really concern ourselves with gifts. We concern ourselves with what God has told us to do, and we help people. The gift aspect, the manifestation of the Spirit, is up to God. We can rely on Him to manifest because He is God and He is very predictable. He will do exactly what He says He will do.

The fact that we believe He will do what He says He will do is our part of faith. It all comes together, so when you experience it, you can use it, even if you backslide. Once you experience God in a certain way, you know what He will do.

If you know that God loves people and that He wants people well and not sick, then you can minister to people. If you should backslide, then you would still know that God loves people. You would still know that God doesn't want people sick, and you could still pray for people. They could still get healed because your faith in God and His love for them is still just as strong, even though your walk with Him isn't as close as it was before.

Usually by the time you hear of some preacher falling, that wasn't the day he fell. It usually was way before that and he was on this path going downward, and then finally it caught up with him. It's not that God just puts up with it or that God hides it.

God is slow to jump on something because He gives people time to turn around. It is usually after so long a time before He actually exposes something. When He does expose it, it is not to get at the person He's exposing. It is to protect the Body of Christ and hopefully to turn that person around.

That's why a person who operates in a gift can backslide, and the gift will still work. Why? That's because they still have to step out in faith, and they still know what they knew before.

That's good and bad. It's good for the people, but many times if the person doesn't recognize that, then he may think, "Well, I must still be okay with God because He's still healing people when I pray for them." In reality, he's not still okay with God. It's just that God loves people.

Once you experience God in a certain way in one of these various manifestations, it gets very easy to experience Him that way from then on, pretty much at will. The key is getting that first experience. Get it that first time where you say, "Okay, God is using me to do this."

Maybe you have been used to interpret a message in tongues in Church. That wasn't just a one-time thing. You may have been taught that the Spirit came on you and interpreted, and now He's gone. That's not true. The Spirit abides within you. He does not leave; He is still there. That same Spirit that allowed you to interpret that is still there. Last time He may have initiated it, but once you experience it, then you can initiate it.

That is one of the problems with the revival movement. Everybody thinks it's up to God to send revival. The first time revival breaks out, people may say, "Wow! That was awesome!" However, from then on, they are responsible to stay revived. It's not a matter of, "Okay. That was good, but now it's gone. Let's just sit back and wait until another wave comes around." No.

This goes back to John chapter 5, and the Pool at Bethesda. Jesus heard about the man at the pool. It was said that at a certain season an angel came down and troubled the water. They were all waiting for the water to get troubled. Do you realize the whole time that they were sitting around waiting for the water to get troubled, the one who was sending the angel to trouble the water was walking around in the temple? They could have gone to Him and gotten healed at any time. They didn't have to wait until the water was troubled.

Our problem is that we want to wait for the troubling of the water rather than be connected with the One that can trouble the water at any time and keep it troubled.

Here is the key for us: He says, "Out of your belly shall flow rivers of living water." That's the troubling of the water. If living water is coming out of you, it's troubled. All that means is that you stir the water up; that's all it means. That's why He tells you, "You stir up the Holy Spirit that's in you.

You stir up the water that's in you and when you stir up the water, it will be troubled. People will get healed, blessing will come out, tongues will come out, and interpretations will come out. All of these things will start to happen because you decided to cooperate with God who is always on.

John Lake went to Africa in 1908. He left here on the first day of April and it took him about six weeks to get there. He got into Cape Town around May 14. His family, seven children and his wife, and two other people went with him. They were in Africa for about six months, and on December 22 of that year his wife passed away.

There was a lot of controversy over it. There was speculation as to the reason she died. During that time, he called her death, "Satan's master stroke," because they were so in love and so connected.

He was left with seven children, and the youngest at the time was eighteen months old. There he was in a foreign country with no backing and nobody to support him; he had nothing. His wife passed away while he was off on a trip, and he came back to find out that they had already buried her.

He had some other problems going on with the kids, so it really affected him. He began, as usual, by spending a lot of time with God and praying in tongues. Then God gave him an interpretation of a message, and he wrote it down. He called it "Guidance." It was an interpretation of a message in tongues that was given to him, privately, while he was praying in other tongues.

The following was given to John Lake through tongues and interpretation after the death of his first wife, Jennie, in South Africa on Dec. 22, 1908:

Guidance

O, Soul, on the highway, from earth unto glory
Surrounded by mysteries, trials, and fears;
Let the life of thy God, in thy life be resplendent;
For Jesus will guide thee, thou need'st never fear.

For if thou wilt trust Me, I'll lead thee and guide thee
Through the quicksands and deserts of life, all the way.
No harm shall befall thee; I only will teach thee
To walk in surrender with Me day by day.

For earth is a school to prepare thee for glory;
The lessons here learned, you will always obey.
When eternity dawns, it will be only the morning
Of life with Me always, as life is today.

Therefore, be not impatient, as lessons thou'rt learning;
Each day will bring gladness and joy to thee here;
But heaven will reveal to thy soul, of the treasure
Which infinitude offers, through ages and years.

For thy God is the God of the earth and heavens;
And thy soul is the soul He died to save;
And His blood is sufficient, His power eternal;
Therefore rest in thy God, both today and always.

You will notice that what he was praying in tongues was being prayed out as an interpretation of them. It was the Spirit of God praying through him and glorifying God. It was magnifying God and glorifying Him. At the same time it was comforting him, exhorting him, and helping him to cope with the situation he was going through.

Notice: this wasn't a message that was given to him by somebody else. He was praying in tongues to God, magnifying God, and in the process of magnifying God, God was talking to him and answering the need of his situation.

Through his own prayer, tongues, and interpretation, he was getting the answer, the solace, and the comfort that he needed. No one else was bringing it to him. It came out of the rivers of living water that were going out of him and coming back into himself.

Look at what David went through. In 1 Samuel chapter 30, starting with verse 1, it says,

> 1 And it came to pass, when David and his men were come to Ziklag on the third day, that the Amalekites had invaded the south, and Ziklag, and smitten Ziklag, and burned it with fire;
>
> 2 And had taken the women captives, that *were* therein: they slew not any, either great or small, but carried *them* away, and went on their way.
>
> 3 So David and his men came to the city, and, behold, *it was* burned with fire; and their wives, and their sons, and their daughters, were taken captives.
>
> 4 Then David and the people that *were* with him lifted up their voice and wept, until they had no more power to weep.
>
> 5 And David's two wives were taken captives, Ahinoam the Jezreelitess, and Abigail the wife of Nabal the Carmelite.
>
> 6 And David was greatly distressed; for the people spake of stoning him, because the soul of all the people was grieved, every man for his sons and for his daughters: but David encouraged himself in the LORD his God.

When David and his men got back, their lands and the city were burned. David's wives, and all of the wives, sons, and daughters of all of his mighty men of valor were taken away captive. It said that David and the men that were with him cried. They cried until they could cry no more tears. Then, it said that after all of that, "David began to encourage himself in the Lord."

They went through the process of grieving. Grieving is normal. They cried and they grieved, but then they went to David. Notice it didn't say, "The men gathered around David and said, 'Don't worry David. We'll go and get them back.'" No, the men were ready to kill him.

They said, "Look what you've done to us. Look what you've brought us to. We were out fighting for you and now our families are gone."

David had no one there who was coming to him and encouraging him, so he encouraged himself in the Lord. The way he did that was he began to write a psalm and sing to himself to encourage himself.

As he sang the psalm, he heard himself say how he'd gone through troubles, but his God was with him. He knew that his God would help him to overcome those troubles. It says that he would continue to serve God all the days of his life. That came by inspiration. I'm not saying that David spoke in other tongues. I'm just saying that the Spirit of God with David began to flow out of him and he began to encourage himself, because there was no one else there to do it.

Whenever you think you're alone, and whenever you think you've got no one to encourage you, you always have yourself. From within yourself, you can pull out the wisdom, the counsel, the encouragement, and the comfort of God, by the Spirit, by praying in other tongues.

The Bible is very clear. If you want a gift, and you desire it, you go after it; you seek it. All of these gifts are manifestations of the Spirit, and He wants to manifest Himself. He will manifest Himself to you for your need, for yourself, as well as for anybody else.

Back in the late '60s or early '70s, Oral Roberts went to Tulsa. He had made all kinds of decisions and everybody said, "Oh, this is going to cost you the ministry."

Being a Pentecostal preacher, he said that he had prayed in tongues all of his life. He went to a certain area of Tulsa and started walking around. As he was walking around this field, he prayed in tongues. He stopped and said, "What am I doing here?" He started saying, "I need the interpretation of these tongues. What's going on?" He prayed out the interpretation, and the interpretation he described was all of Oral Roberts University. He built ORU, the Christian University, there.

Every time a problem would come up, they would say, "What are we going to do about this?" He would say, "Hang on; I'll get back with you." Then, he would go and he would pray in tongues, and then he would pray out the interpretation. He would tell them the interpretation and that would be the answer for the problem, and then they would move on. For maybe 30 years, he did that very thing of praying in tongues, interpreting it, and doing business according to the interpretation of the tongues. That's how ORU was built.

Personally, I believe that a lot of the problems that ORU experienced in the later years was because there was a ceasing of tongues and interpretation of the guidance of God telling them what to do. This is nothing against him, but there comes a time, if you surround yourself with the wrong kind of people, you start getting wrong counsel. You will move toward business more than ministry. When you do that, things change.

You have to understand what gets you to the point where you are. It may not always be the exact same thing that will get you to the next point, but you never totally change the direction. In other words, what you started with, you stay with. You stay with the same idea because that is how God uses you in that area.

There are a lot of things that change even in what we're doing. My whole purpose with the Bible School was to equip ministers for the field. My goal was not to have a Bible School that was accredited, in the sense of having someone say, "Okay, you're a Bible School." It had nothing to do with that. The whole purpose was to equip ministers for the field as quickly as possible. For people who want degrees, there are other schools for that. We're not doing that. We are building a school.

My goal is to get to a place where I don't charge tuition. I don't like tuition. That's why we don't charge a fee to come to these meetings. They're open and anybody can come to them. We don't charge a fee for being here.

That's the way I want the Bible School to be. I want it to be on a donation basis. I really don't want to have to charge tuition, because we want the message to get out, and we want to train people. We are in the process of setting it up that way. That is not the conventional business wisdom of how to do things, but it is spiritual.

It's not about how much money we can acquire or anything else. Honestly, the way I feel about it is that as long as I can get to where I'm going next, and get to eat a meal regularly, and have a roof over my head if I need it, that's good. My purpose is not to see how much I can acquire, but to see how far I can go in the spirit realm.

I want to see how much I can accomplish for the Kingdom of God, so it's not about how much money I have; it's what we can do. That's the purpose. That's why we're pushing to do things a little differently.

Sometimes it seems like we don't know what we're doing, and it's because we don't. We are finding out by the Spirit as we move forward.

I look at the church world, and if it is supposed to be producing Jesus-like Christians, it isn't. Why would I want to do things the way they've done them? That's the beauty of the situation we're in. We can do things the way we see them in the Bible and the way we know that God wants us to do them.

We want to fulfill Ephesians. We want to make sure that we help present to Christ a pure, glorious, spotless, and without wrinkle church. We're not going to do that by copying things that other people have done that produced the wrong results.

I'm going to get into some of these things because I really want us to get to the practical application aspect of it.

TONGUES AND INTERCESSION FOR OTHERS

We are looking at Tongues and Intercession. Notice, this has to do with groaning, crying out, weeping and travailing. In Romans 8:26, it says,

> 26 Likewise the Spirit also helpeth our infirmities: for we know not what we should pray for as we ought: but the Spirit itself maketh intercession for us with groanings which cannot be uttered.

"Likewise the Spirit also helpeth our infirmities: for we know not what we should pray for as we ought." Notice that it says, "…we know not." That is a little deceiving, because the Apostle John said, "We know all things." That was written later. When Paul used the word "know" here, he was saying that we don't know with our minds, but we do know with the mind of the Spirit. What we need to do is get what is in the mind of the Spirit into our minds. That's called renewing the mind.

There are all kinds of aspects that fit together regarding renewing of the mind, but I am absolutely convinced that the best way is by praying in tongues and interpreting them out.

Watch what he says next: "…but the Spirit himself maketh intercession for us with groanings which cannot be uttered." The Spirit of God, Himself, is making intercession for us.

Since we don't know how we ought to pray for things, He has to pray for things. Now, how is He going to pray for these things? He is in us, and He knows us. He actually says this in verse 27,

27 And he that searcheth the hearts knoweth what *is* the mind of the Spirit, because he maketh intercession for the saints according to *the will of* God.

We have always looked at this as an outward thing. We are going to pray in other tongues and intercede by the Spirit for other people. Sometimes you get into what people would call a "spirit of intercession" and you start praying, and say, "I wonder who that was for?"

Maybe you didn't know who it was for when you prayed. It is good if about 90 percent of your praying and intercession in tongues is for other people. You can direct your tongues toward a situation. You say, "They're calling for help, and I don't know what the problem is. I don't know what's going on. I just know that something isn't right," and you don't know how to pray. How do you pray? You pray in tongues.

You say, "I am going to pray in tongues, and I am purposely going to direct it toward that situation, because God knows what that situation is." Then, you start praying in tongues and you intercede. The thing is that you'll start praying that way, and it will take on a life of its own. In other words, it will move into other areas, and sometimes you'll even know what it's about in the lives of others.

It depends on how much God can trust you. The more God can trust you to keep secrets, the more He will reveal secrets. If you've got to tell everything God shows you about other peoples' lives, He probably won't show you much. He will probably just keep it in tongues and you won't have a clue what's going on.

When I was in Africa in '97, we got stopped by government troops. I was with another pastor, and they put us in the back of a truck. As we were driving, we saw several cars with open doors, and things strewn out. They were shooting people; it was a bad situation. We didn't know what their plan was or what they were going to do to us. We didn't know if we were going to be shot; we didn't understand them.

I was in Kenya at the time. We were put in the truck and were driven some distance, not knowing if they were going to take us over a hill somewhere and shoot us.

I had about $3,000 in cash on me. At that time the average yearly salary for people in that area was about $300. That was like a ten year pension plan for somebody.

It was daytime there but nighttime here. At that exact moment, my wife was awakened here in the States and began praying in tongues for me. She knew it was for me but didn't know the situation we were in.

At that point they took me straight to the airport, and then they went back to the guest house where we were staying and they gathered up all of my things. It is never a good feeling when somebody else gathers your things. They brought them to the airport, and then made me buy a ticket to leave out early. They forced me to get out.

When I got back, my wife and I started talking and I was telling her about the situation and what had gone on. Then, we started comparing notes. At the exact time that I was put in the truck, and they started driving away, and when that pastor and I started praying in tongues, my wife was awakened and she began praying in tongues. I firmly believe that because of that incident, we were spared. I believe that was intercession. The pastor and I were doing it for ourselves and she did it for me. I believe that is why we were spared at that time. We have seen all kinds of incidents like that.

Sometimes your intercession will be for other people. At some point, you're just going to have to trust God that what is happening is Him.

As you're praying in other tongues, your mind will try to wander. That is okay because your mind is not involved. It says that you pray with your spirit so your understanding is unfruitful at that point.

As you're praying in other tongues you may get what I like to call, "flashes." You may just get a picture, but "poof," it's gone. The split second that you see it, you know everything about it. There's a split second where it just "flashes." It's like looking at a picture.

It's as if you took a picture out of your photo album. You can take that picture out and somebody else can look at it and all they see is the picture. If you look at it, you can see what's not in the picture, because you were there.

When you're praying in other tongues and this picture flashes, you may see just this picture at that point, but it's like you know the whole situation, because you were there. It will be just for a moment, a split second. Boom! It's like an instant download where you know everything about that situation. That is the Spirit of God showing you what you're praying about.

That's why it's good to keep your mind focused and not let it wander. The carnal mind, the un-renewed part of your mind, wars against the Spirit. Isn't that what He tells us? As the un-renewed mind wars against the Spirit, your un-renewed mind is going to be unruly.

Whenever you decide and say, "I'm going to pray in tongues," your mind is going to say, "Oh, I don't want to do that. I want to go and watch this TV program," or "I want to go and do something else." You have to start to discipline yourself to say, "Okay, I'm going to pray in tongues, and I'm going to do it for an hour." You think, "An hour, I can do it for an hour." You get to praying and, you're praying in tongues, until you think you've prayed for an hour. "Okay....five minutes?" Then you'll go again. The key is to build up, and maybe you don't start with an hour. Maybe you start with five minutes, and then you go to ten minutes and you build it up to where you can keep that same intensity over a period of time.

As soon as you start praying in tongues, you set yourself and say, "Okay, I'm going to pray in tongues." The problem is that when you get there and you start praying, your mind is not involved and because of that, everything in the world will come into your mind. You'll be sitting there praying in tongues and as soon as you start praying, you'll think, "Did I turn the stove off? Is the stove off? I better go check." Everything tries to draw you away to stop you from doing that, and get you back into the natural. Why? That's because the carnal part of your mind is still controlled by Satan.

The carnal part of your mind still thinks in line with this world, which is at enmity against God. The devil does not want to give up any ground. He does not want you to get farther into the Spirit. He wants to keep you, like Jude said, in the sensual, soulish, realm of the soul. That is in the reasoning realm. Why? When you're reasoning, the devil can help direct you. He can give you reasons. He can give you things that make sense. He will say that it is logical to think this way, but God doesn't think logically; He thinks spiritually.

What people don't realize when they read the sermons and messages given by John Lake, as I said before, they were all usually prayed out in tongues first and interpreted. Even when he gave instances in his life, he may not have mentioned tongues, but that instance was a result of praying in tongues.

John Lake gave this story once:

He said, "I was driving down the road and the Spirit of God spoke to me." He was in Oregon driving on a two lane road going around a mountain. He said, "As I was going around this curve, I heard the Spirit of God telling me to get on the wrong side of the road. Now, logically that made no sense, because if there was a car coming around the other side, we would hit head on." He said, "I had heard that voice so many times, that I knew instantly to obey it, so I did. I switched lanes and got over." He said, "Right after I switched lanes, a truck came around the curve in the wrong lane. Had I stayed in the right lane, had I reasoned it out, we would have hit head on, but because I listened to the voice of the Spirit and did what I was told, I was in the other lane, and I missed the truck." He said, "Then, I got back over."

The reason he heard the Spirit of God was because he was sensitive to the Spirit which came about due to praying in other tongues.

That is another benefit of speaking in other tongues. It keeps you alert and makes you sensitive to the Spirit of God. I'm not talking about getting weird, but it will make you sensitive, and you will do things.

One of the things that I've noticed in my own life, especially over the last couple of years, is that I let things happen a lot more than I did when I was starting out. What I mean by letting things happen is that I trust God, and I know that He is directing my steps.

This is one of the things that really annoys my wife, because I'll say, "I'm going to do this." "Why are you going to do that?" "I don't know." I'm not saying I hear the voice of God. I just say, "I don't know; this is what I want to do." She will say, "It makes no sense," and I say, "Yes, I know." "Why would you stop there as opposed to here? Why the change?" "I don't know. I just know I should." When I do, then there's somebody there, and we talk.

Lately, when I go into places, somebody will say, "You're Curry Blake." I think, "Really? Am I? Are you sure?" Then I say, "Yes," and then we start talking. If I had stopped where I normally stop, I wouldn't have seen them, and I wouldn't have been able to talk with them, and usually, there's a prayer involved. It has gotten to be that way more often lately, and it is almost always in places that I don't normally go. It's almost always, as one might say, "Accidental," or "Coincidental." No, that was God directing my steps.

I believe that was very similar to the way Jesus operated as He went about. He had certain things in certain places where He had to be, but mostly, He wandered around. In His mind He wandered, yet at the same time in the overall plan of God, He was right where He was supposed to be when He was supposed to be there.

Our problem is we try to figure things out and say, "Well, that doesn't make sense, so I'm not going to do that." Sometimes it's the "not making sense" part that is your best testimony.

I'm not telling you to just float around. I'm saying that as you pray in tongues you'll be sensitive and it's easier for the Spirit of God to maneuver you into places. You don't even know He's doing it until afterward.

It's like the old saying, "Luck is what happens when preparation meets opportunity." The more you practice, the better you get at something. The whole idea is that the more sensitive to the Spirit you are the better things will go.

People look at me and say, "Wow, look at your life. Your life is blessed." It is blessed and the reason it's blessed is because I'm more sensitive to the Spirit of God and to where He is moving me.

I don't feel any different than I've ever felt. I don't hear the voice of God saying, "Turn here, or go there." With me, it's more like we are one together. Because of my study of the Word of God and my understanding of the Word of God, I firmly believe the Scripture in 1 Corinthians 6:17. It says,

17 But he that is joined unto the Lord is one spirit.

"He that is joined to the Lord is one spirit with the Lord." He and I are one, together. I believe He can tell me to turn and I'll feel like it's me wanting to. Why? We're in this together.

This is usually why people notice that God is talking to them. Suppose you're going down the road and God says, "I want you to turn here and go that way." Maybe you're not sensitive to it, so you try to keep going forward, and God says, "I'm saying that we are turning." That "hit," or sudden awareness, is "Oh, you want me to go this way."

The reason you notice it is because you bump into God, but if you're yoked with Him, you don't bump into Him. When He starts to turn, you start to turn, automatically because His yoke is your yoke, and you walk together. There is that oneness of walking together. Sensitivity to that comes through speaking in other tongues and doing it on a regular basis in your normal life, not just whenever you have a crisis.

Most people only pray in tongues or only pray to God when they're in a crisis. When everything's good, they just leave things alone. They could be a lot better if they would continue to pray in tongues.

God's best is not just to get you from one crisis to the next. God's best is that you walk with Him and avoid the crises. Then, if you find yourself in a crisis, you know that the reason you're there is to help somebody else.

TONGUES AND INTERCESSION FOR YOU

We want to take these piece by piece. We have already been through Romans chapter 8, verses 26 and 27, but I want to go back and look at that again before we look at verse 28. I am going to read those so that you get the whole context here.

> 26 Likewise the Spirit also helpeth our infirmities: for we know not what we should pray for as we ought: but the Spirit itself

maketh intercession for us with groanings which cannot be uttered.

"Likewise the Spirit also helpeth our infirmities…" These infirmities are our weaknesses, and our lacking, you might say. This is the Spirit of God, Himself, working within you to pray for you, because He knows what is going on in your life.

The way He prays through you is through your own lips, so a lot of times if you're not praying in other tongues, you're hurting yourself.

One of the things I want to emphasize is that many times when we pray in other tongues, we're praying for other situations and for other people. God can sometimes give you pictures and different things of what you're praying for, and your mind will sometimes try to wander. It's good to keep it focused.

You can even focus on listening to yourself praying in tongues. Don't let your mind wander. The flesh wants to wander, and it wants to dictate things, so stay focused. You can even read while you pray in tongues, because the mind is not involved. I would dare say that if you can't read and understand what you're reading while you're praying in tongues, you probably have not fully received the Baptism of the Spirit. A lot of it is you making it happen.

It's just good to know if it's truly the Spirit of God working through you in other tongues. A good test to make sure it truly is the Spirit of God in you is to read while you pray in tongues, and make sure that you still understand what you read.

There is so much to this, and obviously, we're not going to cover it all in a seminar that only lasts a couple of days. We have to realize that the depth of the Spirit is such that we can take one piece of this and talk about it for a week, easily, and never exhaust it. That is because it is Biblical, it is scriptural, and yet it is experiential at the same time.

One of the reasons that God uses tongues when you are praying for other people is that you don't need to know everything about their situation. If you did know the entire situation, you might pray a prayer that is not as big as God wants it prayed. If you knew every detail of that situation, you might pray more of a selfish prayer rather than praying the will of God. Many times you don't know exactly what you are praying for.

I loved Dr. Lake's stand on praying in tongues, and his teachings are quite different from a lot of the teachings that you hear.

Another of the great preachers was John Wesley. He said, "It appears as though God can do nothing on this earth except first he gets a man to pray." Almost all of the great men of God believed that, and they have said it in various ways. It is up to the believer to identify a need and then pray.

I firmly believe, because there is such a union between the Spirit of God and the Body of Christ that God wants to work on this earth. He has placed us here, and He expects us to operate by His Spirit to accomplish what He wants accomplished here.

God doesn't do things like man does. There are very few things that are more frustrating than for someone to give you a job to do, and while you're doing it, they send somebody else in to do that job, and you weren't told about it ahead of time. The person just shows up and starts doing the job. You ask, "Well, I'm doing this. Why are you here?"

God is not like that. He doesn't usurp authority that He has already given. As a matter of fact, He's very big on not usurping authority. The Bible says, "The heavens belong to God, but the earth has He given to the sons of men." He is working through a body on this earth to accomplish what He wants accomplished. He has relegated Himself to operate through man, because He gave the earth to man.

Could He just come in and bully His way through? Yes. It wouldn't be hard, but instead, He comes in by His Spirit and has men pray. Many times they don't even know what they are praying for, because they're praying by the Spirit about a situation. Praying by the Spirit releases that situation, and it may be a situation that has nothing to do with you. It could be a situation that has to do with a governmental change in another nation.

There are so many aspects of speaking in tongues and praying in tongues. I believe that God, seeing the situation, says, "This situation is forming, and I need a Christian to pray about that, right now." The Holy Spirit will stir up somebody to do something or find a Christian who's praying in tongues, and say, "Oh, it's that one. We're going to use that tongue for this situation."

There is nothing to say what that is until God says what it is. You can make any sound you want, and God is going to say, "Ah! I'm using those sounds today to mean a certain thing in that situation." Why? That's because He is God. Even if what you were praying wasn't a language, it has the sounds of a man speaking who has authority on this earth. God can take that and use it for that situation.

Many times you don't know what is going on, but it doesn't matter. You don't have to. That's the beauty of it. I believe that as you pray, God can use that. I also believe that many times what we're walking in is the result of past generations that have prayed. Their prayers have been stored up and are coming to pass.

I believe that as we pray in other tongues, God can say "Here is what I want you to say. I want you to say it right now, and when I need it I'm going to call it. I'm going to need it 150 years from now."

There were prayers prayed by the Moravians, prayers prayed by John Wesley, and prayers prayed by the Apostle Paul that I believe are coming to fruition today, because they prayed in tongues or prayed in different languages. He set those on a shelf; it's almost like they are time-release capsules. He will say "This is for that situation. I have a man to pray it and when I'm ready, I can release that thing and it will be there."

I am trying to get you to the point where you don't limit God because he's already made preparation for the situation you're in right now. Look at God and say "Whatever situation I'm in, I can deal with it now," or "It's already been dealt with. Regardless, it's fixed today."

Verse 26 said, "But the Spirit itself maketh intercession for us with groanings which cannot be uttered."

Romans 8:27 and 28 says,

27 And he that searcheth the hearts knoweth what is the mind of the Spirit, because he maketh intercession for the saints according to the will of God.

28 And we know that all things work together for good to them that love God, to them who are the called according to his purpose.

We know that verse 28 is a Scripture that is always pulled out and used out of context. We are going to put it into context. Let's just take this apart, piece by piece:

First of all, let's look at it in reverse. "To them that are called according to His purpose..." All things don't work together for the good to everybody. "Well, did you hear about so-and-so? He had a terrible car wreck." "Well, you know all things work together for the good." No! That is not what he is talking about. It only works together for the good to those that love God and are called according to His purpose.

God can turn things but not everything that happens is God's plan. If everything that happened was God's plan, He wouldn't have to turn things to make them right. Everything that happens is not God's will. If it was God's will, it would have been right in the beginning and it would have been part of the overall plan.

Verse 28 says, "And we know that all things work together for good to them that love God, to them who are the called according to His purpose." Now, let's go back a step. What are all things that work together? People will say, "Well, a hurricane tore somebody's house up, and that works together for the good…" Can good things come out of bad things? Sure! Can somebody's house get torn up and the insurance build them a better house? It could happen, although I haven't heard of it a lot.

That is not what he is talking about. We have to remember that Paul is talking about spiritual things here. He is not talking about natural things and the whole context here is the Spirit of God. All of Romans 8 is talking about the Spirit of God working within us to bring about God's will.

He says here that all of these things work together, so what "things" is he talking about? They are the things from the previous chapter and from the previous verse. Verse 26 says, "The Spirit helps our infirmities," because we don't know how to pray, "but the Spirit itself makes intercession for us with groanings." We are talking about intercession with groanings.

Verse 27 says, "And he that searches the hearts knows what is the mind of the Spirit, because He makes intercession…" There is that word, intercession, again, "…for the saints according to the will of God."

What works together for our good? It is this intercession that he is praying. What works together for our good are the things that the Spirit of God is praying out in intercession for us. That's what is working together for our good. Why? That's because He knows the things that are the will of God, so He is praying the will of God into being in our lives.

It's not saying that every problem that comes along is the will of God. It is saying that the will of God is what the Holy Spirit prays and makes intercession for. We know that all of these things work together for our good. What things? It is talking about the intercessions that He is doing. He is making intercessions with "groanings which can't be uttered."

It's not every problem that you face that is working together for your good. When people die in car wrecks, it doesn't work together for their good. He is not talking about events. He is talking about the Spirit making intercession by the Spirit.

How does the Spirit make intercession for you? It is out of your own lips. Why? That's because He is praying for you.

How do you pay your bills? You pay them out of your own bank account. You write your check for your own bills. Why? That's because it comes from you.

Out of your belly will flow rivers of living water. Those rivers come out of you and the Holy Spirit prays for you and makes intercession for you as you pray in other tongues. Can He use another person to intercede for you? Of course He can. They are usually connected to you, but He can use somebody who doesn't know anything about you.

The number one way He prays for you is through you. That way you are the only one responsible if you don't have something. You say, "Suppose someone wanted to intercede for me and the Holy Spirit wanted to intercede for me. Maybe it didn't happen because I didn't let Him pray in other tongues through me," or "If somebody else is supposed to be interceding for me and they don't, then it's their fault that I don't have what I should have from God." You're not allowing the Spirit of God to work through you to ask for you.

James 4:2 says,

> 2 …ye have not, because ye ask not.

The fact is that God put Himself inside you to pray through you, to ask for you. If you don't have what you need, it is because you have not asked.

Too many times we shut down how God wants to work through our lives because we don't pray in other tongues. It's not just a matter of praying, but it's a matter of it being for our own benefit. We don't allow Him to make the intercession through us because we get tied up in the affairs of the world. When we are entangled in the affairs of the world, we're just not spiritually minded. We lack in those areas because we have not given the focus on praying in other tongues that the Bible gives us. We are going to look at how it's done.

The number one thing in Corinthians that Paul was talking about was tongues. All the problems that came up had to do with tongues. Do you know why? That's because they were doing it so much. In that very book, 1 Corinthians 14:39, he said, "Don't forbid it." He could just as easily have said, "Just stop. It's not that big of a deal anyway. Just stop it. It's causing too many problems." He didn't say that. He said, "Do it right, but don't forbid it." Why? It was a foundational aspect of their lives, just as it is a foundational aspect of your life. It is the aspect of the Holy Spirit working through you. The number one way that the rivers of living water flow out of your belly is by speaking in tongues.

He said in verse 28, "And we know that all things work together for good to them that love God, to them who are the called according to His purpose."

Look in Galatians chapter 4. We are going to be talking about groaning, crying out, weeping, and travailing. We are going to talk about all of these aspects here. Paul was writing to the Galatians who had backslidden. Starting in verse 19, it says,

> 19 My little children, of whom I travail in birth again until Christ be formed in you,
>
> 20 I desire to be present with you now, and to change my voice; for I stand in doubt of you.
>
> 21 Tell me, ye that desire to be under the law, do ye not hear the law?

"Of whom I travail in birth again until Christ be formed in you..." This is not a one-time deal that he is praying for them. He said that he travailed.

We've been friends with David Hogan for many years now. He says that there is a group of women who work with him, and they're like mothers in the church. He says that whenever they have a big problem coming in that they don't know how to solve, maybe somebody has died or they need prayer power, he goes and calls this group of women together.

They come together in this hut bringing a rug in under their arms. They all come in, put this rug down, and then get down beside each other on that rug. They all get on their faces before God; they don't get up until the problem is solved.

They pray in other tongues. Many times he has been there praying as well. From time to time, he will hear different ones praying in tongues, and sometime they are speaking in English. They don't speak English. To them, English is the tongue that David speaks.

They get on their faces, having made the commitment that they will not get up until it's done. They stay there, and they know when it's done in the Spirit, because of the release that they have in their spirit.

Romans chapter 8 has a lot about the Spirit of God and how He works in us. Let's start with verse 19.

> 19 For the earnest expectation of the creature waiteth for the manifestation of the sons of God.

> 20 For the creature was made subject to vanity, not willingly, but by reason of him who hath subjected the same in hope,

"For the creature" means all of creation, as we know it. This was talking about the earth, and how everything about it was subjected to the sense realm, you might say, but not willingly. The earth did not decide to be subjected to Satan. Man gave the earth to Satan at that point. It was not subjected willingly, "…but by reason of him who has subjected the same in hope."

> 21 Because the creature itself also shall be delivered from the bondage of corruption into the glorious liberty of the children of God.

Paul was writing here to the Romans and this was around 40 to 60 years into the Church. This was after the cross, so technically, Paul was writing during the same time period that we are in now. Things didn't change at Acts 28 when that was written, and all of a sudden there was a whole new time period. No. It all started with the New Covenant in Jesus.

His resurrection started a whole new thing. Now we're in that whole new thing. The people Paul was writing to were in the same Covenant that we're under. It's the same time period; nothing has changed.

Here he says that "The creature itself also shall..." That means that it is in the future. We know that when Jesus said, "It is finished," He had finished His work, but there was still a "shall" that needed to be done. In other words, everything was not done.

There are still some things left to be done. It says, "This creature shall be delivered from the bondage of corruption into the glorious liberty of the children of God."

> 22 For we know that the whole creation groaneth and travaileth in pain together until now.

The word *groaneth* is the Greek word *sustenazo*. It is pronounced *soos-ten-ad'-zo,* and it means *to moan jointly.* This was translated in the KJV as: *groan together.*

The word *travaileth* is the Greek word, *sunodino*. It is pronounced *soon-o-dee'-no,* and it means *to have pangs in company; simultaneously with.* This was translated in the KJV as: *travail in pain together.*

The words "*groaneth*" and "*travaileth*" in the Greek are somewhat similar but far enough apart in the dictionary that there are some differences.

There are similarities and they are like synonyms, with the same meaning but different words used. They can also mean *to sympathize with, or in expectation of relief from suffering.* Even though creation is travailing, it expects a relief from the travailing.

Romans 8:23 says,

> 23 And not only they, but ourselves also, which have the firstfruits of the Spirit, even we ourselves groan within ourselves, waiting for the adoption, to wit, the redemption of our body.

You will notice that the Greek word for "*groan*" here is quite different, 200 words different. It is *stenazō*, and it means *to murmur, pray inaudibly: with grief, groan, grudge, sigh.*

We are still waiting for something. That's what some groups of believers don't get. Jesus has finished His work, but there are some of us who are still waiting. This is not the way it is always going to look. There is something coming that is better. I firmly believe that for something better to come, we have to grow up in order to allow that to come in. He said, "We are waiting for the adoption, to wit, the redemption of our body."

The inaudible prayers are "groanings which cannot be uttered." Paul was saying, "We groan within ourselves with groanings which can't be uttered." He was saying that what the Spirit does is make intercession for us with "groanings which cannot be uttered."

Paul is tying the groanings that we do with the intercession that the Spirit does. If we are not doing these groanings, the Spirit can't intercede through these groanings. We are co-workers together with Him; we are fellow laborers together. He is our helper. He is not the doer for us.

This is the way He helps you: just as you begin to speak in tongues, the sound of your voice starts the motion, but He forms the words.

We are switching to John chapter 11. The reason I put these together is so that you can take them in context.

John chapter 11, starting in verse 1,

> 1 Now a certain man was sick, named Lazarus, of Bethany, the town of Mary and her sister Martha.
>
> 2 (It was that Mary which anointed the Lord with ointment, and wiped his feet with her hair, whose brother Lazarus was sick.)

3 Therefore his sisters sent unto him, saying, Lord, behold, he whom thou lovest is sick.

4 When Jesus heard that, he said, This sickness is not unto death, but for the glory of God, that the Son of God might be glorified thereby.

You can see from this Scripture why people say, "You can be sick for the glory of God." Well, only if you're healed. It's the healing that brings the glory of God—not the sickness. God didn't make him sick so He could heal him in order to give glory to Himself.

5 Now Jesus loved Martha, and her sister, and Lazarus.

6 When he had heard therefore that he was sick, he abode two days still in the same place where he was.

He didn't say, "Hang on; let's just wait here." It just said that He stayed there.

7 Then after that saith he to his disciples, Let us go into Judaea again.

8 His disciples say unto him, Master, the Jews of late sought to stone thee; and goest thou thither again?

9 Jesus answered, Are there not twelve hours in the day? If any man walk in the day, he stumbleth not, because he seeth the light of this world.

10 But if a man walk in the night, he stumbleth, because there is no light in him.

11 These things said he: and after that he saith unto them, Our friend Lazarus sleepeth; but I go, that I may awake him out of sleep.

Notice that He already knew Lazarus was dead.

12 Then said his disciples, Lord, if he sleep, he shall do well.

Once again, they show that they were thinking in the natural and Jesus was thinking in the spiritual.

13 Howbeit Jesus spake of his death: but they thought that he had spoken of taking of rest in sleep.

14 Then said Jesus unto them plainly, Lazarus is dead.

Jesus didn't like saying the word "dead." He hardly ever said it. He only said it when people were so dense that He had to say it so He could get it across to them. Usually, He said, "Asleep." It was like when He said, "Why are you mourning? The damsel is not dead as you suppose but she just sleeps." They were all laughing, and told Him, "We know she's dead. Who do you think You are?" He didn't like to say that people were dead.

15 And I am glad for your sakes that I was not there, to the intent ye may believe; nevertheless let us go unto him.

"I'm glad for your sakes that I wasn't there." Why? If He had been there Lazarus would have been healed and wouldn't have died. If he hadn't died, there wouldn't have been a raising.

16 Then said Thomas, which is called Didymus, unto his fellow disciples, Let us also go, that we may die with him.

This is the one that is always called "the doubting Thomas." We always think of him as "doubting Thomas" instead of the one willing to be the first martyr. We always look at the negative instead of looking at the positive. He didn't say, "Well, I don't believe." He said, "Let's go die. Let's go with Him; we're going to die, too. They will stone us like they are going to stone Him." He was willing to go. Amen? When people talk about him, it's always, "doubting Thomas." It should have been, "brave Thomas."

17 Then when Jesus came, he found that he had lain in the grave four days already.

People always say, "Jesus should have gone right then, but He waited until after Lazarus died so He could raise him up." No, it says, "He stayed there two more days." Lazarus was sick, so Mary and Martha sent out a messenger. It took the messenger some time to get there, apparently two days at least. He was still alive when the messenger left.

Jesus stayed there another two days, because He already knew Lazarus was dead. When Jesus showed up, Lazarus had already been in the grave for four days. There was no need for Jesus to be in a hurry.

People always put it down saying, "God told Him to wait there until after he died so He could raise him up." No, he was already dead by the time He heard about it. All He did was wait two more days to make sure that nobody could say, "Well, he wasn't really dead." He had been dead four days, so that was really dead. He had already started to smell.

18 Now Bethany was nigh unto Jerusalem, about fifteen furlongs off:

19 And many of the Jews came to Martha and Mary, to comfort them concerning their brother.

20 Then Martha, as soon as she heard that Jesus was coming, went and met him: but Mary sat still in the house.

21 Then said Martha unto Jesus, Lord, if thou hadst been here, my brother had not died.

Isn't it amazing that the first thing she did was accuse Him? She said, "If You had been here, he wouldn't have died."

22 But I know, that even now, whatsoever thou wilt ask of God, God will give it thee.

23 Jesus saith unto her, Thy brother shall rise again.

She was telling Him, "If you want to, you can raise him from the dead." He said, "Your brother will rise again."

24 Martha saith unto him, I know that he shall rise again in the resurrection at the last day.

She said, "I know that he shall rise again in the resurrection at the last day." Do you see how she was wavering? She was going both ways here. One minute she was saying, "Oh, I know God will do whatever You ask." Then she was saying, "I know he will be raised someday."

Jesus talked about him rising. She should have at least thought, "Yes, I know. Let's go right now! Come on!" After she said, "I know he'll rise again at the resurrection, at the last day," verse 25 tells us what Jesus said to her.

25 Jesus said unto her, I am the resurrection, and the life: he that believeth in me, though he were dead, yet shall he live:

Jesus was saying, "I am the resurrection. What are you waiting on? The resurrection is here." We always put that in a spiritual connotation, but He was talking to the sister of a dead man.

26 And whosoever liveth and believeth in me shall never die. Believest thou this?

27 She saith unto him, Yea, Lord: I believe that thou art the Christ, the Son of God, which should come into the world.

Jesus asked her, "Do you believe this?" She agreed, saying, "Yes, Lord. I believe You are the Christ. I believe You are somebody special."

28 And when she had so said, she went her way, and called Mary her sister secretly, saying, The Master is come, and calleth for thee.

It says, "She went her way." She turned around and walked off. She probably wasn't expecting Jesus to raise her brother at that point. She went to her sister, Mary, and said, "The Master has come and He calls for you." It doesn't say He called for Mary. Maybe that was left out, but it doesn't say that.

29 As soon as she heard that, she arose quickly, and came unto him.

30 Now Jesus was not yet come into the town, but was in that place where Martha met him.

31 The Jews then which were with her in the house, and comforted her, when they saw Mary, that she rose up hastily and went out, followed her, saying, She goeth unto the grave to weep there.

32 Then when Mary was come where Jesus was, and saw him, she fell down at his feet, saying unto him, Lord, if thou hadst been here, my brother had not died.

She was more or less saying the same thing that Martha said.

33 When Jesus therefore saw her weeping, and the Jews also weeping which came with her, he groaned in the spirit, and was troubled,

The Greek word *groaned* here is *embrimaomai*. It is pronounced *em-brim-ah'-om-ahee* and it means *to snort with anger; to have indignation on*. That is not the same word that refers to how we groan in the spirit. This was translated in the KJV as: *straitly charge, groan, murmur against*.

The word for troubled is *tarasso* (tar-as'-so); *of uncertain affinity; to stir or agitate (roll water)*. This was translated in the KJV as: *trouble*.

Groaned there meant: *to snort with anger*. This was not Jesus weeping. He was not looking at them, and saying, "Oh, that's so sad." He wasn't saying that.

Groan literally means: *to have indignation on*. He was getting upset. It means *to blame, to sigh, to sternly enjoin*. In other words, He was locking in on this situation. It is also translated: *to charge, to groan, to murmur against*.

He was groaning within Himself. He was snorting with anger; He was getting fed up. He was getting mad in the Spirit, and He was troubled. The word *troubled* here meant literally *to stir up or agitate, as to roll water*. It was like "*troubling*" the water.

What was Jesus doing? He was stirring up that gift that was in Him. He was getting upset. Notice that He got mad in the Spirit, and then He stirred up the Spirit; He agitated the Spirit. Why? He was getting ready to raise the dead.

What does that require? Usually, it requires the gift of faith, and it requires the gift of miracles. There is no indication that Jesus operated by gifts. He had laid down everything that made Him different from anybody else. He only operated in what we have. He was able to stir up the Spirit to meet the challenge of the situation and to do that, He had to get fed up.

If you've been to the DHT, you have heard me say that John Lake said these very things. He said that there are 15 different elements to the secrets to divine healing. One of them is to get fed up. In other words, you have to get mad about these situations.

You have to realize that what is happening is not right, it is not the will of God, and it is not going to happen anymore.

As long as you have the attitude, "Oh, I'm so sorry for you. This is awful. Oh, God, please touch this person." Forget it! That is not how healing occurs. Healing occurs whenever you stand in Jesus' place and minister for Him. You say what He would say. He wouldn't say, "Oh God, please touch this person."

You say, "In the Name of Jesus, I command you, devil, back off! Leave this person! Be healed, now!" When you stand there and say that your attitude changes, your voice changes, and your tone changes. Why? That's because you're not begging God to heal. You don't ask God to do what He's already done. "By His stripes you were healed." He's already done it. Now, it's just a matter of getting that problem off of them.

That problem should have already left them alone. It didn't, so you have to get fed up and chase it off. Usually, that requires that you get upset. When people get upset, they tend to get loud. The loudness is not what does it. It's the fact that getting upset and getting fed up stirs you up to get loud. The loudness is a result of being stirred up.

You can get stirred up and be loud or you can get stirred up and be quiet. Once you learn how to get stirred up, you also have to learn how to do it quietly, especially if you're in a hospital, because you don't get to yell and scream in a hospital. You can't just be yelling and screaming and think that is going to do it. You have to get fed up, and you have to get stirred up.

Paul told Timothy, "Stir up the gift that is within you." He was telling Timothy, "Timothy, stir it up. Agitate the water; stir up the Spirit within you." Jesus said, "If any man thirst, let him come to Me, and I will give him to drink."

When it said, "Out of His belly shall flow rivers of living water," it was speaking of the Holy Spirit which had not yet been given, because Jesus had not yet been glorified.

What was He doing here? He was stirring up the water of the Spirit that was in Him to get the job done. Do you see how natural it is? By natural, I mean natural progression.

Notice that when Jesus groaned in the spirit it was not out of weakness. It was not out of sorrow, and it was not out of sympathy. He was mad. If you go to the Strong's Concordance, there is a certain level of word definition that they give you. If you go deeper and look it up in Thayer's Bible Dictionary, you can get varying levels. It gets a little more specific.

In the Strong's it says, "*To snort with anger, to have indignation on,*" but if you go to Thayer's it actually says, "*To snort like a war horse, about to go into battle.*" That gives it a whole different connotation.

When it said, "He groaned in the spirit," it did not mean that it came out of His soul; this was not emotion. He groaned out of the spirit, not out of the soul. Inside He began to snort like a war horse ready to go to battle. He was getting agitated inside saying, "No, this is not happening. This is not staying this way because this is not right." That's what you have to get ahold of.

The groaning in the spirit that Paul was talking about can come on you. This is part of the travailing. When Paul said, "I travail in birth again," part of that had to do with the troubling inside where you start to agitate, and stir up, and get fed up.

You will start to feel that travailing and it will take on a physical representation. It starts in the Spirit and it will generally overtake you.

The problem is that most people start in the soul and as they get the soul agitated, they get worked up, so they can't tell if the spirit is worked up. If you get the spirit worked up, He will usually work up the soul. If you start in the soul, you're never sure if the spirit gets engaged. If you start in the spirit, the soul will engage.

The problem is that many church services are soulishly oriented. They start in the soul and never get to the spirit. They can have a great service, good music, and excitement but it's all emotional. It is all soulish, and it is not spiritual. That is why I have said over and over again that I refuse to work people up. It is easier to just preach the Word. I love to watch when the Pentecostal people get excited and the preacher yells. I love it, but I don't do it. That is just not me.

The reason I believe that I have the personality I have is because I don't want to get you emotionally charged. I want to preach to you and have you make a conscious decision to walk in the things of the Word of God. I want this to be built into you in the spirit, so then you can make that choice. It will then flow over into your soul, and what is going on inside should make your soul happy. That's when you get ahold of it.

If I just came in and gave you some feel-good preaching and got you worked up, we could have a good service, but by the time you got home, it would be gone. If I can get this built into you, then it will flow over into your soul.

If you don't know me personally, I'm a happy person. Life is good, and I enjoy life. I don't know how it could get better. It's just good. It is not that I'm just happy. It is that I'm joyful. Happiness has to do with your external surroundings, but joy comes from inside. No matter what's going on around you, you can still have that sense of expectancy and that joyfulness.

That is the way that I live. I live out of my spirit, not out of my soul. Because I live out of my spirit, my soul gets to join in, but if I lived out of my soul, my spirit might never engage. In that case, a lot of things just wouldn't happen.

Watchman Nee was a Chinese Christian author and church leader. He was born in 1903 and died in 1972. If you have read anything of his, you would know that he talks about the latent power of the human soul. He talks about how most manifestations that take place in churches are not spiritual but soulish manifestations.

If you made a video tape of what most churches do, especially during the worship and into the preaching, and if you took it piece by piece and described the people and then took the same cameras and went to a concert, the people would have the same thing going on. Some of the manifestations might be different, but the manifestations would happen. Why? That is because it is soulish and not spiritual.

The purpose of a band is to work you up, give you good entertainment, and get you excited. Unfortunately, the main purpose of what people call "worship" in churches has nothing to do with worship toward God. It has nothing to do with connecting with God. It has everything to do with making you feel good so you'll come back again. It's soulish and not spiritual.

We have a piano, all of the instruments, and everything we need for a worship team; we just don't have a worship team. We have talked about it, and my wife thinks that we need a worship team. I said that I agreed because people need to worship but, honestly, I don't get my worship at church. I worship more in my car than I do anywhere else, and there are certain CD's that I listen to.

I know people want worship in church and that's good. I was praying about it and what came out was that I have got to teach worship before we get a worship team. I have to get our church fellowship able to worship God without that so that when we do get it, it will be pure worship.

I really believe that by the Spirit of God we should have true worship and not just piggy-backing, as we would say. We don't want it to be so that you just come in and get soulishly attached so that you can just flow with the music.

The idea is that we have to worship God and once our worship is right, the team will come. I just have to teach on it first, and the longer I wait before I teach on it, the further off I'm putting a worship team. I'm not in a big hurry to get it done; I want to make sure it's right. We have to worship in spirit and in truth, and not just with song.

We have to worship from the spirit and we have got to be able to do that anywhere. If electricity went out in most churches, they couldn't do worship. It's all based on the electric piano, the electric organ, and the electric guitars. I have been in Africa where all of the power goes out regularly and it doesn't slow them down a bit. It is awesome. They keep right on going.

I stayed in a home with a family, and no matter what we did all day long, every evening we would all gather around in a circle before we ate dinner, and we would start singing. As we would start singing, the other members of the family would come in. We would all stand around in a circle, worshiping God for 30 to 45 minutes.

Every now and then the father would stop and point to somebody who would give glory to God for something that had happened that day. One would say, "I want to thank God that He did this. I want to thank God that He is working in me this way," and then they would go back into singing. The father would stop again and point to somebody to give praise. They did that as a family. It wasn't at church; it was in a family. That is why things happen over there like they do.

Our blessings have become our curse, because we've learned to rely on them. Our luxuries become necessities to us, and we start looking at those things instead of always giving thanks and praise unto God and making sure that we can stay focused, no matter what. I could do power-point presentations, and I'd like to do some of those, but I am very keen on making sure that everything we do, we can do anywhere. I can do without electricity; I can worship in a dark room, sitting around quietly.

I was in Bentonville, Arkansas, and we were preaching in a hotel meeting room when a storm came up. This was before we learned to take authority over those things. The storm came up and the power went out and the only light in the room was an exit sign. We asked everybody to stay put because it was not the time to start moving around in the dark.

I moved underneath the exit sign where I could see my Bible and tried to read from it. I couldn't see it well, so I finally put it down and kept preaching. I don't need a Bible to preach. I have it in my mind, so I preached for another hour. The power came back on, and we went right on and had a healing service.

Why? I refused to let a little storm shut down the Word of God. You have got to get it in you and you have got to be able to do it anywhere, anytime, no matter what. If they come in and take out your instruments, what are you going to do? Are you still going to be able to worship? You still have your ten string instrument, your hands, with you and you use it wherever you go. You have to get beyond the peripheral. It has to be internal.

Christianity is internal and can be anywhere, anytime, under any circumstances. I can go overseas, where they speak other languages. When they start worshipping, I don't need to know the words that they're singing.

It is like when I go to a Russian church and it's all in Russian. I don't even know how the words are pronounced unless I hear them singing them. I stand there and sing in tongues, praising and worshiping God.

I'm one in Spirit with them, and most of the time I get the feeling that even my tongues take on the Russian accent and the Russian way of speaking, because we are one in Spirit. That's the way it's supposed to be; we are one. Amen.

GROANING AND TRAVAILING

We are talking about groaning, we are talking about travailing; we're talking about groaning in the Spirit, weeping, praying, and all of the various manifestations of the Spirit. We have to tie these together. Usually, it has to do with tongues or is a part of the overall being of the Spirit within us coming out.

Let's look at John chapter 5. We're just going to tie this in together, showing you the similarities here. Start at verse 1.

1 After this there was a feast of the Jews; and Jesus went up to Jerusalem.

2 Now there is at Jerusalem by the sheep *market* a pool, which is called in the Hebrew tongue Bethesda, having five porches.

3 In these lay a great multitude of impotent folk, of blind, halt, withered, waiting for the moving of the water.

4 For an angel went down at a certain season into the pool, and troubled the water: whosoever then first after the <u>troubling</u> of the water stepped in was made whole of whatsoever disease he had.

You can see the connection between troubling of the water and healing. It didn't matter who they were and it didn't matter what they had, they got healed. The fact that there was a pool of water, and an angel came down and troubled it, and that whosoever got healed of whatsoever, should prove to you that the key point in healing is not the disease or the sick person.

In the church today, people think that it's what this person did or what they didn't do. They think it's not God's will today, because this person sinned or they didn't have faith.

It's always about God and the sick person. Many times, people think it's about the disease, and that it's a punishment or a character builder. Honestly, when people get really sick, they don't have good character. Selfishness comes out. I'm not saying anything negative about them. I'm just saying that's what happens. When people hurt, they are not fun to be around. Pain, especially constant pain, tends to put people on edge which makes them generally agitated and upset.

Notice in verse 4 it said, "The angel troubled the waters." The word troubled is underlined in your manual. That is the Greek word "*tarasso,*" and it means *to stir or to agitate.* You do realize that is exactly the same word we saw in John 11:33.

> 33 When Jesus therefore saw her weeping, and the Jews also weeping which came with her, he groaned in the spirit, and was underline{troubled},

"He groaned in the spirit and was troubled." Notice that when He groaned in the spirit, He was seeing, knowing, and getting fed up with something. Being troubled, He was stirring up the spirit within Him; He was agitating the water of the spirit. We connect that with John 5 where it talks about how the water was troubled and when the water was troubled, somebody got healed. Whenever Jesus troubled the spirit within Him, somebody got raised from the dead. It is the same word, same idea, and same understanding.

We are going back to where Jesus was raising Lazarus from the dead in John chapter 11. In verse 34 Jesus asked,

> 34 …Where have ye laid him? They said unto him, Lord, come and see.

It may seem a little confusing there, but I just put John 5 in there, parenthetically, to tie the two together. Let's go on in John, chapter 11:

> 35 Jesus wept.

36 Then said the Jews, Behold how he loved him!

37 And some of them said, Could not this man, which opened the eyes of the blind, have caused that even this man should not have died?

38 Jesus therefore again <u>groaning</u> in himself cometh to the grave. It was a cave, and a stone lay upon it.

That is the same kind of groaning that Paul talked about in Romans 8:23, when he said, "…even we ourselves <u>groan</u> within ourselves." It was the same kind of groaning.

39 Jesus said, Take ye away the stone. Martha, the sister of him that was dead, saith unto him, Lord, by this time he stinketh: for he hath been *dead* four days.

40 Jesus saith unto her, Said I not unto thee, that, if thou wouldest believe, thou shouldest see the glory of God?

41 Then they took away the stone *from the place* where the dead was laid. And Jesus lifted up *his* eyes, and said, Father, I thank thee that thou hast heard me.

At that point there was no movement. How did Jesus know that God heard Him? That's because Jesus knew God and knew that God had heard Him. He didn't wait for Lazarus to come to the door and say, "God, I am glad you heard me." Jesus wasn't wondering, and He was not hoping. He was believing and praying. He said, "I thank thee that thou hast heard me."

42 And I knew that thou hearest me always: but because of the people which stand by I said *it,* that they may believe that thou hast sent me.

The only reason He prayed was so that the people that stood by might believe that God had sent Him. He wanted the people to know that He was connected to God.

> 43 And when he thus had spoken, he cried with a loud voice, Lazarus, come forth.

"He cried with a loud voice, 'Lazarus, come forth.'" Notice that He didn't say, "Father, please heal Lazarus, and raise Him from the dead. Father, do something."

He commanded Lazarus. He said, "Father I am talking to You so these people can hear Me talking to You, so they'll know I'm connected to You. I am thankful to You, and I am glad You hear me. I know You always hear Me. I just wanted to thank You." Then he turned and spoke directly to the problem. Not once did He ever talk to God about the problem. He never talked to God about Lazarus.

> 44 And he that was dead came forth, bound hand and foot with grave clothes: and his face was bound about with a napkin. Jesus saith unto them, "Loose him, and let him go."

Jesus told the man that rolled away the stone to loose him and let him go. The man probably wondered what was going on with Lazarus. The bodies were prepared like mummies. Mummies were stiff, and had a case around them. How did he stand up? Obviously, something went on in the tomb that we were not privy to. Lazarus stood up and moved to the door. It doesn't say how that happened, but he moved to the door.

Then, Jesus told them, "Loose him, and let him go." Jesus himself makes intercession for us.

Look at Romans 8:34,

34 Who *is* he that condemneth? *It is* Christ that died, yea rather, that is risen again, who is even at the right hand of God, who also maketh intercession for us.

This was Paul writing to the Romans. Remember in Romans 8:26, it said, "The Spirit itself maketh intercession for us," and here it says, "Christ…who also maketh intercession for us." Now, you have Jesus and the Spirit working together in harmony to make intercession for you.

Jesus is seated at the right hand of the Father, but He also lives in you. The Bible talks more about the Spirit being in you than Christ being in you. Admittedly, they are one and the same and they're connected, so they're in union, but the idea is that the Spirit in you makes intercession, and then your High Priest takes that intercession and ever lives to make intercession for you. What you pray out by the Spirit goes to Jesus, and Jesus makes that intercession before the Father.

The good thing about that is that you may not have much faith in your prayers, but you can have faith in Jesus' prayers. What He's praying is what you just prayed. He says, "Did you hear that Father? I pray what that person just said."

Jesus Intercedes For Us. We Intercede for The Lost.

In Hebrews 7:25, it says,

25 Wherefore he is able also to save them to the uttermost that come unto God by him, seeing he ever liveth to make intercession for them.

Let's go to page 24. We're going to talk about crying aloud. We're going to look at some of the various aspects like we mentioned earlier.

It Says to Cry Aloud

Psalms chapter 55, verses 16-19, says,

> 16 As for me, I will call upon God; and the LORD shall save me.

> 17 Evening, and morning, and at noon, will I pray, and cry aloud: and he shall hear my voice.

"Pray, and cry aloud." There is a time and a place for these things. There are certain meetings for certain things. There are teaching meetings, there are evangelistic meetings, and there are just believers' meetings where you come together to operate in the gifts of the Spirit and to flow in the gifts of the Spirit. There are prayer meetings where the purpose is to come together to pray either for a specific thing or for everybody to bring their problems in to pray against these things. Everybody will agree with them and get them taken care of.

Our problem is we try to play different games by the same rules. Different games have different rules. There are believers' meetings and then there are unbelievers' meetings. One of the reasons why the Church does not grow very much is because we treat every meeting for believers like an unbelievers' meeting. We'll have a room full of people who are saved, like we have every Sunday, then one person will come in that we are pretty sure is not saved. All of a sudden, the entire service will go toward evangelism. Everything will drop to the lowest denominator, rather than rising up.

A couple of years ago, I was in South Africa, either in Durban or Cape Town. I was preaching one night and it was a healing service. Usually at a healing service, I try to preach something about healing. I had been teaching the DHT all week.

When I got up to speak that night, it was strange because I knew the direction that I was going. I knew that it had nothing to do with healing. I thought, "Okay, this is going to be different. Since it wasn't their faith that counted, it didn't really matter what I preached. I knew what I was going to do, no matter what.

I got up and I went to Colossians. Basically, I did a simple exposition of Colossians. It's a short book so I just went through it verse by verse and hit some highlights on it. I didn't go through each detail in every verse. I just hit the main highlights.

The main thing was about you being connected with God, being connected with Jesus, and that fullness of the Godhead dwelling in Jesus. Now, Jesus dwells in you, and the fullness of God dwells in you. You are supposed to walk with all of this life coming out of you. It was a precursor for the New Man, basically. I preached, and I told the people, "I'm really not preaching toward unbelievers. This is meant for believers. I know there are many unbelievers here, but this is for believers."

I just preached, and I said, "This is the life you are supposed to live. This is what's in you and this is how you should be living the Christian life." We had more people healed that night during the preaching than we had during all of the services. They got healed just listening about the life of God within them. The amazing thing was that the people started praying for each other.

As we did that, somebody came and got me and said, "Brother Curry, would you come over and talk to this family?" I said, "Yes." I went over and spoke to the whole family of six or eight people. I said, "Yes, what can I do for you?" They said. "We just wanted to shake your hand and say thank you." They had brought their child in for prayer and for healing. While we were ministering, the child got healed.

Also, they wanted me to know that before I started preaching that night, they were not saved. While I was preaching, they said, "We want that life." They got saved by listening to the life that's available to live. I didn't get into trying to avoid hell. I didn't get into judgment and punishment. I didn't get into any of that. It was just, "This is what Jesus died to provide for you," and they grabbed hold of it. The whole family got saved and their child got healed.

The reason I am saying this is because there has to be a point where we start having meetings specifically for certain things. That's one of the reasons why, eventually, we will go to two services here. The early morning service will be for believers, because the unsaved people usually come to the later service.

We're going to have the early morning service for believers, and that's where we're going to get into details. That's where we're really going to train. We are going to get into what the people would call "the meat of the Word." We're really going to get into that, and then we are going to take a break, and then we'll have worship.

Then, we're going to have the 11 o'clock service, and that will have a more evangelistic tone to it. The beauty of it is that the people in the early morning service will stay over, and then they will help me minister to the people who come in. They can listen to a "lesser meat-filled service" because they have already been fed. Then they will stay over to help other people. That will be part of their training as they grow up. That's what we will be doing in the future.

The purpose of this is so that in our meetings we will come to a point where we are ready to do what we need to do in a meeting of believers. Then we can launch into who we're supposed to be. In other words, we get to practice some of the things we are talking about. It can't all be just preaching and saying, "Bless you," and then everybody goes home. There has to be a point where we are walking in the things we are learning. It's not like you go home and *maybe* put it into practice, but you actually do it while you are here.

At the DHT, the Divine Healing Technician training, I pray for people all during the week, but the last service is for the people that went through the training. We bring the sick up and they pray for them. That way they get to practice right then, and they get to see people healed right then under their own hands. They get activated for healing before we leave.

This goes back to where it says, "I will pray and cry aloud." Unfortunately, we have come to a place where we are too respectable. When we got man's respect, we lost God's respect. We would rather please man than please God.

There are things that we're going to have to do. The whole purpose is to break through the veil of the flesh that doesn't want you to do these things. For instance, the veil of the flesh—your fleshly body, your soulish aspect, your soul, your un-renewed mind—doesn't want you to pray in tongues. Why? It doesn't enjoy it. It's not fruitful. It doesn't get anything from it, and it gets bored while you are praying in tongues.

You have to set a time. When you start to talk about it, and say, "I'm going to do this," your mind starts thinking, "No. I don't want to do this. I want to do this other thing." As soon as you settle down to pray, then all of a sudden your mind starts thinking: "Did I turn the stove off?" or "Was that the telephone?" Your mind will start saying anything. It's like when a little child says, "Can we go? Are we done yet? Let's go play. Let's go do something else."

You have to take control over your mind, so that you can settle down. Usually, in the beginning, it will take you a long time to get to a place where you can focus on the things of the Spirit. Most people never get there. Most people just come in, pray a couple of prayers, and then they go back out. It is totally soulish, and it has no Spirit connected with it.

If you are involved with the world, if you've got a lot of interaction with the unsaved people in everyday life, then it can take you a little longer to get to a place where you can focus on the things of the Spirit.

You need to get all of the other things out of your mind, so you won't be so distracted. There comes a point where you have to be focused and be able to block those other things out and say, "I am taking this amount of time. I am going to do this."

In the beginning, it is a discipline. You set the time and you say, "I am going to do for this for a certain period of time." After a while, what starts as a discipline then becomes a habit, and then once it becomes a habit, then the third stage is you have to become what the Book of Acts talks about and that is how people get addicted to the Word.

As much as I read while preaching, and being around people telling them about the Word, I am still so trained that the last thing I do before I go to bed is read. Even though I do that all day, I still feel that addiction to read before I go to sleep. If I don't read, I will lie awake for hours, battling back and forth. I should just sit up, read, and get it over with.

At first it's a discipline. Then it's a habit. Once it is a habit, then it becomes an addiction. When it becomes that kind of addiction to the Word, it is a good thing. That's what you want. It helps you and it draws you into the things of God.

It's the same thing when you pray, especially when you are praying in tongues. Again, your mind is unfruitful, but it is your spirit that prays. You have to set yourself to do this because your mind will always try to lead you off into something else.

The other thing is that you determine when you are going to pray. You decide. Most people are either morning people or they are night people; they are one or the other. You should be able to do what you want to do, when you want to do it, and you ought to be able to discipline yourself to be able to do that.

My life is very hectic. It is routine in little doses, and then it gets to where it is not routine. I'll be here for a week or two, and then I'm on the road for a week or two. When I'm on the road, it's a totally different life. I'm in motels at night, and I drive all day. When I get to the next motel, I'm in a different city. After that motel, there is a different motel, and I'm driving to the next place. I'm constantly going, so there's no routine.

It's very hard for me to get into a routine of even exercising or anything like that. I have all of the equipment I need; I just don't have the time. I can't take the equipment with me, so I have to try and work it out. The best thing I can do is go for a walk. Even when I'm on the road, I try to get the time to walk a little; I have to do that. Because my life is not a routine, I have to be able to set myself to do what I need to do when I can do it.

My mind is always going, and if I'm at home, it is actually harder for me to fall asleep there than when I am on the road. When I am traveling, especially when I get on a plane, I say, "I am going to be on the plane for the next 18 to 21 hours. I will sleep this much time, I will write this much time, and I will read this much time." That way I can set myself and discipline myself to do those things.

You have to look at your clock, and say, "Okay, I have to sleep now." You don't feel like sleeping, but you decide to sleep. You have to realize, your spirit is in control. You have to take control of your soul and you have to take control of your body. You have to tell your soul and your body what you want it to do.

If you are a night person, you should be able to discipline yourself to be able to say, "I am going to get up at six o'clock in the morning." That is really early for you, but you say, "I am going to pray for an hour. I'm going to do it like I mean it."

Don't just get up and stand half asleep, and mumble a prayer. No, you've got to do it like you would do it at your peak hour. You have to learn to do it. Why do you have to do this? That's because there's going to come a point, if you are serious with God, and you are building yourself up in the Spirit, where God is going to need you to do something for somebody. I guarantee you it's going to come at an inconvenient hour for your normal life. It will come when you are not ready. You have to live ready.

You have to be ready and be able to do whatever you need to do. That is why you have to pray in tongues today. You say, "Why? Life is good." That's because you don't know what tomorrow will bring. You don't want to wait until tomorrow to do it. If they call you and say, "Hey, somebody just dropped dead," you don't want to say, "Well, call me back in three days." You can't do that. You have to be ready right then. Get ready now and build up so that tomorrow, if you don't have time to get built up, you can release what you've already got.

You may have a hard time getting up in the morning. When I first started, I had a hard time. Now, I have gotten into a place where I am good almost any time of the day. When I am up early, I am wide awake. I am up and gone.

When my kids were growing up, I stayed up late at night after they went to sleep. That was the quiet time, and I could write, and read, and do other things I couldn't do during the day. Now, I can really shift anytime to do what I need to do.

When I first started, especially in the morning, it was hard because I was more of a night person. I actually had to set myself to be able to get up, and stay awake, and pray like I needed to. I figured the best thing to do in the beginning was to pray in tongues in the mornings. Like I said, when you pray in tongues, your mind is not fruitful. Your mind will want to go back to sleep while your spirit is praying.

I decided the best way for me to stay awake was to get on my knees and start praying. I would wake up two hours later. Then, I would try sitting. Lying prostrate before the Lord did not work for me. As soon as I would lie down, I would go to sleep.

I had to try all of these different things. It was really hard for me to stay awake, so I decided that I would stand on the edge of the bathtub. If you stand on the edge of the bathtub, you can't fall asleep. If you do fall asleep, you are going to crack your skull because you are going to fall. I had to stand on the edge of the bathtub until I trained myself to stay awake. I stayed awake from then on.

You have to do what you have to do, but at some point you have to make the decision and say, "I am going to do this." Somebody's life or somebody's miracle is waiting for you. It is really simple. They are waiting for you to get disciplined, to get built up, and to live for something greater than yourself. Amen? That's the bottom line for Christianity.

Let's get back to where we were. He was talking about the wailing, the travailing, and the crying aloud. Starting in verse 17 of Psalms chapter 55, it says,

> 17 Evening, and morning, and at noon, will I pray, and cry aloud: and he shall hear my voice.

That was three times a day that David prayed.

> 18 He hath delivered my soul in peace from the battle *that was* against me: for there were many with me.

> 19 God shall hear, and afflict them, even he that abideth of old. Selah. Because they have no changes, therefore they fear not God.

Isaiah chapter 54, starting with verse 1, says,

> 1 Sing, O barren, thou *that* didst not bear; break forth into singing, and cry aloud, thou *that* didst not travail with child: for more *are* the children of the desolate than the children of the married wife, saith the LORD.

"Sing O barren, thou that didst not bear; break forth into singing." What was he telling them? He was saying, "O "barren one," the one who couldn't bear a child, "break forth into singing." Why? "You are rejoicing before you see the child." Did you hear that? That's faith when you rejoice beforehand because you call those things which "be not as though they were."

If you're going to call those things "that be not as though they were," you have to act like things are before they are.

He said, "…break forth into singing, and cry aloud." There it is again, "…cry aloud."

"Thou that didst not travail with child: for more are the children of the desolate than the children of the married wife, saith the LORD." This was talking about bringing forth spiritual children, predominantly.

In Isaiah chapter 54, starting in verse 2, it says,

> 2 Enlarge the place of thy tent, and let them stretch forth the curtains of thine habitations: spare not, lengthen thy cords, and strengthen thy stakes;

Notice, he was talking about enlarging and growing, even though he was talking to barren people. In other words, he was saying, "Look, cry, and speak. Bring forth these things. Act like it is true. Get a bigger tent. Get a bigger place."

If you want to have an orphanage, have a place for the children before they show up. People say, "When the children start showing up, then I will get a place." It is too late then. You build it, and they'll come. That is what faith is. Faith prepares ahead of time. Faith makes the nest before the eggs are ready.

> 3 For thou shalt break forth on the right hand and on the left; and thy seed shall inherit the Gentiles, and make the desolate cities to be inhabited.
>
> 4 Fear not; for thou shalt not be ashamed: neither be thou confounded; for thou shalt not be put to shame: for thou shalt forget the shame of thy youth, and shalt not remember the reproach of thy widowhood any more.

Now, look at Isaiah chapter 58. This is on Page 25 of the manual. This is just giving you some ideas of where He said to cry aloud. He was talking about praying to God and speaking things out. Notice what they were crying aloud. They were not saying, "Oh God, help us." They were speaking forth these things and calling these things into being. He says in verse 1,

> 1 Cry aloud, spare not, lift up thy voice like a trumpet, and shew my people their transgression, and the house of Jacob their sins.
>
> 2 Yet they seek me daily, and delight to know my ways, as a nation that did righteousness, and forsook not the ordinance of their God: they ask of me the ordinances of justice; they take delight in approaching to God.
>
> 3 Wherefore have we fasted, *say they*, and thou seest not? *wherefore* have we afflicted our soul, and thou takest no knowledge? Behold, in the day of your fast ye find pleasure, and exact all your labours.

Notice what fasting is: fasting is not so much about afflicting the body as much as it is about afflicting the soul. Why? It's not your body that gives you problems when you fast, at least not for the first three or four days. After that, your body starts to give you problems, but for the first three or four days, it is entirely your soul.

Let me give you a secret. If you want to eat, all you have to do is declare a fast. As soon as you declare a fast, almost everyone you know comes around and wants to take you out to eat. Isn't that right? If the homeless people got ahold of this, there would be no more hunger in America. Amen? As soon as you decide, "I am going to fast," everybody calls you up and says, "Hey, what are you doing for lunch? Where are you going?" If you're ever lonely or low on money, just declare a fast and somebody will take you out to eat. That's just the way it works.

He says, "Wherefore have we afflicted our soul, and thou takest no knowledge?" In other words, "God we are hurting ourselves, and you are not paying attention." "Behold, in the day of your fast you find pleasure, and exact all your labors."

> 4 Behold, ye fast for strife and debate, and to smite with the fist of wickedness: ye shall not fast as *ye do this* day, to make your voice to be heard on high.

It says "You shall not fast like you do this day, which is to make your voice to be heard on high." In other words, "Don't fast to make Me hear you." Yet, that is exactly why almost every church that I've ever been around fasts. They say, "We're going to fast to get God's attention." Here it says that is not why you fast.

If you fast to get God's attention, it's exactly like a child throwing a temper tantrum, and saying, "I'm going to hold my breath until I get my way." I've got news for you. Let him. If he holds it long enough, he'll pass out and there won't be a problem. You can't kill yourself by holding your breath, so don't worry about it. I am not getting into childrearing, but you're going to have to break that will.

Isaiah 58:5-6,

> 5 Is it such a fast that I have chosen? a day for a man to afflict his soul? *is it* to bow down his head as a bulrush, and to spread sackcloth and ashes *under him?* wilt thou call this a fast, and an acceptable day to the LORD?

> 6 *Is* not this the fast that I have chosen? to loose the bands of wickedness, to undo the heavy burdens, and to let the oppressed go free, and that ye break every yoke?

Notice this is not fasting toward God in that sense. It is fasting to break these things, and it is fasting to afflict your soul so that you can be effective in setting the oppressed free. Fasting is to fix you—not to fix God. Fasting is to kill you, so to speak. It is for you to die to self so that Christ who is in you can be seen.

You don't fast to get God's attention or fast in a way to try to get God to do something. People say, "We're going to twist God's arm by fasting. If we fast long enough, He will give us what we are asking for." No. What you do is fast so that you die enough to get His will in your life and to live out His will through your life. He says for us to break every yoke.

> 7 *Is it* not to deal thy bread to the hungry, and that thou bring the poor that are cast out to thy house? when thou seest the naked, that thou cover him; and that thou hide not thyself from thine own flesh?

In other words, he is asking, "Isn't the reason you fast is to cook your food and take it to the hungry?" When most people fast they say, "Oh, don't get me around food. I'm fasting. When I'm fasting, I don't get around food." Fasting is not so you can avoid food, but it's for you to cook food and then, when you decide not to eat it, you can take it to the hungry.

If you are not eating only because you're staying away from food, there's no virtue in that. Virtue is being right there and saying, "No, I refuse. I'm in charge of my body. I am in charge of my soul. Body and soul shut up. You are not eating. The poor and the hungry are going to eat this." Then, you take it to them.

When you're there talking to them, say, "I cooked this, and I brought it for you. I am not eating. You're going to eat." Why do you let them eat and you not eat? While their mouths are full, yours is not. You can talk to them while they eat. You can preach, you can witness to them, and tell them things. It's not just so you can go and have a meal together. You take food for them to eat and while they're eating, you witness to them.

We are still in Isaiah chapter 58. After you have fasted like that, verse 8 says,

> 8 Then shall thy light break forth as the morning, and thine health shall spring forth speedily: and thy righteousness shall go before thee; the glory of the LORD shall be thy reward.

In other words, "He has got your back."

> 9 Then shalt thou call, and the LORD shall answer; thou shalt cry, and he shall say, Here I *am*. If thou take away from the midst of thee the yoke, the putting forth of the finger, and speaking vanity;

The "putting forth of the finger" means pointing the finger at people.

> 10 And *if* thou draw out thy soul to the hungry, and satisfy the afflicted soul; then shall thy light rise in obscurity, and thy darkness *be* as the noonday:

11 And the LORD shall guide thee continually, and satisfy thy soul in drought, and make fat thy bones: and thou shalt be like a watered garden, and like a spring of water, whose waters fail not.

"The LORD shall guide thee *continually*." It doesn't say every now and then. It says, "*…continually*." This is in the Old Testament, yet this is one of the key promises of being in the New Covenant. The original Greek says, "*Constantly led or consistently led*." Every day, those that are constantly led are the sons of God. It is a key thing to be continually led.

Most people think, "Well, God led me to do that," or "I wish God would lead me like He did before." No. Those are special leadings. The everyday leading is what Romans 8:13-14 talks about, which is to kill the deeds of the flesh and do what you're supposed to do.

You don't need a leading to lay hands on the sick, to pray for the sick, to cast out devils, or to do anything else, because you already have a commandment that says to do it. You don't need a leading to obey a commandment. Remember that. A commandment is the leading to obey it. If it wasn't a commandment it would just be called a suggestion. It is not a suggestion; it is a commandment.

"And the LORD shall guide thee continually, and satisfy thy soul in drought, and make fat thy bones." Now, that is not as bad as it sounds. What he means is that He's going to take care of you. You're not going to go hungry and you're going to be healthy and strong. "And thou shalt be like a watered garden, and like a spring of water, whose waters fail not."

12 And *they that shall be* of thee shall build the old waste places: thou shalt raise up the foundations of many generations; and thou shalt be called, The repairer of the breach, The restorer of paths to dwell in.

There were prophecies spoken about us 25 years before I was born. They have been spoken by different people, and they have come to pass. We have had prophecies spoken over us for the last 35 years.

Even these meetings are the result of these prophecies to "restore the paths to dwell in, and to be a repairer of the breach," and to bring things back to the way they were. We've become so modern in many cases that we have forgotten the foundations of the Church.

> 13 If thou turn away thy foot from the sabbath, *from* doing thy pleasure on my holy day; and call the sabbath a delight, the holy of the LORD, honourable; and shalt honour him, not doing thine own ways, nor finding thine own pleasure, nor speaking *thine own* words:

> 14 Then shalt thou delight thyself in the LORD; and I will cause thee to ride upon the high places of the earth, and feed thee with the heritage of Jacob thy father: for the mouth of the LORD hath spoken *it*.

So far, we've talked about crying aloud, we've talked about groaning within, about being troubled, and even talked about travailing to some degree. We are going to look at travailing in more detail.

Travail: An Intense Prolonged Struggle

In Isaiah 66, starting in verse 6,

> 6 A voice of noise from the city, a voice from the temple, a voice of the LORD that rendereth recompence to his enemies.

> 7 Before she <u>travailed</u>, she brought forth; before her pain came, she was delivered of a man child.

8 Who hath heard such a thing? who hath seen such things? Shall the earth be made to bring forth in one day? *or* shall a nation be born at once? for as soon as Zion <u>travailed</u>, she brought forth her children.

9 Shall I bring to the birth, and not cause to bring forth? saith the LORD: shall I cause to bring forth, and shut *the womb?* saith thy God.

In verse 8, it said, "As soon as Zion travailed she brought forth her children." God was waiting because He was waiting for Zion, in this case the Church, to travail to bring forth her children.

It was like when Daniel prayed. It said that as soon as Daniel prayed, his prayer was heard and the angel was sent with the answer, but it took 21 days to get through. Why? It wasn't on God's part, and it wasn't on Daniel's part. The problem was the enemy that stood in-between.

For some reason, when Christians seem to experience a delay in an answer, the first thing they want to do is blame it on God. Either it's not His will so He hasn't answered, or they think that they don't have enough faith. In reality, "It's in the mail." It's on its way, but we get impatient.

We are the microwave generation. We want this now. If it's not now, it must not be working. You get frustrated if you can't get your food in 30 seconds. You think, "What's the matter with this thing? It has been 30 seconds and my food ought to be hot by now." Think back to where we came from. At least you don't have to heat it on a rock. Some things take a little time.

Jeremiah chapter 30 says,

5 For thus saith the LORD; We have heard a voice of trembling, of fear, and not of peace.

6 Ask ye now, and see whether a man doth travail with child? wherefore do I see every man with his hands on his loins, as a woman in travail, and all faces are turned into paleness?

Jeremiah was referring to men travailing like a woman. We know this has to be spiritual. We know that men cannot give birth to a child. He was saying, "I am seeing these men crying to God just like women do when they're in travail. It is coming from inside and it's not just a physical travailing. It's a physical travailing birthed in spiritual travailing and inwardness."

Let's look at 1 Corinthians chapter 2:1-16. I am turning this back toward tongues because that is our topic here.

1 And I, brethren, when I came to you, came not with excellency of speech or of wisdom, declaring unto you the testimony of God.

2 For I determined not to know any thing among you, save Jesus Christ, and him crucified.

3 And I was with you in weakness, and in fear, and in much trembling.

4 And my speech and my preaching was not with enticing words of man's wisdom, but in demonstration of the Spirit and of power:

We would ask why? Verses 5 and 6:

5 That your faith should not stand in the wisdom of men, but in the power of God.

6 Howbeit we speak wisdom among them that are perfect: yet not the wisdom of this world, nor of the princes of this world, that come to nought:

Notice, He was talking about a wisdom that he speaks, but it's not the wisdom of this world. James says that there are two types of wisdom: there is an earthly wisdom which is devilish, and then there is a divine wisdom which is godly.

He was saying, "I came to you with wisdom, but it was not wisdom like man has. It was not earthly wisdom, it was not devilish wisdom, but it was divine wisdom." Now watch what he said: "Yet not the wisdom of this world, nor of the princes of this world, that come to nothing."

> 7 But we speak the wisdom of God in a mystery, *even* the hidden *wisdom*, which God ordained before the world unto our glory:

"But we speak the wisdom of God in a mystery." Do you hear that? The wisdom of God is spoken in a mystery, "Even the hidden wisdom, which God ordained before the world unto our glory."

Here's what you have to realize. You think you have discovered God but in reality, He has been waiting for you to show up. His plan includes you. He planned way ahead for you to get here. He knew you were going to be here.

This is not a surprise to Him. He planned this before the foundation of the world. You are not going to take Him by surprise. That's why God never gets in a hurry. There is no surprise and no crisis to Him; there's no emergency to Him.

When you think in terms of the working of miracles, they're only miracles to us. They're not miracles to God. When you can do anything, then nothing is a miracle. Think about that. It's not a big deal to Him. It is only a big deal to us. Even though it's not a big deal to Him, He made the provision for the working of miracles for every believer. That's how much He takes care of us.

He says, "Even the hidden wisdom, which God ordained before the world unto our glory." It is not even unto His glory but unto our glory. Why? It is to give us a part in His great plan.

> 8 Which none of the princes of this world knew: for had they known *it*, they would not have crucified the Lord of glory.

"Which none of the princes of this world knew…" They didn't know this plan, "…for had they known it, they would not have crucified the Lord of glory." In other words, had they known what the crucifixion was going to bring about, they surely wouldn't have done it.

Do you think that the devil would care if the crucifixion just got you saved? If that's all it did so that when you die, you get to be with God, why would he even care?

The devil hated the crucifixion because if Jesus hadn't left, He couldn't have sent back His Spirit. Before that, the devil had to deal with one man walking around filled with the Spirit of God. Now, all men can be filled with the Spirit of God.

On the day of Pentecost, instead of dealing with one Jesus, he was dealing with 120 that were like Jesus. All of a sudden, it was a whole lot harder for the devil to keep his hands on and know what all was going on. It was hard enough trying to stop the One. He couldn't stop Him. What was he going to do with the 120? Soon, there were 3,000 more.

Then daily, there were those that were added to the church "such as should be saved." Those who were added to the church got filled with the Spirit. Why? That's because that was the norm. Each one was speaking in other tongues, and they began exhibiting displays of power.

That was what Jesus was trying to get to, and that's why the devil didn't want that to happen. Had he known what was going to take place, he would never have crucified Jesus. It would have been much better for him to just let Jesus go on living His life and letting Him do what He did.

Instead, the devil, not knowing what would happen, let his henchmen kill Jesus, and because of that, the Gospel spread. Amen? If he had known, he wouldn't have done it.

He says in verse 9,

> 9 But as it is written, Eye hath not seen, nor ear heard, neither have entered into the heart of man, the things which God hath prepared for them that love him.

We have always heard that quoted, and it used to be true, but that's an Old Testament quote. It's not true anymore. In verse 10 he says,

> 10 But God hath revealed *them* unto us by his Spirit: for the Spirit searcheth all things, yea, the deep things of God.

"God hath revealed them." What has He revealed? He has revealed, "The things that God has prepared for those that love Him." These are things that "eye has not seen and ear has not heard."

People read that and say, "Oh, nobody knows what it is going to be like over there. Eyes haven't seen and ears haven't heard of the mansions that God has prepared for us." That has nothing to do with what this was talking about. He was telling them, "You have no idea what God has prepared for you." That was because in the Old Testament, they didn't have any idea. They had no clue what the resurrection was going to bring about.

"God has revealed these things to us…" How? "God has revealed *them* unto us by his Spirit." Why do you think He wants His Spirit in you? He wants His Spirit in you so that you can know "the Spirit that searches all things, yea the deep things of God."

11 For what man knoweth the things of a man, save the spirit of man which is in him? even so the things of God knoweth no man, but the Spirit of God.

12 Now we have received, not the spirit of the world, but the spirit which is of God; that we might know the things that are freely given to us of God.

"Now we have received, not the spirit of the world, but the Spirit which is of God." Why? It is so that we might know "the things that are freely given to us of God." Why does God want you to have His Spirit? That is so that you can know all of the things that He has given to you.

How are you going to know these things? John said, "We already know them." How do we know them? We have them in us. How do we get them in us? Again, the mind of the Spirit knows these things. He prays the perfect will of God out of your life, through you praying in other tongues.

In Session 2, we read from Isaiah chapter 28, verses 10 and 11,

10 For precept *must be* upon precept, precept upon precept; line upon line, line upon line; here a little, *and* there a little:

11 For with stammering lips and another tongue will he speak to this people.

I'm trying to build this "precept upon precept," and lay it "line upon line." I am always taking it back to our foundation. As you pray in other tongues, especially when you interpret them out, you are not only being built up in the Spirit, but your mind is being fruitful, also. That's because you are understanding as you interpret. You're not being unwise.

Paul told the Ephesians, "Don't be unwise, but wise knowing the will of God." How do you know the will of God? The Spirit is going to pray the perfect will of God out through you. All you have to do is interpret it and then you will know the will of God. You can work that out in your entire life.

Again, it goes back to praying in other tongues and that's why it is so important. He said we have the Spirit so that we can know the things that God has given to us, and not just given them to us, but freely given. These are not things we have to work for.

You have to realize that we get what we get because Jesus did what He did. We don't get what we get because of what we do. We get what we get because of what Jesus did. That's called grace.

Say someone wanted to bless me with a high powered sports car. "Here are the keys. It's yours." I want to pass it on and bless my 10-year-old grandchild. I want to bless him the very best I can, so I give him this sports car. Can I give it to him? Yes. Can he drive it? No. Why? He's not mature enough to handle it.

There are things that God has provided for us. They are available. They're done; they're set. If I want to partake in that, then I have to be ready for that. It's not about deserving it. This is where people miss it. They think, "Okay. If I do this, then God will give me that because I deserve it. I have worked for it." If you have done something to earn it, then it's no longer a gift; it's wages. God's not going to be beholden to anybody. He's already done so much for you. No matter what you do, He will never owe you a thing, yet you owe Him everything.

It is like when you want to get into the Olympics. I could maybe talk to somebody and get you a place on an Olympic team. I might be able to get you on the track and field team. If I approached you and said, "I got you on the team; you are in," you would say, "That's awesome." However, if you just kept sitting there on the couch saying, "That's good. I can't wait," you are not going to be prepared. I might be able to get you on the team, but if you go out there without being prepared, you're not going to win. You're going to look like an idiot.

On the other hand, you don't deserve to win just because you trained a lot. A lot of people train hard, but they don't train the right way. You have to run, so as to win.

I don't look to God and say, "Okay, God, I am going to fast and after I fast, You are going to give me a gift." No. I say, "I fast so that I can shed myself, so I can operate effectively in this gift."

God's not waiting to give me the gift. He gave me the gift when He gave me Christ. There are still so many layers of me that maybe you can't see the gift, but as I die and I start peeling off the layers of me, then the gift can be operated because it's closer to the surface.

It is not that we deserve the gift. The gift's there. You lack nothing in that sense. You were born again complete in Christ.

I am switching over into the "New Man" teaching. You are born again complete in Christ. Just because you're born again complete doesn't mean you can function fully in all of it. Why? You have to renew your mind. There are disciplines that you are going to do, and if you don't, you will never fully function to the potential God ordained you to function in.

In 2 Timothy chapter 2, verses 20 and 21 it says,

20 But in a great house there are not only vessels of gold and of silver, but also of wood and of earth; and some to honour, and some to dishonour.

21 If a man therefore purge himself from these, he shall be a vessel unto honour, sanctified, and meet for the master's use, *and* prepared unto every good work.

The Bible says, "In every house there are vessels of honor and dishonor." If you're going to be a vessel of honor, then you will purge yourself. Do you get that? You purge yourself. It's not that God does it. Why? God says, "I've given you My name, My Word, and My Spirit. I've given you gifts. I've given you power. I've given you everything. What are you going to do with it?" What do we want to do? We want to have a party. We want to enjoy it and bask in it, rather than use it for the purpose for which it was intended.

We have to realize what we have. We have to grow up to be able to use it. It's not that God is waiting for you to attain something so He can give it to you. He's waiting for you to shed something so that you can function in what's He's already given you.

It's not a reward. God is not rewarding you with gifts. He's already given you that reward. He has already given you these things. Now, it is up to you to shed enough of yourself so that only Christ can be seen.

He says in verse 13,

> 13 Which things also we speak, not in the words which man's wisdom teacheth, but which the Holy Ghost teacheth; comparing spiritual things with spiritual.

"Which things also we speak, not in the words which man's wisdom teaches, but which the Holy Ghost teaches." These are not words that man teaches (man's wisdom), but words that the Holy Ghost teaches. I guarantee that this is a direct reference to praying in tongues. This ties right in with what Paul told the Romans, comparing spiritual things with spiritual.

> 14 But the natural man receiveth not the things of the Spirit of God: for they are foolishness unto him: neither can he know *them,* because they are spiritually discerned.

15 But he that is spiritual judgeth all things, yet he himself is judged of no man.

16 For who hath known the mind of the Lord, that he may instruct him? But we have the mind of Christ.

"For who has known the mind of the Lord, that he may instruct him?" This is an Old Testament verse. Then he says: "But we have the mind of Christ."

"Who has known the mind of the Lord?" He just said it. He was saying, "Who knows the mind of the Lord, except the Spirit?" Who knows the mind of the Lord, except the Spirit which is in him? This Spirit of God is in you. He knows the mind of the Lord. That's why he says, "But we have the mind of Christ."

If we have the mind of Christ, that mind of Christ is there, and who knows that mind? The Spirit knows. How do you get the Spirit to get the mind of Christ out of your spirit into your mind? You do that by praying in other tongues. You renew your mind with the Word of God.

Romans 12:1-3.

1 I beseech you therefore, brethren, by the mercies of God, that ye present your bodies a living sacrifice, holy, acceptable unto God, which is your reasonable service.

2 And be not conformed to this world: but be ye transformed by the renewing of your mind, that ye may prove what is that good, and acceptable, and perfect, will of God.

3 For I say, through the grace given unto me, to every man that is among you, not to think of himself more highly than he ought to think; but to think soberly, according as God hath dealt to every man the measure of faith.

You have to renew your mind, but you speak in other tongues. You pray these things out, you interpret them, and as you interpret them, you get the mind of Christ in your mind as well as in your spirit. That's the purpose of this.

He knows the mind. He prays the mind of God, and He prays the perfect will of God for you, and that forms you to look like Christ. It is this travailing in Spirit that brings that forth. You can travail for yourself, which most people end up doing at some point, or you can travail for others.

The idea is that in a fellowship, the body should be travailing for one another. If you do that, then you will definitely not pray selfishly.

TONGUES: A TIME AND A PLACE

We're reading from 1 Corinthians chapter 14 starting with verse 18. You need to mark these in your Bible. Paul was writing to the Corinthians. Remember, these were the carnal Corinthians, the ones who were messed up. He said,

> 18 I thank my God, I speak with tongues more than ye all:

"I thank my God, I speak with tongues MORE than you all."

> 19 Yet in the church I had rather speak five words with my understanding, that *by my voice* I might teach others also, than ten thousand words in an *unknown* tongue.

"Yet in the church…" He was talking about the assembly coming together. Then, he said, "…I had rather speak five words with my understanding, that by my voice I might teach others also, than ten thousand words in an unknown tongue."

People have taken that verse to put down tongues. Paul was not putting them down; he had just said, "I thank my God, I speak with tongues more than you all." He wasn't putting them down. He was just saying: "Look, there's a time, a place, and a way to do things. In a meeting with believers, it is easier and better to teach than it is to try to get a tongue and to try to teach by interpretation."

It's much better to be able to pray in tongues, interpret it out, and then follow Dr. Lake's example. He was able to bring those things out all at one time in a message. Whenever you bring those out like that, you're not including the tongues. You're just giving the interpretation. Since tongues with interpretation equal prophecy, you will be preaching prophetically and bringing forth the will of God and the mind of God. The following is a quote from the manual:

"The Apostle Paul stated plainly that he spoke with tongues more than all of the Corinthians (who were known for speaking in tongues more than any other group), but he said that in a church gathering, he would rather speak in a known language.

"This clearly shows that Paul spent extensive time speaking in tongues during his normal daily life. This shows the difference between private use of tongues and public use of tongues."

Paul spoke in tongues more than all of the Corinthians, who were known for speaking in tongues. If he had to get onto them for doing it the wrong way, then Paul must have spoken in tongues a lot. This proves that he spoke in tongues more in his daily life, and shows that there are private and public uses of tongues.

Notice he said that in a congregation he had rather speak in his known language rather than in tongues. He had just said, "I speak with tongues more than you all," which proves that the tongues that he was talking about were in his private time during his daily life.

Obviously, he had more revelation than anybody else of his day.

In Mark 16:15-20,

15 And he said unto them, Go ye into all the world, and preach the gospel to every creature.

16 He that believeth and is baptized shall be saved; but he that believeth not shall be damned.

17 And these signs shall follow them that believe; In my name shall they cast out devils; they shall speak with new tongues;

18 They shall take up serpents; and if they drink any deadly thing, it shall not hurt them; they shall lay hands on the sick, and they shall recover.

19 So then after the Lord had spoken unto them, he was received up into heaven, and sat on the right hand of God.

20 And they went forth, and preached every where, the Lord working with *them,* and confirming the word with signs following. Amen.

In Mark 16 are some of the statements about tongues that you know. In verse 17 it says, "In my name shall they cast out devils; they shall speak with new tongues." We've already talked about this. A lot of this has been coming out and we don't even have to look at it here, but I've given you the Scriptures to go back over.

Go to the next page, page 30. We're going to look at 1 Corinthians chapter 14 in depth. I'm trying to point out some things.

Remember what Paul said in 1 Corinthians 14:18:

18 I thank my God, I speak with tongues more than ye all:

Remember that. Make a note of it.

Somebody might say, "Well, tongues aren't very important." The Apostle Paul apparently thought they were. He spoke in tongues more than anybody else at that time.

In 1 Corinthians 14:21 it says,

> 21 In the law it is written, With *men of* other tongues and other lips will I speak unto this people; and yet for all that will they not hear me, saith the Lord.

We know this is out of Isaiah 28. We have already read about the word "lips" in the Hebrew which is the word, *śâphâh or śepheth*. It means *a spout out of which something flows* or it can mean *a dam*.

The Greek word for lips in 1 Corinthians 14:21 is *"cheilos"* and it means *a form; a lip as a pouring place*. It means literally *a margin (of water), meaning a lip or a shore*.

Then, in Acts chapter 2, it says,

> 1 And when the day of Pentecost was fully come, they were all with one accord in one place.

> 2 And suddenly there came a sound from heaven as of a rushing mighty wind, and it filled all the house where they were sitting.

> 3 And there appeared unto them cloven tongues like as of fire, and it sat upon each of them.

> 4 And they were all filled with the Holy Ghost, and began to speak with other tongues, as the Spirit gave them utterance.

5 And there were dwelling at Jerusalem Jews, devout men, out of every nation under heaven.

6 Now when this was noised abroad, the multitude came together, and were confounded, because that every man heard them speak in his own language.

7 And they were all amazed and marvelled, saying one to another, Behold, are not all these which speak Galilaeans?

8 And how hear we every man in our own tongue, wherein we were born?

9 Parthians, and Medes, and Elamites, and the dwellers in Mesopotamia, and in Judaea, and Cappadocia, in Pontus, and Asia,

10 Phrygia, and Pamphylia, in Egypt, and in the parts of Libya about Cyrene, and strangers of Rome, Jews and proselytes,

11 Cretes and Arabians, we do hear them speak in our tongues the wonderful works of God.

12 And they were all amazed, and were in doubt, saying one to another, What meaneth this?

13 Others mocking said, These men are full of new wine.

14 But Peter, standing up with the eleven, lifted up his voice, and said unto them, Ye men of Judaea, and all *ye* that dwell at Jerusalem, be this known unto you, and hearken to my words:

15 For these are not drunken, as ye suppose, seeing it is *but* the third hour of the day.

16 But this is that which was spoken by the prophet Joel;

17 And it shall come to pass in the last days, saith God, I will pour out of my Spirit upon all flesh: and your sons and your daughters shall prophesy, and your young men shall see visions, and your old men shall dream dreams:

18 And on my servants and on my handmaidens I will pour out in those days of my Spirit; and they shall prophesy:

19 And I will shew wonders in heaven above, and signs in the earth beneath; blood, and fire, and vapour of smoke:

20 The sun shall be turned into darkness, and the moon into blood, before that great and notable day of the Lord come:

21 And it shall come to pass, *that* whosoever shall call on the name of the Lord shall be saved.

22 Ye men of Israel, hear these words; Jesus of Nazareth, a man approved of God among you by miracles and wonders and signs, which God did by him in the midst of you, as ye yourselves also know:

We have already read most of this, but the main thing I want to go back to is verse 4.

4 And they were all filled with the Holy Ghost, and began to speak with other tongues, as the Spirit gave them utterance.

Most people would say, "That's as the Spirit moves you." It didn't say as the Spirit moves you. It said, "...as the Spirit gave them utterance." Notice, it says, "They were all filled with the Holy Ghost, and they began to speak with other tongues."

"And they began to speak…" Who began to speak? All of those who were filled with the Holy Ghost began to speak. The Holy Spirit gave them the utterance as they began to speak.

You still have to move your lips, your tongue, and your mouth. They are still your vocal chords. The Holy Spirit doesn't take control of you; that's not His job. His job is to help, not to be a dictator. He is not there to commandeer you.

Go with me to page 32. This is basically all Scripture.

Acts chapter 10, starting with verse 43:

> 43 To him give all the prophets witness, that through his name whosoever believeth in him shall receive remission of sins.
>
> 44 While Peter yet spake these words, the Holy Ghost fell on all them which heard the word.
>
> 45 And they of the circumcision which believed were astonished, as many as came with Peter, because that on the Gentiles also was poured out the gift of the Holy Ghost.
>
> 46 For they heard them speak with tongues, and magnify God. Then answered Peter,
>
> 47 Can any man forbid water, that these should not be baptized, which have received the Holy Ghost as well as we?
>
> 48 And he commanded them to be baptized in the name of the Lord. Then prayed they him to tarry certain days.

"To Him give all the prophets witness," speaking of Jesus, "that through His name whosoever believeth in Him shall receive remission of sins. While Peter yet spoke these words, the Holy Ghost fell on all them which heard the Word." Listen to what was happening. While Peter was preaching, the Holy Spirit fell on them that heard the Word.

"And they of the circumcision," the Jews there, "which believed were astonished, as many as came with Peter, because that on the Gentiles also was poured out the gift of the Holy Ghost."

Do you realize that we have gone almost halfway through the book of Acts and are in chapter 10 before they ever realized that the Gentiles could be saved? Before then, they had to be proselytes and come into the Jewish religion. Here was a first time. Notice, this is what was key: "…on the Gentiles also was poured out the gift of the Holy Ghost. For they heard them speak with tongues, and magnify God."

How did they know they had the gift of the Holy Ghost? It tells us right there. "For they heard them speak with tongues, and magnify God." Notice: it was speaking in tongues that proved to the Jews that the Gentiles could be saved. Before that, as I said, they had to be accepted into the Jewish religion as proselytes.

"Then answered Peter, can any man forbid water…" Notice, they hadn't been baptized yet. There is a process, or a progression in the Spirit, and we see this in Galatians 4:6. He says,

> 6 And because ye are sons, God hath sent forth the Spirit of his Son into your hearts, crying, Abba, Father.

We can say that it is a two-fold process: there's a step one and step two.

Step 1. You get born again. (First, you've got to be a son, then as a son you ask for the Holy Ghost.)

Step 2. You get filled with the Baptism of the Spirit. The Holy Ghost descends into a son (a newborn Christian), the Christian is filled with the Spirit, and then begins speaking in other tongues.

For many people step one happened at one time and step two happened 10, 15, 20 or maybe 40 years later. That is not God's plan. God's plan is for it to be like it was in the Book of Acts. He shows us that the second they believed, the Holy Spirit fell on them. Bam!

What were they hearing? Well, they heard the preaching of Jesus as the Christ. I'm sure that they brought out everything about His going and sending back the Spirit. That's what happened to them on the day of Pentecost. I'm sure they were hearing all of that, so the minute they heard that, they said, "Oh, that sounds good!" Bam!

God was not waiting for them to attain a certain level of spirituality before He gave them the Holy Ghost. Like I said before, He gives you the Holy Ghost, not because you deserve it, but because you need it. You need Him to come into your life. He's trying to get the Holy Spirit to fill you as quickly as possible.

Wrong teaching, wrong doctrine, and wrong understanding have kept us from being filled in many cases, and in some cases it was even taught against.

He says in verse 45 that they realized, "…as many as came with Peter, because that on the Gentiles also was poured out the gift of the Holy Ghost." We know that the gift of the Holy Ghost can be poured out, so we know it was the Baptism of the Spirit he was talking about.

"For they heard them speak with tongues, and magnify God." They considered the gift of the Holy Ghost, or the receiving of it, to be demonstrated by speaking in other tongues.

In verse 47 of Acts, chapter 10 he said "Then answered Peter, can any man forbid water, that these should not be baptized, which have received the Holy Ghost as well as we?" We know now that they had not yet been baptized. In a matter of seconds, these people got saved and baptized in the Holy Ghost. Even before they got a chance to get baptized in water, they got baptized with the Holy Ghost.

In verse 48 of Acts, chapter 10 it said, "He commanded them to be baptized in the name of the Lord. Then prayed they Him to tarry certain days." In other words, "Okay, we're saved, we're filled with the Holy Spirit, now stay here and teach us for a while."

Now go to page 33. Acts chapter 19 verses 1-6 says,

1 And it came to pass, that, while Apollos was at Corinth, Paul having passed through the upper coasts came to Ephesus: and finding certain disciples,

2 He said unto them, Have ye received the Holy Ghost since ye believed? And they said unto him, We have not so much as heard whether there be any Holy Ghost.

3 And he said unto them, Unto what then were ye baptized? And they said, Unto John's baptism.

4 Then said Paul, John verily baptized with the baptism of repentance, saying unto the people, that they should believe on him which should come after him, that is, on Christ Jesus.

5 When they heard *this,* they were baptized in the name of the Lord Jesus.

6 And when Paul had laid *his* hands upon them, the Holy Ghost came on them; and they spake with tongues, and prophesied.

"And it came to pass, that, while Apollos was at Corinth, Paul having passed through the upper coasts came to Ephesus." Later on, he wrote the Book of Ephesians to them, so these were the people he was talking to.

"And finding certain disciples, he said unto them, Have you received the Holy Ghost since you believed? And they said unto him, We have not so much as heard whether there be any Holy Ghost. And he said unto them, Unto what then were ye baptized? And they said, Unto John's baptism." What was amazing is that they only heard part of John's message. They heard John's message of baptism to repentance, but John also said, "There's One coming after me that's going to baptize you with the Holy Ghost and fire."

How did they not hear that? All they heard was John's baptism. It doesn't say that they were John's disciples. It just says that they were baptized with John's baptism. Apparently, some other disciples came in who had heard about John's baptism, had baptized them, yet didn't tell them John's entire message. They didn't tell them about the Baptism of the Holy Ghost because they said, "We haven't even heard about the Holy Ghost. We didn't know there was one."

He asked, "Unto what then were you baptized?" They said, "Unto John's baptism."

Then Paul said, "John baptized with the baptism of repentance, saying unto the people, that they should believe on Him which should come after him, that is, on Christ Jesus. When they heard this, they were baptized in the Name of the Lord Jesus. And when Paul had laid his hands upon them, the Holy Ghost came on them; and they spoke with tongues, and prophesied."

They had been baptized with the baptism of repentance, but as soon as they heard about being baptized in the name of the Lord Jesus, they said, "Yes, let's do that." Paul laid his hands on them, the Holy Ghost came upon them, and they immediately began speaking with other tongues and prophesying.

There are approximately 21 instances regarding this that I will be going over at some point. I will show you how this all works together.

There are groups that would say that what he was talking about here, the Baptism of the Spirit, was when you got saved and were baptized into Christ. All of the terminologies have to be put together. People will say, "Well, when you get born again, that's the Baptism in the Spirit. You're baptized into Christ and that's it, because it is said that there is one baptism."

Actually, there are more baptisms; there are seven baptisms, but I think only three or four of them apply to Christians today. The others were all Old Covenant/Old Testament baptisms.

There is much talk about being baptized in the Spirit. Some have a hard time explaining Acts 2 and how that happened and why. They say, "Well, that's when they got born again," but yet you've got Jesus saying much earlier, "You're clean now through My Word." You've got all of this written and there's still a lot of debate over it.

Here's the thing: Scripture tells us what it is. I'm not talking about human debate; let's just go with what Scripture says. In verse 2, Paul was talking to the Ephesian disciples, "He said unto them, 'Have you received the Holy Ghost since you believed?'" Some translations actually say, "Did you receive the Holy Ghost when you believed?" and people say, "Oh, see! Right there is proof."

Here's the question: if the Baptism of the Holy Ghost, Baptism of the Holy Spirit, and the new birth are one and the same, why would Paul ask them if they had received it when they got born again? Do you see? The fact of this one statement where he is asking if they received it when they got born again proves that there are two separate experiences. That statement in and of itself is enough, not to mention Acts 2 and all of the other Scriptures.

Let's just put that to rest. If you are born again, then you can still receive the Baptism of the Spirit and when you do, it should be, according to Scripture, evidenced by speaking in other tongues and/or prophesying and therefore magnifying God.

The Bible says that we are sealed with that Holy Spirit of promise. What better way to know that you are absolutely saved, delivered, and accepted by God than to also have the Holy Spirit speak through you? You will know that it is the Spirit of God dwelling in you. It shouldn't be a sign to you, but that affirmation from God Himself that says, "Yes, I dwell in you."

Compare verse 6 in Acts 19 that we just read above, with verse 6 in 2 Timothy 1:6 where Paul was talking to Timothy.

Acts 19:6,

> 6 And when Paul had laid *his* hands upon them, the Holy Ghost came on them; and they spake with tongues, and prophesied.

In 2 Timothy 1:6,

> 6 Wherefore I put thee in remembrance that thou stir up the gift of God, which is in thee by the putting on of my hands.

That is what I was saying earlier. What he was referring to here was not "a" gift. It was "THE" gift of the Holy Ghost that he was talking about.

Paul was telling Timothy to speak in tongues more, which would stir up the gift of the Holy Spirit.

Let's go to 1 Corinthians and get into chapters 12, 13 and 14.

In chapter 12, Paul begins writing to the Corinthians and he says,

> 1 Now concerning spiritual *gifts*, brethren, I would not have you ignorant.

The original Greek for "*concerning spiritual*" is *pneumatikos* which means *concerning spirituals*. "Now concerning spirituals, brethren, I would not have you ignorant."

2 Ye know that ye were Gentiles, carried away unto these dumb idols, even as ye were led.

3 Wherefore I give you to understand, that no man speaking by the Spirit of God calleth Jesus accursed: and *that* no man can say that Jesus is the Lord, but by the Holy Ghost.

4 Now there are diversities of gifts, but the same Spirit.

5 And there are differences of administrations, but the same Lord.

6 And there are diversities of operations, but it is the same God which worketh all in all.

You have to remember that the Corinthian Church was messed up. They had all kinds of things going on. They had sin going on in the Church; they had sin that even the heathen didn't do. They were really sinning. Paul had to write to them to tell them how to correctly operate the gifts of the Spirit which proves, "Where sin abounds, grace does much more abound."

Sometimes you have to step back a little and look at things to get an overall picture. Paul was writing to them and he gave them one of the main keys in 1 Corinthians 14:27-30,

27 If any man speak in an unknown tongue, let it be by two, or at the most by three, and that by course; and let one interpret.

28 But if there be no interpreter, let him keep silence in the church; and let him speak to himself, and to God.

29 Let the prophets speak two or three, and let the other judge.

30 If any thing be revealed to another that sitteth by, let the first hold his peace.

Paul was saying, "If you're going to speak in tongues let it be one or two, at the most by three but only if there's an interpreter. By the way, if there's not an interpreter present, then keep silent. If somebody gets a message from God, then let him give it out if there's an interpreter, but if not, let him keep it to himself." He then says, "If somebody else gets something, let him hold back and let the other one give it."

He was talking about how you are supposed to treat one another and how this is supposed to operate. Later on he even says in verses 39-40,

39 Wherefore, my brethren, desire earnestly to prophesy, and forbid not to speak with tongues.

40 But let all things be done decently and in order.

"Let everything be done decently and in order." There are groups that have used that Scripture to kill gifts because they say, "Decently and in order means it doesn't work at all and don't do it here because it's not in order here." If gifts are not in order in your church, you're not at a church. You are at a social club and you need to leave it.

I want you to get this because this amazed me. Paul actually told them how to operate the gifts. He told them, "If you're going to speak in tongues, the limit is two, at the most by three, and then only if there is an interpreter." He was telling them how to operate the gifts. That means that humans are in charge of how the gifts are operated.

If God were in control of how the gifts operated, why would He tell man how to be in control of them and how to operate them? He wouldn't. He would have just said, "Hey, don't worry about it. God's in control. Just let God take control and whatever happens is God." He didn't say that.

He said, "There is order to this." Why? That's because we are co-laborers with God. We work with Him. We're joined to Him. We have our part to do, and He has His part.

God never tells you to turn your will loose. He doesn't tell you to empty your mind and be in a void and just float, letting God do whatever He wants to do. The Bible never says that. It says for you to submit to the will of God. He says for you to have your mind renewed to the will of God. He tells you to be wise and know the will of God so that you won't be doing things that are not God's will.

God is very pragmatic in this and He tells people how to operate these gifts. It is not a matter of just raw emotionalism, which half the time isn't even the gifts operating anyway; they are just soulish things going on.

The key is to be in union with God. God did not give you the Holy Spirit just so you could have an exciting service.

These gifts are our tools. Dr. Sumrall used to say, "These are our weapons." We have to realize how to use them, which means we have to be able to use these weapons like a doctor would use the tools in surgery. He has his tools laid out and systematically goes through and uses what needs to be used at the right time.

Our lives were blessed because we got to spend time with Dr. Lester Sumrall. I wasn't even in ministry at that point. Dr. Sumrall was one of the people who really brought spiritual gifts back into the church. He trained under a man named Howard Carter, who wrote some of the first books on the gifts of the Spirit. Howard Carter learned how to operate the gifts of the Spirit while he was in prison in England during World War I as a conscientious objector. He was a preacher who wouldn't go to war so they put him in jail.

In the prison where he was, there was a crack in the ceiling of his cell right above his bed. When it rained, the rain would drip through that crack onto him. He couldn't move his bed and he couldn't sleep anywhere else. He had to lie there getting wet. He was a godly man, a preacher at that point, and he was praying. He was saying, "God, you've got to do something about this. I can't take this. I'm lying here in water, I can't get out of the water, and You've got to do something."

Finally, God spoke to him and said, "YOU do something." "God, what do You want me to do? There's nothing I can do." God said, "What can you do?" He said, "I can't do anything. All I can do is stay here and pray." God said, "You can talk." He said, "Yes." Then, God said, "Talk to the rain and tell it not to come back into your cell."

The rain was dripping through the ceiling onto him and he stopped in the middle of his prayer and said, "You stop! Go back out, and don't come back!" He said that as he lay there, he watched the rain come down, stop in mid-air, and then go back to the ceiling. Even though the hole didn't close up for the rest of the time he was there, when it rained it never came back into his cell. He said, "That's how God opened up the gifts of the Spirit." Then, he started working in them.

Up until that time, the gift of the word of wisdom wasn't even called that. They just called it the gift of wisdom. They said, "Oh, Solomon had that and it meant that he was wise." They said that the gift of knowledge, or the gift of the word of knowledge as we would call it, was just being smart and knowing the Bible. They naturalized all of these gifts, but it was Howard Carter that actually brought this into fruition to be able to say, "No, this is a specific activation by the Spirit of God. God gives them to man and man operates them."

Dr. Sumrall started teaching on these gifts and that's where we got our understanding of the gifts, originally. I believe, by the Spirit of God, He has added to that and has brought some things to fruition in our life. That was true even with the Corinthians. We know that the Book of Corinthians was written to carnal Corinthians. Let's go to 1 Corinthians and we'll look at chapter 3 starting in verse 1. Paul was writing to them and he said,

1 And I, brethren, could not speak unto you as unto spiritual, but as unto carnal, *even* as unto babes in Christ.

"And I, brethren…" He called them brethren, so we know they were born again, "…could not speak unto you as unto spiritual, but as unto carnal, *even* as unto babes in Christ."

2 I have fed you with milk, and not with meat: for hitherto ye were not able *to bear it,* neither yet now are ye able.

3 For ye are yet carnal: for whereas *there is* among you envying, and strife, and divisions, are ye not carnal, and walk as men?

The way one translation reads is "…and walk as mere mortal men?"

Paul was writing to the Corinthian Church saying, "You are carnal, you're in the flesh, you've got sin, and all these things going on. He tells them, "I can't give you meat. I can only give you milk." This is in chapter 3, and then, 9 chapters later, he gives the only full list of the gifts of the Spirit. He had just told them, "I cannot give you meat," and yet he writes about the gifts of the Spirit to them while he is telling them what is going on in their church.

What you have to remember is that 1 Corinthians is not 1 Corinthians. The one named 1 Corinthians is really 2 Corinthians and the one named 2 Corinthians is actually 3 Corinthians. Since we don't have the original 1 Corinthians, they just made it easy and called 2 Corinthians the first one and 3 Corinthians the second. W e didn't want to call it the second and third, because then you would always be going back and looking for the first one and you wouldn't be able to find it.

Originally, they wrote to Paul first, and then Paul wrote back to them. Then, they wrote back and forth, sending their letters.

They wrote to Paul and said, "When we come together, we've got these things going on in the church, and we don't know what's happening.

Everybody is speaking in tongues. People are speaking in foreign languages and they don't know what they're saying. Then somebody will stand up and say, 'Well, this is what they're saying,' yet they don't even know that language and they're supposed to be interpreting."

Paul said, "That's okay. Concerning spiritual things I don't want you to be ignorant, so here's what's going on. God gave us these gifts by His Spirit." Then, he goes through the list of them. "There's a word of knowledge, there's a word of wisdom, there's faith, there's the working of miracles, etc." He lists them and explains them.

I just read about when Paul went to the Ephesians. He found out that the baptism they had been baptized with was John's baptism. They had not been baptized with the Holy Spirit. They had been baptized by John and they didn't have the Holy Ghost; they didn't even know anything about the Holy Ghost.

Paul was telling them, "You've got all of these gifts, and you've got tongues." He was saying, "You have been born again, and you have received the Spirit. You just don't even know what you've got. You've got all of these gifts going on, and God is working these things through you. He's there, and you're doing these things by faith. You're stepping out and God's moving on you, but you have to realize that gifts are given."

Fruit is grown, but gifts are given. That is the amazing part. He gave us all of these gifts.

In one of the longest books in the New Testament, Paul wrote to the most carnal, messed up church and described the gifts of the Spirit to them. He didn't write that to the most spiritual church. Paul didn't tell them, "You have been good. You have gotten the teaching and you've done it. Now, I'm going to reveal some secrets to you. I'm going to give you some meat. I'm going to give you some things I haven't given to everybody because you're special and you deserve this, and I want you to know about the gifts. If you're spiritual enough, God may give you one of these gifts." No. He didn't say that.

Instead, he said, "You are a bunch of carnal Corinthians. You're messed up, and you've got sin going on that is not even mentioned among the heathen; you're sinning more than the heathen and that's bad." Then he said, "You've got all of this going on, and in the middle of that, God is working in your midst. I don't want you to be ignorant. I want you to know what's going on," and He starts to describe it.

Do you realize that the most complete list of the gifts was given to the most messed up church? Do you think there may be something to that? Why? Why would He give the gifts to the most messed up church? They had the biggest need. He gives gifts because you have a need. The gifts meet a need. It's not a reward for you to play with; it meets a need.

I'm using the best terminology I can to get the point across. The gifts of the Spirit are literally bursts of divine energy that have certain characteristics. The bursts of divine energy working through a person to speak in other tongues has the characteristic that brings about speaking in tongues, as we would say, diversities of tongues.

The same Spirit that can manifest Himself as a burst of energy in tongues, can manifest Himself as a burst of energy in faith, or can manifest Himself as a burst of energy in a word of knowledge. A word of knowledge is like, "Boom," and you know something. You ask yourself, "How do I know that?"

You can just picture these carnal Corinthians who had no clue what was going on. There might have been some man sitting there, who had been baptized in the Spirit, and he had spoken in other tongues. Apparently they spoke in other tongues a lot.

I really believe that one of the reasons why so many gifts were operating is because they were speaking in other tongues so much that it was activating all of these things. Miracles started happening, and they didn't even know what they were doing.

Suppose that in the middle of speaking in tongues, this man suddenly says, "Wait a minute, I know this," and then he stands up and says, "There's somebody breaking into your house, right now. There's somebody stealing things out of your house." The person just knows. "How do you know that?" "I don't know. It was a thought." "Well, that's crazy. Let's go and check it out." They would go and check it out, come back and say, "Wow, how did you know that?" He couldn't know that humanly. That was a word of God's knowledge imparted to him and that's how he knew it right then.

You saw that with people like William Branham. He could tell you everything but you had to be generally within a few feet of him or walk within his presence. There were times when he would look out and he would see something over them, and as he saw it, he would call people up and start knowing everything about them.

We're going to see how far we can stretch you here. I have to preface it with this:

Do you remember Elisha and Gehazi? Naaman the leper went to Elisha to be healed. Naaman fought against what Elisha told him to do, but eventually he did it and then he said, "I'm so glad I'm healed. I want to give you all of these things." The prophet said, "No, I'm not taking a thing from you; go your way." Naaman left and Gehazi, the servant of Elisha, went after him and said, "Excuse me. My master said he has decided he would like a few of those things." Naaman loaded him down and then Gehazi went back. The first thing the prophet said was, "Where did you go?" Gehazi said, "Oh, I don't know. Why?" He was dealing with a prophet. The prophet said, "Don't you know that my spirit went with you?"

Now, think about that. These are things that you don't hear about in church, because when you start talking about this, all of a sudden people start getting really nervous and they start trying to call it something else.

I've had so many people write to me. I had one lady write to me over a period of time; actually, I conversed with her several times through email. She said, "I go to a denominational church and the gifts aren't allowed there." My first thought was, "What are you doing there? You should leave."

Everybody has this idea that they are the missionary that's going to bring it in. If you do that, you're in rebellion. Do you realize that? Generally, we have to accept that God has placed that person over that church, and if you're trying to do something they don't want to do, you're in rebellion. You should leave and go somewhere where what you believe is accepted. It's that simple.

This woman kept writing to me saying, "They don't want this. I started seeing these things, knowing these things, and I started telling the people about them. As soon as I started telling these people about these things, they started calling me a witch. I said, 'But I'm not a witch.'" She said, "I pray. God tells me these things. I don't want to know them. God just tells me." She said, "Now I've learned to just keep my mouth shut, but I see things happening. I know they are going to happen before they happen. I just don't tell anybody. When it happens, I feel guilty because I didn't warn them. If I do tell them, they call me a witch." I said, "You've got a choice: stay or go. Stay and keep silent, or leave and find a place that can use and appreciate the gift that God has given you." We haven't been in communication, so I don't know what she did.

Getting back to what the prophet said, "Didn't you know that my spirit went with you?"

Let's fast forward to the early 1900s, around 1910. John Lake was in South Africa and he was on his platform in the Apostolic Tabernacle. They would all get together before the service to pray and they would all start praying in other tongues.

As he was praying in other tongues, some people brought up a prayer request for a young lady in a mental hospital in Wales. He said, *"Okay, we'll pray."* He read the details to them and then he knelt down and started praying.

He said, *"As soon as my knees hit the platform, I was in the Spirit."* He said, *"Immediately, I saw myself flying."* This was before airplanes. He said, *"I saw myself flying over the mountains, over South Africa, going straight up the Continent. I could see it, I detailed it, and I made mental note of what I was seeing. I detailed everything, all the way up. I saw the body of water, and I saw England coming up. I went over England, and I went into Wales. When I got to Wales, the city that they had given me on the prayer request, I landed at the end of a street. I was standing at the end of street and I walked down. I knew what house to go to because I recognized it,"* even though he'd never been there. He said, *"I walked to the door and there was this old ring on it that they used to knock on the door. I knocked on the door. They opened the door. I walked inside, went straight up to this young girl's room, opened the door, walked inside, put my hand on her, and I cast the devil out of her. The next thing I knew as I opened my eyes, I was back on my platform in South Africa."*

He said, *"It takes three to four weeks, for mail to get from Wales to South Africa."* Three weeks later, he got a letter saying on this date this girl was instantly delivered. Nobody saw him; nobody saw anything. He wasn't there in the flesh; he was there in the Spirit.

This is from a man who spent most of his free time praying in other tongues.

Praying in other tongues bridges the gap between the natural and the spiritual and lets you step across into either one, depending on where you are at the time and what you are doing.

We've had a couple of instances of this.

We had a situation about two years ago. We had some people come through from California. They wanted to talk to me but I was off on another trip. They said, "We wanted to come by and thank Brother Curry for coming to our home group/Life Team and teaching the Life Team. We are really thankful he could stay there for two weeks."

Number one, I'd never been there. Number two, if I had been there, I couldn't have stayed two weeks. They said, "He taught us, and took us through the whole DHT and answered our questions and everything. We just wanted to thank him." We have this documented. I had never been there.

What is the answer? First of all, that was at a time when God really started pushing me toward what I felt was a real impression to start praying in other tongues and doing it constantly. This ties in with several other instances that took place around that same time.

When I got back from my trip, the first question they asked me was, "When were you in Southern California, how did you get there, and what was going on? This is crazy." I took this information in and asked, "God, what is this? What's going on here? Is there somebody out there that looks like me, going around saying he's me?"

Sometimes you don't ask for things, but they're just given to you. Sometimes you ask and you forget about asking, and they just show up. Did you ever notice that? The more you try to figure out a solution, it's like the farther away it gets, and as soon as you give up on it and say, "Okay, I'm not going to think about this," then the answer comes. That's exactly the way the Spirit of God works in you.

Remember in the Book of Acts when Peter was in prison and they were all praying for him? It said that, all of a sudden, he was let go. He came out and went to the gate where they were having a prayer meeting for his release. He was beating at the gate when the girl ran out and saw him. She went back to the others and said, "Peter's angel is at the front gate."

That girl had no faith that their prayers were being answered. He showed up and she didn't say, "Oh, you're free!" Instead, she ran back in and said, "It's his angel." Apparently, the Jewish belief is that a person's angel looks like him.

Let's go back to what happened in Southern California. I couldn't get there. They needed the information; they needed to know the teaching. What happened? Did they not know that my spirit could be out there, but in the form of an angel that looked like me and it could actually teach them?

I just told you that I had to stretch you, and I probably lost half of you right there.

I didn't ask for that. I didn't plan for that. I didn't believe for that. The need drew it. Do you understand?

This happens; it's exactly what the prophet said, "Didn't you know that my spirit went with you?"

There are a whole lot of things that are really taken out of context. They are wrong and you shouldn't get involved in them, but there is an aspect of transference of spirit. Mainly, it has to do with you becoming like them so that you do what they do, and you take on their attributes. You can hang around with the wrong people and you'll pick up their mannerisms and you'll take on their spirit. That's why you have to be careful with whom you associate.

The same thing happened with David Hogan.

I was on an Indian Reserve, Lac La Ronge, in Saskatchewan, up in Canada. It was a neat place in the middle of the woods. Basically, it was a trailer house that had a fence around it because there were bears there. I walked to the front door and there were claw marks on the front door. There I was with my bags, just off the plane. I was looking at this door and I was asking, "How did these get here?" "Well, those are from a bear that tried to get in." "Oh, really? Where's the hotel?" We were in the middle of the woods and it was really out there.

I went into the bedroom which had a bed that was made out of wood. They had cut a tree and then built the frame from it. It had a mattress and everything. It was a good place and it was neat. Over in the corner was nothing but open space.

About 5:30 in the morning, I started to wake up. That's when the sun is just starting to come up. You can see shadows and you can make out shapes in the room. I woke up, I looked across from me, and I saw David Hogan. He was sitting there on a tree stump (that was not in my room). He was sitting with his legs crossed and when I looked over at him, I was thinking, "They didn't tell me you were coming." I was thinking that he was in my room because he was there. Hollywood did not think up holograms; God did.

He was sitting there with his legs crossed. I looked at him, and said, "David!" He said, "Yep. As soon as you get back, you need to come and see me." I said, "Okay." Then, poof! He was gone.

Then, after I got back into town, I was thinking like Mary. I was pondering these things in my heart. I wasn't about to tell anybody about it; I was thinking about it.

We went to a meeting up in Arkansas and I got a chance to meet with David. We sat down. I said, "I've got to ask you a question." He said,

"Yeah, that was me." I said, "What was you?" He said, "That was me. I needed to talk to you." I said, "Okay." Then I asked, "How do you do that?" His answer was: "That's how we do it in Mexico. We can't get on the phone lines because they tap our phone lines. If they find out where we're going to be, they'll take us, and they'll do things to us. If they know I'm out of the country, and out of the way, they'll burn down our churches, and they'll kill our pastors. The only way we meet is by setting the meeting in the Spirit, and then, whoever's supposed to be there, shows up. If you don't have the Spirit, you don't know where we are so you can't find us. If you do have the Spirit, the Spirit will lead you."

I am just trying to give you some experiences. I don't get to talk about this much. When I do the DHT, my job is to take people who have no experience in healing and get them to functioning in healing. I can't come in and talk about some of the neat things I've seen, such as visions and things like that.

If I did start talking about them, then all of a sudden, some would say, "I haven't had a vision, so that's not me. It will work for you because you're somebody special and I'm not." No, it's not that at all. It's the Spirit. The same Spirit that is in me is in you. We all have the same Spirit, so it all it comes down to this—how much are we letting Him out?

In meetings like this, I get to talk about other subjects a little bit more than I get to do at the DHT. The idea at those meetings is to not draw a distinction between the people and me. It is to draw us together and say, "If I can do it, you can do it." Hopefully, you've been through the DHT. If you have been through a DHT, you have heard my testimony about when I got run over. The testimony of my daughter is also in the DHT. Those testimonies are in the DHT, because those testimonies are foundational.

With the DHT, the idea is to draw us together, whereas in these meetings, I'm trying to draw you out. Do you understand? I'm trying to draw you out so that you can stretch yourself and it can be more than just saying, "Here's what I can do or what you can do." It's what the Spirit of God can do, through us.

Let's go back to talking about communicating in the Spirit.

David has to set the meetings in the Spirit, like I said, but the idea is that they all pray in tongues a lot; that's what they function on. They work together, and by working together, their spirits are joined together. That's the point. That's why husbands and wives can be in different places and the husband can be in trouble and the wife can know it. Why? That's because there's a connection. Why? Usually it's because you spend time together. It is the same thing with twins. Something can happen to a twin and the other one can feel it. Why? There is that spiritual connection.

Ten years ago, I flew home from a meeting. I had three or four guys with me. As soon as I got off the plane, this lady called me and told me her name and said, "I am in Hot Springs, Arkansas." I said, "Okay." Then she said, "You need to come here. I've got a meeting set up and you need to come." I said, "I'm just getting off of a plane. I'm going to go home, and then we'll figure it out." She said, "No, you need to come. I've already bought you a ticket and you need to go over, get your ticket, and come on." I responded by saying, "Look, lady. I don't know who you are, but I don't like this." She said, "Listen, I have set up some things and you need to come. This is by the Spirit of God." I said, "Okay." My guys all went back home, and I got another plane ticket and flew to Hot Springs.

When I got off the plane in Hot Springs, she had me picked up. Then, we drove out to the middle of nowhere; it was way out. There were dirt roads. There was no way I could have found it; it was a good thing she had somebody pick me up. We were out in the middle of nowhere, and we ended up at this little cabin. All of the property would fit into a big room. It was more of a house, but it was just a one room place.

We went inside. This lady had this thing set up for me to teach the DHT for three days. When I walked in the door, I started looking around. I saw the faces of people that I grew up watching on television. She heads up a national prayer assembly that's in Washington D.C. She used to have an office right outside the White House. She had connections with Benny Hinn and with Oral Roberts. She also had connections with Rex and Clement Humbard, who put Kathryn Kuhlman on television.

I walked into this room and literally, I was stunned. There were people there that made me say, "Wow! These are people I grew up hearing about."

I went in, and started introducing myself. Then, she said, "Okay, Brother Curry is going to teach us this." For three days I was standing there teaching these people. They all wanted to hear our message, but they didn't want to come to an open meeting. It was easier to get a closed group like this together. Very honestly, I just stood there for a second, kind of amazed. I wanted to say, "I want to hear you preach."

While I was preaching and teaching the DHT, every day, at least two or three times a day, there was a knock at the door. The lady would go over, and open the door. It would interrupt things because the door was right there.

The first day there was this young man and his wife at the door. He looked in and asked, "What's going on here?" She said, "We're having a Gospel meeting." "Oh, okay," and they just walked in. She said, "It's by invitation only." He said, "All I know is that two days ago I was in Georgia and God said to pack up my family and head this way. When we got to Hot Springs, He said, 'Go this way; now, go that way; turn down this dirt road.'" Then he said, "I had no idea where I was going. All I know is that this is where God said to come." They showed up at those meetings and sat there for the rest of the three days.

We had two people every day, for the next three days, to just show up like that. These were people who were literally in tune with the Spirit to where they could hear the Spirit tell them where to go. It was amazing to me because you could barely get to this place on purpose, let alone by accident. I mean, these people had to hear God say turn here, go there, and all of that. By the time the DHT was over, the place was packed. We had a lot of people in there.

When David started telling me about how they set their meetings in Mexico, I realized that that's exactly how those people got there. It wasn't a matter of an invitation. David didn't send out an invitation by mental telepathy. He literally set the meeting and then, by praying in the Spirit, the people were in tune. Their "tuning forks" picked that up, and they went there.

I'm absolutely convinced that how much you pray in tongues depends on how in tune your "tuning fork" is. The more you pray in tongues, the more sensitive you become to the Spirit of God and the more your "tuning fork" lines up with certain things. I believe it will take you certain places and have you do certain things.

Again, if you've been to the DHT, you know some of this, but I've got to bring this in because it ties into it. Go to Ephesians chapter 4, starting with verse 8,

> 8 Wherefore he saith, When he ascended up on high, he led captivity captive, and gave gifts unto men.

It says, "He gave gifts unto men."

> 9 (Now that he ascended, what is it but that he also descended first into the lower parts of the earth?

10 He that descended is the same also that ascended up far above all heavens, that he might fill all things.)

11 And he gave some, apostles; and some, prophets; and some, evangelists; and some, pastors and teachers;

12 For the perfecting of the saints, for the work of the ministry, for the edifying of the body of Christ:

13 Till we all come in the unity of the faith, and of the knowledge of the Son of God, unto a perfect man, unto the measure of the stature of the fulness of Christ:

"For the perfecting," or maturing, "of the saints, for the work of the ministry, for the edifying," building up, "of the body of Christ: Till we all come in the unity of the faith, and of the knowledge of the Son of God…" As I've said before, this is where it talks about coming in the unity of the faith. We're going to have the Five-Fold Ministry until we all come to the unity of the faith and until we all come to the knowledge of the Son of God.

The knowledge of the Son of God is not the knowledge that Jesus is the Son of God, because he's talking to the Church, and the Church already knows that. If you don't know that, you're not in the Church. The knowledge he's talking about is the Greek word *epignōseōs*. It is a variation of the word *epignōsis* (pronounced ip-ig'-no-sis), and it means, literally, *the exact experiential knowledge that the Son of God has*. It's not the knowledge of Him; it's His knowledge working through you and living out through your life. That's the purpose of the Five-Fold Ministry. It is to equip you.

God supplies your every need. Isn't that right? Philippians 4:19 says,

19 But my God shall supply all your need according to his riches in glory by Christ Jesus.

God supplies your need, but He gave you the Five-Fold Ministry to equip you. That's not redundant.

It's just like the military. The government supplies all of your weapons; the drill instructors equip you and teach you how to use the weapons you've been given. The Five-Fold Ministry does not give you anything—God gives it to you; He supplies it. The Five-Fold Ministry equips, meaning it trains you and shows you how to use what you've got. God supplies; the Five-Fold Ministry equips.

We're going to have this equipping until we all come to "the knowledge of the Son of God," until we all know what He knows and experience it. "Unto a perfect man," until the Body of Christ (until we), come to a perfect man, "unto the measure of the stature of the fullness of Christ." He doesn't leave us any room to wonder what the perfect man is—it's the measure of "the stature of the fullness of Christ." The Five-Fold Ministry is to grow us up and get us to a place where we grow up into "the stature of the fullness of Christ."

Look at verses 14 and 15 of Ephesians chapter 4. They tell us why.

14 That we *henceforth* be no more children, tossed to and fro, and carried about with every wind of doctrine, by the sleight of men, *and* cunning craftiness, whereby they lie in wait to deceive;

15 But speaking the truth in love, may grow up into him in all things, which is the head, *even* Christ:

"That we *henceforth* be no more children, tossed to and fro, and carried about with every wind of doctrine." That's what happens to children; They are they're tossed to and fro, "by the sleight of men, *and* cunning craftiness, whereby they lie in wait to deceive; But speaking the truth in love, may grow up into him in all things, which is the head, *even* Christ." We're going to grow up into Him, into "the stature of the fullness of Christ."

We're going to have this Five-Fold Ministry until we grow up. We're not going to need the Five-Fold Ministry in heaven; we're not going to need to be equipped in heaven. We're equipped here to do the work of the ministry <u>here</u>. This growing up, this maturing, happens <u>here</u>, not over there.

Let's go to 1 John chapter 3.

> 1 Behold, what manner of love the Father hath bestowed upon us, that we should be called the sons of God: therefore the world knoweth us not, because it knew him not.

> 2 Beloved, now are we the sons of God, and it doth not yet appear what we shall be: but we know that, when he shall appear, we shall be like him; for we shall see him as he is.

"Behold," (that means take notice, look, see) "what manner of love the Father has bestowed upon us, that we should be called the sons of God: therefore the world knoweth us not, because it knew Him not."

"Beloved, now are we the sons of God, and it doth not yet appear what we shall be…" Do you hear that? "Now we are the sons of God, and it doesn't yet appear what we shall be…" Watch this: "But we know that, when He shall appear, we shall be like Him; for we shall see Him as He is."

The way I was always taught is that it was saying, "When He shows up, we're going to be changed and be like Him." That is not what that says.

It says literally, "We know now that we're the sons, and we don't know what it's going to be like, but we do know that when He appears we're going to be like Him." It doesn't say we're going to be changed to be like Him. It says we're going to be like Him when He appears. We've got to grow up to look like Him before He can appear.

He says, "But we know that, when He shall appear, we shall be like Him; for we shall see Him as He is." James tells us in chapter 1, verses 23-26,

23 For if any be a hearer of the word, and not a doer, he is like unto a man beholding his natural face in a glass:

24 For he beholdeth himself, and goeth his way, and straightway forgetteth what manner of man he was.

25 But whoso looketh into the perfect law of liberty, and continueth therein, he being not a forgetful hearer, but a doer of the work, this man shall be blessed in his deed.

26 If any man among you seem to be religious, and bridleth not his tongue, but deceiveth his own heart, this man's religion is vain.

James said that we look into a perfect mirror, the perfect law of liberty. As we look at this, He said, "Be doers of the Word and not hearers only, thereby deceiving your own heart." He was saying, "If you're a hearer only, you deceive yourself. If you're a hearer and not a doer, you're like a man who looks in a mirror and when you walk away, you forget what you look like."

Notice, he was linking looking into a mirror to looking at the Bible. When you look at the Bible, what do you see? You see Jesus. When you look at a portrait, a painting, you see the painting; you don't see yourself. Here he said, "If you're a hearer and not a doer, you look in the mirror and, when you walk away, you forget what you saw in the mirror." Why? That's because the mirror is who you are.

The Bible isn't just a picture of Jesus; it is a mirror of you. When you look in the Bible and you see Jesus, who are you seeing? You are seeing you. Why? You're going to "grow up into Him in all things."

The Five-Fold Ministry is to "grow you up" to look like Jesus, into "the stature of the fullness of Jesus Christ." Now, we are the sons of God, but we are going to grow up, and as we grow up, we are going to look like Him. The Five-Fold Ministry is to grow us up to look like Him. He can't technically show up until we look like Him and until we all have the knowledge of the Son of God.

The key is in 1 Corinthians where he wrote to the carnal Corinthians. He said, "You need gifts." Jesus didn't need gifts. Why? He operated in the fullness of the Spirit. The Spirit still worked through Him. It was the same result; it was how the result happened that was different.

"The whole creation groans waiting for the manifestation of the sons (plural) of God."

This world is waiting for us to show up like Jesus; that's what the world is waiting for. Why? Because, when we do, then we will start to alleviate its groaning and start saying, "No, that stops. No, this doesn't happen. Storm, you die. You do not cause damage." Why? Then we start walking as sons of God. Isn't that what Jesus did? He calmed the storm.

As we grow up, we need help. The more we grow, and the more we walk in the fullness of the Spirit, like Jesus did, the fewer bursts of the power of gifts we need. You don't see gifts in Jesus' life—you see the fullness of the Spirit. The result is the same, but you're growing up and maturing into it, whereas before, He did it for you.

As you grow, He quits doing it so much for you and you start working in union together with Him. Now, as you do that, you need gifts less. The less you operate in gifts, the more fullness of the Spirit you operate in. You get fewer bursts but more fullness.

In other words, you don't just come to church and say, "Let's see if a gift works. Bam! That was awesome!" No. You start by asking,

"What do you need?" "I need healing." "Be healed!" See the difference? Now you're walking like Jesus. You're not walking like children who have to wait for a burst of power. You're the cause of the power, in the sense that you are directing the power.

The key is that the Spirit of God in a Christian should be no less powerful than the Spirit of God was in Christ. We're to do the same works and greater. Why? That's because there are more of us. Now, there are more that He should be able to flow through. We're facing a defeated enemy, whereas Jesus had to face the devil full on. Even when He had to face the devil full on, in full power, the devil wasn't a problem for Him. If we are facing a devil who has been defeated, how much easier should it be for us to just step on him? Amen?

Paul says, "All things have been put under His feet, yet we don't see all things under His feet." Why? That's because the church has not grown up and put things under His feet. It says, "He is seated until His enemies become His footstool." When His enemies become His footstool, then we're going to hand it over to Him, and He's going to hand it over to God, and the kingdoms of Christ will be the Kingdoms of our God. All of that will then come together, but we have to grow up first, which is why this thing is taking so long.

You can be a world class body builder and have all of the genetics to be a young Arnold Schwarzenegger, or any of the other body builders. You can have the genetics for that, but let me tell you, Arnold Schwarzenegger had more than genetics. He had the right diet, he had the right exercise program, and he had the right discipline to make those things happen.

Many people have perfect genetics and yet end up being couch potatoes. Why? That's because they don't have the right diet, don't have the right exercise program, don't have the right discipline, and don't have the right attitude to make it happen. If you don't have a good exercise program, you are not going to develop strong muscles. If your diet is not the healthiest one, you're not going to develop the best strong, healthy muscles.

If every Sunday you feed yourself junk food and then you think that you're going to live the next week as a spiritual giant, an over-comer, guess what? It isn't going to happen. It's going to slow down the growth of the Body. Why? We are joined together; we are all parts of the Body. That's why it's so important. The stronger each person gets, the stronger we all get.

If you pray in tongues for an hour every day, we'll all be stronger. The more you do it, the easier it will get for me to do it. The easier it gets for me to do it, the easier it will get for somebody else to do it. Why? We are connected in the Spirit realm. We're talking about growing up into Christ and functioning as the Body of Christ.

I'm not taking away from the gifts of the Spirit. We just have to realize what the Bible tells us. I'm going to say this very carefully: the Bible applies to certain people at certain times. I know that is a dangerous statement. What I mean by that is that you can't just tell a person, "You must repent and come to Christ," and then they say, "Okay, I repent. I come to Christ, and I receive Him. What do I do next?" You say, "Next, you must repent and come to Christ." They say, "I just did that. What do I do now?" You say, "Repent and come to Christ."

Repenting and coming to Christ only applies to people who have not repented and come to Christ and continued to walk with Him. It only applies to people who have not done that. If you are doing that, then repenting and coming to Christ doesn't apply to you; you've already done that. Now, you walk with Him.

That's why He says, "If you hunger and thirst after righteousness, you shall be filled." Once you're filled, you're not hungering and thirsting anymore. Why? That's because you are filled.

I hear these people all the time that sound so spiritual: "I'm a God chaser," or " God, we're thirsty; we hunger after You," or "God, we're desperate for You." Look up the word "desperate." It means *without hope*. When somebody says, "God, I'm desperate for You," what that person is saying is, "God, I'm without hope for You."

I'm not desperate for God; I'm not a God chaser. As a matter of fact, even when I wasn't with God, I wasn't a God chaser. He chased me until I surrendered. I didn't chase Him. We've all gone our own way, we've all been led astray, we've all gone the way of the world, but God chased us. How many times do we hear, "Pray for my son. He's running from God." Who's doing the chasing? God's doing the chasing. We're not chasing God. God's chasing us.

"Well, we're trying to find the God who hides Himself." If God wanted to hide Himself, all He had to do was not send Jesus. He was already hidden for the most part. God is not hiding Himself; He is revealing Himself.

The last book in the Bible, the one everybody's afraid of, is the Book of the Revelation. It's not the book of the hidden. God wasn't hiding Himself. It's the revelation, the revealing of Jesus. "Well, I can't understand that book." "You can't understand the book that says it's a revelation, a revealing?" Just read it and be blessed; read it and understand.

There has to come a point where we actually start believing the Bible, start talking like we believe it, and start talking like sons. Jesus never talked about lack. He never said, "Oh, God I hope I've got enough faith for this. Oh, God, I hope there's enough anointing left in me to get this one done. You know, I've been working all day and pouring out the anointing on everybody; I just need to back off and get refilled." He didn't say any of that.

© 2012 Curry R. Blake – John G. Lake Ministries

The easiest thing in the world is to preach the message most people preach. It is hard to preach this message. What I mean by that is it's hard to go against the flow, but on the other hand, I couldn't preach anything else because I've seen it. I can't change and I can't preach another message because this is what the Bible says. I can't imagine a life where I'm always constantly chasing God.

At some point it's easy to say, "What's the use? I quit; I just give up." On the other hand, a real life is where we say, "We are joined with Him, and we are one with Him; I am bone of His bone and flesh of His flesh. We're joined together."

One time Paul talked about marriage. He said, "I'm going to use marriage as an example of what you being connected to God is like. The Body of Christ is joined together but the whole Body is joined with Him." We talk about us being joined together, and that's true, but we're joined to Him. That's why He says when a man gets married and leaves his mother and his father and he joins to his wife, they are no longer two, but one. Yet, you look at them and they're still two people there. Yes, there are still two, but they are one in union. We're joined together with the Body of Christ. There is this union. That's what people don't get.

We were up in Challis, Idaho, years ago, and it was up in the mountains. Idaho is a beautiful, awesome place. It was four hours from the nearest Wal-Mart. Now, when you're four hours from the nearest Wal-Mart, you're in the middle of nowhere. We were up on this mountain and we had all of these people waving the banners and doing Jewish dances.

They were bringing all these things in and they had this "Ark of the Covenant" sitting up there. This thing was huge. They were all dancing around and crying to God, "We're going to start the worship. God, come down." They had this big sign up there that said, "Unless You Go With Us, We Will Not Go," which is what Moses had said.

I was looking at all of that and standing there watching all of these people. They were doing everything the prophets of Baal did except for cutting themselves. That was the only thing that was left for them to do. They had all of these preachers up there, and they had this huge "Ark of the Covenant." It was pretty, but it was standing there and they were all preaching behind it. They were all telling God, "Oh, God come down."

I told my team, "I'm not going to preach behind that ark." I said, "I'm a New Covenant ark, and a New Covenant ark is not going to stand behind an Old Covenant ark." I said, "The presence of God is within me now; it's not in that box." I told everybody that was with me, "They're going to move that thing before I get up there. They're going to move it because I am not preaching behind it."

The weirdest thing happened after I told them that. Just before they announced me to preach, a man came out whose name was Michael. He said, "We're just going to move this "Ark of the Covenant" over there out of the way," and they moved it over by the door. After they got it by the door, they announced me and I went up. I said, "You know, you got it almost far enough." I said, "It is still an affront to me." Why? It was because of what they were doing.

I got up there and I laid into them. I was mean. Well, David Hogan was there, so I knew I could be mean with David Hogan there. They were all begging God to show up, so when I got up there I said, "I wonder, what somebody would think if they were driving past here and they were really searching for God. Maybe they don't know God, they're not born again, don't know anything about God, but they want God. They really want Him and they just don't know what to do, so they walk in here.

"When they walk in and hear us doing what we've been doing in here, what would they think? Would they think, 'Wow! I have found people that know God,' or would they think, 'Wow! Here are some people just like me. They don't know God but they're looking for Him. They haven't met Him yet, but I'm just like them.'" I said, "What would make that person want to be like you, because you're like him?" I said, "The truth of the Gospel is to be able to say, 'God lives within me. He moved in and He's never moved out. He walks in me; He talks in me.'"

That's exactly what John Lake showed me through his sermons and teachings. He would get up every morning, put on a suit, and stand in front of a mirror and say, "God is in the man in that suit, and wherever that suit goes, God goes." When I read that, I said, "That is the New Testament Gospel. Jesus died to put His Spirit within me so that I can live His life on this earth."

It takes growing up into that. It's not instant, it's not overnight, and it takes growing up. Now, you're not going to grow up into that if all you hear is, "Hang on; He's going to send someone to rescue us." I'm not saying that isn't going to happen. Please understand, I'm not saying that. I'm just saying that's not the correct mentality. The mentality is, "Yes, let's occupy until He comes. Let's be busy."

The Bible is very clear. It says, "Blessed is that servant, when his master comes, who is busy about his master's business." It doesn't say, "Blessed is that servant that when he comes he finds his servant with all of his prophecy Scriptures in order." It doesn't say that. I'd rather be busy.

The key is to "grow up into Him in all things" so that we live His life. We've got to have the gifts operating in us. As we grow up, we're less enamored with the gifts and more enamored with the life and with the Giver of the gifts.

After you grow up, you have the fruit. That's part of it. Then you have the DNA of the Five-Fold Ministry, and you start to walk and talk like Him, and it's not some weird thing. You don't have to get weird; you can just be normal and walk through life putting hands on the sick and watching them get healed.

This should be your normal life, and this should be a normal expression. You shouldn't have to get weird. You shouldn't have to just keep pulling on something. This ought to be a natural outflow of the Spirit, but to have that, there has to be a change in you.

William Booth started the Salvation Army, and he was an amazing man of God. They would go to the brothels and get the prostitutes saved, and then they would take them to their headquarters. They had dorms for the women and they would house them there. They would train them and drill them saying, "You do this, and you do that, and you say this, and you say that. Here's how you do this, and here's how you win the lost."

They trained them into soldiers. In two weeks, those same women who were prostitutes at the brothels would be standing outside the brothels witnessing to other prostitutes they used to know. They had no fear of falling back into that lifestyle. Why? They were changed.

That's a problem with people today. They say, "Oh, stay away from all of that." Why? That's because they're so afraid that if they get close to it, they're going to go right back into it. Why? People are not so far removed from their old life, in many cases.

You have to kill that thing. Jesus said you have to hate your life. Most people have been offered a good life if they come to Christ. It's true; it's a good life. The offer is not so much that you love your new life but that you hate your old life.

You have to die to live. Too many people are trying to live a resurrection life without ever having died. Preaching the cross is a preaching of death—death to self and everything that's in you. You have to hate your old life and realize that you were dead while you were in it that old life. Now, you have been set free. Once you're set free from that, there isn't any fear of going back into that old life. Why? You don't even like that life. If you find that you still like that life, then you've not been changed.

Your heart can be changed and your head can think, "Well, I could do that," and your heart will say, "What!" and you won't do it, because it's the heart that you'll follow. It takes that change.

That's what William Booth and those people did. They didn't even believe in the Baptism of the Holy Spirit, at that time, and still don't to a large degree. They didn't even believe in it and yet they were able to get people so wrapped up in Christ that there was no doubt that they were saved. That's what we need again.

It's not about, "Oh, God send another revival like the Salvation Army." There's no mention of revival in the New Testament. Instead He says, "Awake to righteousness." Not one time does He say, "Wait until God arouses you," or "Wait until God wakes you up," or "Wait until God sets you on fire!" No! He says, "Awake to righteousness." Once you awake to righteousness, you will not be hungry and you will not be thirsty.

I'm not asking God to send the fire to revive me. I live revived.

"*To revive*" means to *take something that's dead and make it alive.* That happened to me when I got born again. I don't need it today. I am revived; I live revived. The Spirit of God stays in me, He lives in me, He guides me, and He directs me.

Do I always obey everything perfectly? No, but I'll tell you, "This is where my head is. This is what I think about. It's a lot easier when I go with my mind on straight."

What you watch, you become. What you listen to, you'll start to repeat. If you listen to most preachers talk, what comes out of them is garbage. Why? That's because it's what they watch all the time. It's what they listen to all the time, or they go online and pull up sermon notes off "sermonsrus.com." Believe it or not, that kind of information is out there.

I can tell you, "I don't get my messages from anybody but God." I go after God and I say, "Okay, what are we doing here? How can we build the Body of Christ to look like Jesus?" That's when I start praying in tongues, and it's amazing how ideas come. Then we move forward on it.

My kids get a little upset with me at times because I'll say, "We're going to do this," and then they'll say, "You need to think about that because I'm not sure we can do this." Then, the next Sunday I'll get up, on live Internet, to hundreds of people, I'll say, "Here's what we're going to do."

A couple of weeks ago I said, "If you want to join this church, you can join from anywhere you want. You can live anywhere you want, because we can get with you. We can communicate with you; we can email you. We've got JGLM people on every continent, so if you contact us and let us know you want to be a member of this church, we will pastor you. I'll get somebody to contact you, we'll work with you, and you can be a member of this church wherever you are." I said, "Contact us, and we'll connect you to somebody."

As soon as we went off the air, my kids were saying, "How are you going to do this?" I said, "I don't know." "Didn't you think about that before you threw it out there?" "Nope, I sure didn't, but I'll tell you why I got that idea," and I started telling them the following story.

When I was a kid, we lived in an apartment. We had a piano; nobody in my family played the piano. I don't know why we had it, but we had a piano. It was heavy. My dad was a policeman so he had handcuffs. If you put handcuffs with a piano, it's a strange combination.

I was infatuated at that time with a man whose real name was Eric Weiss. Most people know him as Harry Houdini. I was studying Houdini but not his magic tricks. That was just funny stuff. It was his escape stuff that really got me. I got to where if I could get tied up with a rope, I wouldn't stay tied. It wouldn't happen; it couldn't happen. I'm not kidding.

My dad had handcuffs, so I would get his handcuffs. While they were at work, I would handcuff myself to the piano. Then, I would take the key and throw it across the room. Now, that was strong motivation to get out, because I didn't want them to come home and find me still handcuffed to the piano, although they did a time or two.

That's the way I've been all of my life. I will make the choice, throw it out there, and then go after it. If you don't throw it out there, then it's too easy to back off and nobody knows you failed. The best way to do something is throw it out there so if you fail everybody will know and you'll look like an idiot. That gives you a whole lot of motivation to make it happen.

Believe it or not, God has taken that mentality, and blessed it, and used it. If I didn't have that mentality, you wouldn't be sitting here today. It's just that simple.

I choose to believe that what the Bible says we are capable of doing, we are actually capable of doing. You can be the first one to do it, or I can be the first one; I don't care. I know I'm going after it. If you want to go with me, wonderful; let's do this thing together.

Usually, most people are just waiting for the first person to do it and after that one person has done it, then everybody else will jump in. After one person's done it, the level of faith it takes, and therefore the level of reward for faith, greatly diminishes. It's the first ones that do it that we're talking about such as John Lake, Smith Wigglesworth, and those people.

People say, "You shouldn't want that." In Hebrews 11, it talks about the heroes of faith. Why were their names written there? They did things other people wouldn't. People think that Jesus said, "If you want to be great in the Kingdom of Heaven, shame on you! You shouldn't want that." No, that's not what He said, but that's the way it's preached. That is not what Jesus said.

Jesus said, "Do you want to be great? I'll tell you how to be great: serve the most people you can." That's what I've decided to do. I have decided to serve the most people we can and find better ways to do it.

THE POWER OF TONGUES

Some of the things we have been saying may be somewhat of a stretch from what you may have believed before. We do need to be stretched, so we can grow.

We were talking about basically going places in the spirit, even while we are physically in one location. I am trying to show you what is possible. You may not have experienced that but if you haven't, you can. First, you need to believe that it is possible before you actually have faith to step into it.

In 1 Corinthians, chapter 5, Paul was writing to the Corinthian church; it was the same carnal Corinthians. He said,

> 1 It is reported commonly *that there is* fornication among you, and such fornication as is not so much as named among the Gentiles, that one should have his father's wife.

We have talked before about how messed up they were. There was at least one there that was doing this.

> 2 And ye are puffed up, and have not rather mourned, that he that
> hath done this deed might be taken away from among you.

It says, "And you are puffed up and had not rather mourned." Notice that in the middle of all of these gifts operating, he said, "You have this sin going on, and you've got these gifts going on," and then he said, "With all that going on, you are puffed up even when you should be mourning because this sin is going on right in your midst." He didn't say ignore it. He didn't say it is okay and don't worry about it. He said, "You should be mourning because that is going on in your midst."

It said in verse 2, "…that he that hath done this deed might be taken away from among you."

> 3 For I verily, as absent in body, but present in spirit, have judged
> already, as though I were present, *concerning* him that hath so
> done this deed,

Listen to this: "For I verily, as absent in body, but present in spirit." He wasn't saying, "Oh, I'm with you in spirit; I'm there." That's the way we use it sometimes, but he was saying, "Look, I may not be there bodily, but in the spirit, I am there." Watch, I'll prove this: "…concerning him that hath so done this deed."

> 4 In the name of our Lord Jesus Christ, when ye are gathered
> together, and my spirit, with the power of our Lord Jesus Christ,

He was speaking about them being gathered together, "In the Name of our Lord Jesus Christ, when you are gathered together." Then he said, "My spirit is with you with the power of our Lord Jesus Christ." In verse 5, he talked about how to deliver such a one.

5 To deliver such a one unto Satan for the destruction of the flesh,
that the spirit may be saved in the day of the Lord Jesus.

At this point, he said, "To deliver such a one unto Satan for the
destruction of the flesh…" He said, "This person is doing this sin." He
didn't say that it was okay and for them to overlook it. He said, "If this
is going to continue, you deliver this one." He was talking to them
saying, "You deliver this one in your midst over to Satan for the
destruction of his flesh."

Notice the one who is in charge of the destruction of the flesh: Satan.
Not God. Also, notice this: Satan had not even gotten hold of this guy.
He had to be turned over to Satan for the destruction of the flesh.

See how far the Church has come from just biblical standard? The
main reason is because they believe, "Oh, as soon as you sin, bam!
God is going to smite you down." He says, "No, there is time to turn."

If you're a member of a fellowship or a church and you are doing these
things, it will be that body locally that is supposed to woo you back to
Christ, turn you around and say, "That's not right."

Paul went on to say, "You're all puffed up, because you've got gifts
going on. You ought to be mourning. It's time for you to try and get
this person to turn around. He won't turn around, so now you are going
to turn him over to Satan for the destruction of his flesh so that he
might actually repent and come back." In other words, "You're going
to take this protection off of him and send him out. You're not going to
have fellowship with him. That is going to give the enemy the
opportunity to destroy his flesh which, hopefully, will cause him to turn
back to God, repent, and be saved so that he will be renewed back to
God."

The main thing that I wanted to bring out is what he said in verses 3
and 4, "For I verily, as absent in body, but present in spirit, have judged

already, as though I were present, *concerning* him that hath so done this deed. In the name of our Lord Jesus Christ, when ye are gathered together, and my spirit…"

In Colossians 2:5, he said something similar,

> 5 For though I be absent in the flesh, yet am I with you in the spirit, joying and beholding your order, and the stedfastness of your faith in Christ.

The Apostle Paul said, "I am beholding your order." He said, "For though I be absent from you, I am beholding your services." Even though Paul wasn't there, he had connection with them and knew what was going on in the church.

Now, again, I want to reference John Lake. He was in South Africa between 1908 and 1913. While he was over there, they birthed several hundred churches. I think it was a 125 of what they called white churches and over 500 of what they called native churches at that point.

He was doing all of his leadership from the Pretoria area, but he was in Johannesburg. He had churches all over the nation. Whenever a problem was going on, half of the time, before they even wrote to him with a problem, he would write them, and say, "You've got a problem going on."

I have some of his actual writings where he said, "They wrote me a letter saying we have this problem." He would then go and pray in tongues, be there in the Spirit, see the service and say, "You wrote to me and you said this person is causing your problem, but it is not that person. It is this person who is talking to that person that is stirring up all the strife. You need to go and deal with this person." He would send that letter to them, and then they would go and deal with that situation.

They saw him as the senior pastor of all the congregations. They started calling him "The Pastor Who Sees." They would tell the person, "You may be able to lie to so and so, and you may be able to hide it from this one, but you can't hide it from Brother Lake." He would know what was going on, no matter where you were in the congregation, by the Spirit of God.

Again, Dr. Lake said, "These things we did by praying in tongues." That's what brought these things out. That is why I am emphasizing tongues now.

His wife, Jennie, who passed away there in South Africa, was always giving out their food and everything else to the different people that needed help. She was known as "The Missus Who Prays." She was always praying in tongues, always praying in the Spirit, and they would come to her.

They said that if anybody had a problem with receiving the Baptism of the Spirit, they would just go to her house. They would stand outside and listen to her praying in tongues inside the house. She wouldn't even know that they were there, and they would catch what she had. If a person had a problem with receiving, they would just go there. They said that they never knew a person that she laid hands on that failed to receive the Baptism of the Spirit.

This was the big thing that they constantly preached. We look at healing today as the big doctrine, so to speak, but back then, the big doctrine was the Baptism of the Spirit.

Five years before John Lake arrived in Spokane a lady had been praying and asking, "God, what are we missing? What am I missing? What is it that my heart craves?" God spoke to her, and He said, "In five years, there will be a man that will come from Johannesburg, South Africa." God told her what he would do and how he would do things.

At that time, they baptized in what they called Triune Immersion, which means that they actually dunked them three times. They dunked once in the name of the Father, once in the name of the Son, and once in the name of the Holy Ghost. That was the way Dowie did it and that's the way that Lake and the early Pentecostals did it.

God spoke to this lady and said, "This is how he will baptize." It doesn't say that God agreed with it. It just said that's what he would do. He said, "He will do baptism like that and what he will preach is what you need."

Why wait five years? If God was talking to her, why didn't He just tell her? I don't know. When Cornelius was praying, an angel showed up and said, "You need to find Peter and he will show you the way to salvation." The angel was there. Why didn't he just preach? That's because the Gospel hasn't been committed to angels. It has been committed to man.

John Lake showed up in Spokane five years later. This church that invited him was not a Pentecostal church by any stretch. It would be classified today as something similar to a Christian Science church, actually. They said, "We've heard about your healings. Come in here and teach us."

Before he got in the pulpit, he told the pastor, "My message isn't your message. My Christ is not your Christ. We preach a different Christ." The pastor said, "That's all right. You are in the hands of God. You preach your message and you preach all of it." That was gutsy for a pastor to say when a man had just told him, "I am not going to preach what you preach; I am going to preach something different."

Dr. Lake got up to preach and the first message was on the Baptism of the Holy Spirit. When this lady found out that Lake was from South Africa and it had been five years, she was just waiting for the altar call. As soon as he gave the altar call to receive the Baptism of the Spirit, she was the first one up there. Her name was Irene Porpoure. She worked with Dr. Lake for 20 years after that. When he passed away, she actually preached part of his funeral.

She made a statement and said, "I didn't care what he was going to preach. It didn't make any difference to me what he was going to preach. Whatever he was going to preach, I was going to get because God said, 'What he will preach is what you need.'" She received the Baptism of the Spirit. What he preached, first and foremost there in Spokane, was the Baptism of the Spirit.

We look at John Lake and how he was known for healing and we think, "Wow! It was an amazing healing ministry," and it definitely was. What you have to realize is that it wasn't the doctrine of healing that got people healed. John Lake, himself, said that the secret of their success, in what he called the aggressive ministry of healing there in South Africa, was that they taught their workers that they received the power of God when they received the Baptism in the Spirit.

After the Baptism in the Spirit, they could heal the sick and they could cast out devils and they could do it all right then, because when He came upon them and they received that Baptism, they had the power of God to give away.

The church is still 100 years behind where John Lake was 100 years ago, but it's coming up. People are starting to get ahold of it. We need to realize what he was doing, and we need to get back into it.

We try to come in with our own way, and we try to decide on our own. "Well, I don't like that speaking in tongues; that's too weird. I don't like that." That's tough. "Well, I want to get healed. I want God to use me, but I just don't want to speak in tongues." Tough. Go somewhere else. You don't get to pick and choose what you want to do. God decides His plan; you either go along with His plan, or you don't. It's that simple.

We don't get to pick and choose what parts of the Bible we like and what parts we don't. We have to take it, understand it, and walk in it. Usually, we walk in it before we understand it, but there comes that point where we have to make that decision.

I want to cover some basics, and I want to give you some testimonies. I want to give you some examples, because I want you to realize what the Baptism of the Spirit and speaking in other tongues does. Then, I am going to get you activated. We are going to move in what we were doing before, but we're going to take it into different areas. We're going to explain some of it, and take you through some steps.

We already know that 1 Corinthians chapter 12 talks about gifts, and operations, and manifestations of the Spirit. Everybody knows that 1 Corinthians 13 has to do with the love of God and how we are supposed to walk in it. Look again at verse 28 of 1 Corinthians chapter 12. We've already read this but it says,

> 28 And God hath set some in the church, first apostles, secondarily prophets, thirdly teachers, after that miracles, then gifts of healings, helps, governments, diversities of tongues.

That was said about what was in the church. There it is.

Look at the very last verse, verse 31.

> 31 But covet earnestly the best gifts: and yet shew I unto you a more excellent way.

He says, "But covet earnestly the best gifts." It didn't say what gifts were best in the sense of it being a good gift or not. The word used there for "*best*" means *to a greater degree*. He's not saying any one gift in particular. He's just saying, "Go after the gifts; go after them all to a greater degree."

Then he said, "And yet show I unto you a more excellent way." Why? That's because if you focus on gifts, you're going to get like the Corinthians and get puffed up. That is what they did. "Oh, I got this gift. I got that gift. This is what is going on. This is awesome. Look at this. Look at what I can do." If anything, that is what churches are doing.

We see people with gifts, we lift them up, and we exalt them. Then, when they start believing the things that people say about them, we get mad because then they start acting like they are somebody. In reality, we're the ones that put them on the pedestal to begin with. Instead, we should be looking at the gifts or the manifestations of the Spirit to be used as tools.

This is an excerpt from Dr. Lake's sermon called, "How to Enter the Will of God." It says:

"The Lord says, 'They shall lay their hands on the sick, and they shall recover.' But if you do not lay your hands on anyone, they will not be healed. However, if you have faith to believe that you have the Holy Spirit to be used by Him and for Him, your heart and your hands will be ready. He gives us the Holy Ghost to use for God."

You have to realize that God gave you a gift of the Holy Ghost. He didn't give you to the Holy Ghost. You are not His gift; He's your gift. I am not demeaning the Person of the Holy Spirit. I'm saying that we're working together, but we have to get this in order.

You may not realize where God has put you in the overall order of things. There is no physical being on this earth more powerful or higher in the spiritual hierarchy than you are. You ask, "Well, what about an apostle? What about a prophet?" No, those are training gifts. They are trainers that are here to train you. You see, the one that gets trained is more important than the trainer.

We've looked at it like this: on bottom are the believers, then pastors, teachers, evangelists, and prophets, and if we get to the top of this pyramid, there's the apostle. One might say, "If we're really good, we might get promoted up to there." No. If the pyramid was like that, then you would have to turn it around and drive it into the ground. Paul said, "He has taken us, the apostles, to be the very least of everything, and the 'offscouring' of the earth." This is found in 1 Corinthians 4:9-13. We have to realize that apostles are trainers, meant to train the highest position in the Kingdom of God, which is that of a son.

It doesn't say, "The world is waiting for the manifestation of the apostles." It says, "The world is waiting for the manifestation of the sons of God." They won't manifest until the Five-Fold Ministry manifests them. As long as we keep emphasizing gifts and people as opposed to the Spirit of God working through the sons and daughters of God, we will always have it upside down.

Stop putting the Five-Fold Ministry and people with gifts on a pedestal. No one needs to be on a pedestal, because no one is special. Only Jesus is special. When Jesus lives in us, that makes everyone special, and when everyone is special, no one is special. Amen? That's the way it works.

Let's go from 1 Corinthians 12 verse 31 over into 1 Corinthians chapter 13, and you will start to see what he was saying,

1 Though I speak with the tongues of men and of angels, and have not charity, I am become *as* sounding brass, or a tinkling cymbal.

2 And though I have *the gift of* prophecy, and understand all mysteries, and all knowledge; and though I have all faith, so that I could remove mountains, and have not charity, I am nothing.

Paul said, "Though I speak with the tongues of men and of angels, and have not charity (love), I am become as sounding brass, or a tinkling cymbal (or nothing)." He was saying that even if he had the gift of prophecy, and understood all mysteries, and all knowledge, and had all faith, if he didn't have charity (love), he was nothing.

Paul was trying to get them to a point to where they realized that without love it was all for nothing. He was not saying that these gifts don't matter. He was just saying, "If you're going to do them, do them because of love. Don't just do them thinking, "I've got a gift and I'm somebody."

There are people who say, "I've got a gift. The Bible says that a man's gift makes room for him so this is my gift and this is my room." No, what the original Hebrew actually says is, "A man can bribe his way into any position." When it says that a man's gift can make room for him, it actually means that a man can bribe his way into any position. It doesn't have the same connotation when you get back to the original Hebrew.

We are in 1 Corinthians chapter 13, verse 3.

> 3 And though I bestow all my goods to feed *the poor*, and though I give my body to be burned, and have not charity, it profiteth me nothing.

Note that it profits them, but it doesn't profit him.

> 4 Charity suffereth long, *and* is kind; charity envieth not; charity vaunteth not itself, is not puffed up,

Remember, this isn't just talking about an emotion, because true love is not an emotion. It is a commitment. What we see in Galatians is the fruit of the Spirit, but what we are seeing here are the characteristics of God because God is love. "God suffers long." These are aspects of

God. "God is kind. God envieth not. God vaunteth not Himself. God is not puffed up."

5 Doth not behave itself unseemly, seeketh not her own, is not easily provoked, thinketh no evil;

6 Rejoiceth not in iniquity, but rejoiceth in the truth;

7 Beareth all things, believeth all things, hopeth all things, endureth all things.

8 Charity never faileth: but whether there be prophecies, they shall fail; whether there be tongues, they shall cease; whether there be knowledge, it shall vanish away.

"Charity never fails." The words "*never faileth*" in the Greek mean *never quit*. Love never quits. It doesn't say it can't fail in the sense that it can't cease, or maybe not produce what is expected of it. It doesn't have that meaning. It means it will never cease.

Then, he goes right into the next part that says, "But whether there be prophecies, they shall fail (or cease); whether there be tongues, they shall cease." Whenever we have reached full maturity and we have been glorified, these things will cease.

When we talk about that change, it says that corruption will put on incorruption, mortality will put on immortality. We think we can just coast along and at some point it's going to change and all of a sudden we're going to be elevated. That's not what the Scripture says.

Now, I'm not saying that can't happen or won't happen to some degree, because the minute you step into that realm, everything changes anyway. You can't step into that and be the same. He was saying that the Five-Fold Ministry is to get you there first, to grow you up into that.

He says, "Whether there be tongues they will cease." Yes. In this particular instance here, all of these are gifts that operate in the Body, in a congregation. He's saying that at that point you won't need it because you will have grown up and won't need those things to take place.

Then, he says, "Whether there be knowledge it shall vanish." People say, "Well, it says right there that tongues will cease, so they've ceased and we don't have to worry about them." No, if tongues have ceased, then so has knowledge, and we know that knowledge hasn't ceased.

We know, according to the book of Daniel that at the end of days, more knowledge is going to be released and knowledge is going to be even more so. If there is going to be more knowledge, there should be more tongues before it ceases. Why? That's because the more tongues you get, the stronger you get, the faster you grow up, and when you grow up you don't need them anymore. It's like a parachute; you hope you never have to use it.

8 …whether there be knowledge, it shall vanish away.

9 For we know in part, and we prophesy in part.

This is not a spiritual gift seminar, but you have to realize it says, "We know in part and we prophesy in part." Under the Old Testament, if a prophet prophesied something that wasn't of God and if it was proven that he led them off in a different way, then they had the ability to stone that prophet. If he said, "Thus saith the Lord," and it wasn't "Thus saith the Lord," there were some consequences.

Notice here, in the New Testament, it says we judge prophecy. We don't take them out and stone them when they're wrong. Why? That's because we know in part and we prophesy in part.

Some of this is in the "New Man." Here's the difference: under the Old Testament, God moved upon people, but He spoke through them. They didn't understand what He was saying half of the time, but they just said what they heard because He wasn't a part of them. He didn't work with them and work in them for them to decide what to say. He came upon them and He spoke. They just wrote down what He spoke.

That's why Isaiah didn't understand the difference between the suffering Messiah and the conquering Messiah, and he wrote both. That's why when Jesus showed up, they didn't understand it. They saw him coming as a conqueror. They didn't understand the part about the suffering Messiah. When Isaiah wrote that, he didn't even understand what it was about. Why? They didn't have to understand it. All they had to do was be good secretaries and write down word for word what God said. God didn't move from within; He moved upon.

In the New Testament, it's different. It isn't that God is upon us, but He works from within, and in conjunction with us. That's because we know in part, we prophesy in part, so we have to judge prophecy. Under the Old Testament, you didn't have to judge it. It was what it was. In the New Testament, you have to judge it because it's coming sometimes through a tainted vessel, and it's not just word for word what God is saying.

That's why when a tongue is given and there is an interpretation, it's not a translation. It's an interpretation. The person interprets it by the Spirit of God. If that person has certain preferences in doctrine, sometimes those preferences come into play and you have to judge what that person says. You say, "That part of what you are saying is just you. The other part is God." You have to separate that and judge the prophecy. Again, that's something you generally don't see. Here, we're a new congregation, so we're blessed that we get to put these things into play in the beginning.

The first time I ever prophesied in church was at Dr. Sumrall's, which was probably the scariest place you could do it, but I was blessed to be there, and do it, and live to tell about it. We're going to do what we did up there at Dr. Sumrall's.

If you gave a tongue, an interpretation, or a prophecy, when you finished you had to stand there and then Dr. Sumrall would comment upon it. He'd say, "That's right; that's good. Listen to it. Do it," or he would say, "Well, that was stupid." I've heard him say, "I don't know where that came from." You had to stand there and let what you said be judged. Well, again, that's what we are going to do here.

The way they did it there, when Dr. Sumrall was preaching, if you had what you believed was a word from God, and you wanted to give that word, then you moved up to the front row where his sons sat, Frank and Stephen. (Stephen is the one who baptized my son when we were up there.) There was another son who ran the cameras.

They would always leave a seat open on the end. You would go up and sit down, and they would look at you and say, "Have you got a word?" "Yes, I believe so." "Okay, hang on," and then they would motion to their dad. Dr. Sumrall would see it and he would say, "Okay." He didn't stop and say. "Okay come on up." He would keep on speaking.

The whole point of him continuing was because if it was of God it wouldn't go, but if it was of God it would stay. If you sat there for a few minutes and it went away, then you would get up and go back to your seat. That would mean that it was just for you and it was you getting excited in your spirit. Maybe you had a prophetic word that was for you but it wasn't for the congregation.

God knows that if you are fixing to give a word to the congregation and it's not for the congregation, then He will back it off to where you say, "It's gone," and you will go back to your chair.

Dr. Sumrall would just let that work itself out, and he would let you sit there for a while. If he had an opening, he would say, "All right, do you have a word?" "Yes, I have a word." "Okay, come on up." Then you would walk up and he would hand you the microphone. He would stand beside you while you gave the word, whether it was tongues or interpretation. If it was a tongue, he would interpret it almost all of the time. He operated fluently in that.

God told him, "I want you to start a church there in South Bend." He said, "I can't do it. I can't pastor a church." God said, "I want you to start a church." He said, "I can't do it. A pastor has to be able to interpret tongues, and I can't do that." God told him, "The only reason you can't do it is because you haven't asked for it. Ask for it." He said, "Okay, I need to interpret tongues, so please give me the gift of the interpretation of tongues." God said, "Okay. You've got it." He said, "I don't feel like I've got it." God said, "That has nothing to do with it; you've got it. Now, start being a pastor."

From that moment on, when he heard anyone speak in tongues, he instantly knew the interpretation of it, and he could just speak it out. It was like he was hearing it in his own language, and he could just say it. Many times he would stand there and interpret.

We're going to do that as we grow and as we get more proficient in this. This is where you train and where you get to practice. You get good at it here, so whenever you stop somebody in the mall and say, "God has a word for you," it really is God having a word for them. We get to practice here, and then we practice in our Life Teams and our home groups.

As you learn here, you also have to take correction here. If you teach, after you finish teaching, you should stand there. Basically teaching is judged. "What about this and what about that?" "Well, that needs to be fixed." Why? That's because the worst thing you can do is let someone preach some heresy or something, maybe not even that bad, but just off a little bit, and then you say, "Well, that was really good.

Thank you very much. See you next week." Everybody leaves thinking that you agreed with it, even though you didn't.

It is much better to say, "This part was good, and I actually agree with it, but because of this Scripture, I don't agree with the other part." It shouldn't hurt that person. It should help them to grow. It should be for growth, for correction. These are things that you generally don't see in the church, but you will, because it has to come back in that way for the church to grow up.

Now, if you know that what you teach is going to be judged, or if you are going to prophesy, or give a tongue and interpretation and be judged, guess what? You'll be a little more cautious to make sure that what you're saying is right. It shouldn't quench the Spirit, but it should make you examine yourself and make sure of what you're doing.

Make sure you're not just saying something so you can be seen, or that you want to give this dynamite prophecy, the best prophecy anybody's ever heard. You may think that's how you are going to make your mark, or you want to give out some revelation because you've been looking for a revelation. People who look for a revelation, in that sense, usually end up in cults. They usually start some kind of weird doctrine.

I've never looked for revelation. I've looked for ways to help people and in the process of finding ways to help people and meet their needs, God has given revelation. However, I've never gone to God and said, "God I need a revelation to help me make my mark in this world." I don't want to preach things that are different just because they're different. I want to preach what's right.

There are two prayers I've prayed since I was 17 years old. The number one prayer that I have prayed is out of Luke chapter 21: 15.

15 For I will give you a mouth and wisdom, which all your adversaries shall not be able to gainsay nor resist.

I prayed that "God would give me wisdom against which no man can gainsay." That means that I wanted to say the right thing, because I wanted to be correct. It's not that I wanted to be right for the sake of being right. I wanted to be right so I wouldn't lead people the wrong way. That was my second prayer: "God, I never want to lead people on the wrong path. Shut me up before I do that."

A lot of times I've questioned God saying, "God, what about this? If this is wrong, shut it down. Don't even let us go there." Every time I pray that prayer, it's like we burst again. We grow bigger. It's like God saying, "Don't worry about it. This is right. Move forward." We just keep on going forward.

I'm not looking for revelation. My personal mandate is to restore New Testament Christianity back to what the Bible says it is. I really feel like that is our purpose, not that we are the only ones doing this. I believe that's what God is doing throughout the whole Body. I know this is the dispensation of the Gospel that God has given us, and we are moving forward with it. Like I've said, "It's the easiest thing in the world to do because all I do is read the Bible and tell you, "Yes, it means exactly what it says." That's pretty easy. Amen?

Let's go back to 1 Corinthians chapter 13.

9 For we know in part, and we prophesy in part.

10 But when that which is perfect is come, then that which is in part shall be done away.

"But when that which is perfect (or complete or the completion of everything) is come, then that which is in part shall be done away." Why? That's because you'll have the mind of Christ. You will operate in the mind of Christ. You will grow up and be a full-grown, manifested son of God.

I'm emphasizing this, because you have to look at the overall picture. In times past, the church has emphasized Jesus' coming. Basically, the people have this idea: "Let's just wait until He gets here and when He gets here, He's going to fix everything."

There's truth to that, but there's also the idea that we have to meet that, and I believe that these things are going to intersect. I believe that us growing up into Him, and Him fixing things, and Him showing up at that point, is going to happen just picture perfect. I think it's going to intersect perfectly.

I don't think that we are going to be walking around down here for 200 years as sons of God with everything working just right and then Jesus says, "Okay. Now it's time." I really think He's saying, "Come on! Let's get there! Let's get there!" Why? That's because I am ready to come and ready to show up. I believe it's going to happen and "dovetail," as they would say, perfectly together.

I also know that as a part of the Five-Fold Ministry, my job is to train and equip the believers to "grow up into Him in all things."

If a ministry claims to be part of the Five-Fold Ministry, and you leave that place, if you don't look more like Jesus, then they are false teachers, false prophets, and false apostles. Every message is supposed to do two things: (1) make you look more Jesus and (2) make you make decisions to chip away the things of the world and draw you closer to God. Every message should do that. Every ministry of the Five-Fold Ministry should draw you to that.

We talk about this narrow road, and believe it or not, it gets narrower as you go along. It's not that God is saying, "Okay, I'm trying to do these things." No, you just learn that things are not important, and you start stripping away the things that don't really matter.

> 11 When I was a child, I spake as a child, I understood as a child, I thought as a child: but when I became a man, I put away childish things.

"When I was a child I spoke as a child, I understood as a child." He's combining the idea of these things being done away with, along with childhood and immaturity. This is exactly what we've been talking about. "I thought as a child, but when I became a man, I put away childish things."

> 12 For now we see through a glass, darkly; but then face to face: now I know in part; but then shall I know even as also I am known.

> 13 And now abideth faith, hope, charity, these three; but the greatest of these *is* charity.

Now, he goes right into chapter 14. Remember, God did not tell them to write chapter 14; that was man. Man did that so that you could memorize where these are and find them more easily, rather than having to do like the Hebrews who had to memorize everything because they were more of an oral society, and they passed things along by repeating them.

That's why I have not emphasized chapter and verse. Most of the time, my study Bibles at home and my Scripture studies that I've printed out seldom include the chapter and verse, unless it's going into a manual. I keep them in paragraph style and I read them that way, because it doesn't break them up and that makes me not have the tendency to pull a verse out of context and just remember that verse. You could ask me where most of the things are found, and I might not be sure, but I know they are there. Why? That's because it's in me, but in me, it's not chapter and verse.

When God brings to my remembrance what He has said, He doesn't say, chapter 5 verse 3, because He never said chapter 5 verse 3. He can't bring it to my remembrance if He never said it. The Holy Spirit brings to remembrance what He has said, so He doesn't bring that to my remembrance.

Now, if I can remember the chapter and verse, that's great. I have nothing against that but I have not set out to just memorize chapter and verse. I don't do that. I try to take the whole thing in context as a letter, not as chapters and verses. It makes a difference.

Sometimes, when I'm quoting things, it's there; I just can't tell you where it is. There are times when I do remember exactly, because I'm seeing it on the page in my mind. I can picture where it is, on the right hand side of the page about three quarters down. I can see it right there but I can't see the numbers.

In 1 Corinthians, chapter 14, starting with verse 1,

> 1 Follow after charity, and desire spiritual *gifts*, but rather that ye may prophesy.

"Follow after charity." Remember, chapter 12 was about gifts, and chapter 13 was about love. In chapter 14, he goes into details on a couple of things and starts to narrow it down. "Follow after love, and desire spiritual gifts, but rather that you may prophesy." Prefer to prophesy; that's important.

> 2 For he that speaketh in an *unknown* tongue speaketh not unto men, but unto God: for no man understandeth *him;* howbeit in the spirit he speaketh mysteries.

"For he that speaks in an unknown tongue speaks not unto men, but unto God: for no man understands him." That's why he's saying to go after prophecy because tongues and interpretation equal prophecy. Don't just think of prophecy just as prophecy; think of it as tongues with the interpretation. If you get tongues and interpretation they equal prophecy. He doesn't want you just speaking in tongues, because if you just speak in tongues people won't understand it. However, if you can interpret, then that equals prophecy.

If you're going to go after prophecy, you can do "pure" prophecy; you can do tongues and interpretation. Do you see that? Tongues and interpretation, when used together, equal prophecy.

He says, "He that speaks in an unknown tongue speaks not unto men but unto God: for no man understands him; howbeit in the spirit he speaks mysteries." When you're speaking in tongues, you speak mysteries.

> 3 But he that prophesieth speaketh unto men *to* edification, and exhortation, and comfort.

"But he that prophesies speaks unto men to edification (to be built up), to exhortation (to push forward), and comfort." That's what prophecy does. There's nothing in here about the future. It doesn't say prophecy speaks of the future. It says it speaks to men to edify, to exhort and to comfort. Remember, that's what prophecy does.

I could call someone up and say, "I want you to know that God has called you to be a new creation. God has put His mind within you, and God says that by this mind that you will know all things. You don't have need for any man to teach you anything because the Teacher lives in you and abides in you." I could do that and say, "I just prophesied to that person." Why? That's because I have said what God has said. I've edified, exhorted and hopefully, comforted him.

There could be other things that I could say that God would say to me. It might be something else along these lines: "In that situation that's been going on, don't worry about that. God is going to take care of it; He's already got it under control. You don't have to worry anymore."

Why? God is going to take care of it. That would also be prophecy in the sense that it's comforting, because you're going through a problem.

If I were to give you a word and say, "That problem you've been having in your back and the pain that's been going on there, I want you to know, right now, that God has already healed that by the stripes of Jesus, and the pain is going to go. Right now, the pain is going." That is a word of knowledge. See the difference? That's because it is specific, right then. It would comfort, but the purpose would not be for comfort. It would be prophecy in the sense that it is comforting to you to know that God is going to take care of that.

You can see how it works together, but there are all kinds of differences here. Again, this is not a seminar on gifts, so we can't really get into any more details than that.

> 4 He that speaketh in an *unknown* tongue edifieth himself; but he
> that prophesieth edifieth the church.

"He that speaks in an unknown tongue edifies himself." Do you hear that? He does not speak to men, he speaks to God, but he also speaks to and edifies himself. As you speak to God, you edify or build yourself up. You are not edifying yourself or speaking to God; you are edifying yourself by speaking to God. Why? That's because your spirit is created of the same heavenly material that God's Spirit is made from, and whatever blesses Him blesses you.

If you want to understand it with quantum physics, look at the duality theory: whatever takes place in one place, takes place at the other place at the same time. Whatever you do to one thing, it does to the other thing, and since we are seated with Him in heavenly places, if we bless Him, then we are also getting blessed at the same time. Even science doesn't understand it, but they can explain some of it. The last part of verse 4 says,

4 …but he that prophesieth edifieth the church.

That's why he said in verse 1, "…but rather that ye may prophesy." In other words, "I'd rather you prophesy." Why? That way you are not selfish, and you are building up the church.

> 5 I would that ye all spake with tongues, but rather that ye prophesied: for greater *is* he that prophesieth than he that speaketh with tongues, except he interpret, that the church may receive edifying.

"I would that you all spoke with tongues." The people that don't like tongues forget that part. They always say, "Speaking in tongues doesn't really matter; it's the least of the gifts." It doesn't say that. It does say, "I would that you all spoke with tongues."

He was saying, "I thank my God, I speak with tongues more than you all, but I want you all to speak with tongues but rather also that you prophesy." Why? "I want you to build yourself up. I want you to get edified, but I really want you to be useful to the church so that the church may receive edifying."

He didn't nullify what he said about tongues. We should really look at that to say, "If he says he wants us to speak in tongues, then we also should be able to prophesy. If we prophesy, we definitely should be able to speak in tongues." You can't build up the church if you're not built up. You get built up and then God can use you to build up the church.

Isn't that what they always say to you on the airplanes? "If the mask falls down, first put it on yourself before you help the person next to you." Why? That's because if you die, you're not going to be any help to anybody. First, get yourself built up. It's always good.

He goes on to say in verse 5, "I would that you all spoke in tongues but rather that you prophesied for greater is he that prophesies than he that speaks with tongues." Yes, because he is serving more than just himself. It is very simple.

> 5 ...except he interpret, that the church may receive edifying.

He was saying, "When he interprets, the Church receives edifying."

Both times he was going back to the Church; even with interpretation. However, once you speak with tongues and have the interpretation in the Church, then you are equal to the person who simply prophesies. That's because you are not just edifying yourself; you are edifying the whole Body. Again, this goes back to serving.

> 6 Now, brethren, if I come unto you speaking with tongues, what shall I profit you, except I shall speak to you either by revelation, or by knowledge, or by prophesying, or by doctrine?

> 7 And even things without life giving sound, whether pipe or harp, except they give a distinction in the sounds, how shall it be known what is piped or harped?

In other words, there's got to be a reason for speaking in tongues. We don't want to speak in tongues just to speak in tongues, especially in the congregation. It's for a purpose, and that purpose is for the church to be edified.

> 8 For if the trumpet give an uncertain sound, who shall prepare himself to the battle?

> 9 So likewise ye, except ye utter by the tongue words easy to be understood, how shall it be known what is spoken? for ye shall speak into the air.

In other words, it's not landing on anybody; it's not helping anybody.

> 10 There are, it may be, so many kinds of voices in the world, and none of them *is* without signification.

They all have purpose.

> 11 Therefore if I know not the meaning of the voice, I shall be unto him that speaketh a barbarian, and he that speaketh *shall be* a barbarian unto me.

In other words, it's not going to do me any good. If we had a service where I got up and preached to you in tongues and there was no interpretation, you would listen for about five minutes or maybe not even that long. At first, you would be saying, "That's cool." After a short period of time, you would start to read or do something else, because you would not be getting any benefit from it.

At first, it might be a novelty but you wouldn't be learning anything, and you would be thinking, "What am I doing sitting here? I have to be getting something out of this. Is there someone that could interpret where I can at least understand what's going on?"

I like ethnicity in church. There's a church right here in Dallas that I used to go to years ago. It was an Indian church, not a Native American church, but an Indian church. The interior of the church was almost all marble and it was really nice. I've never seen so many shoes in my life. In India, they take their shoes off at the door in many places. They had all of these shoes stacked, and I was thinking, "How do they ever find their shoes?" Half of them looked the same.

The elderly people usually sat in chairs but everybody else sat on the floor and sat cross-legged. They sat there and went through worship, but it was all in their native tongue. I didn't understand a word of it, but I still got blessed. Why? That's because we were of the same Spirit and I could get blessed in my spirit. My spirit was profiting but my understanding didn't profit.

Most people would not go to a church where they are always speaking in another language that they don't understand and there's no interpreter.

Most churches have those little things that they put on your ear and you can hear somebody interpreting or translating what is being said. Why? They know that people won't keep going if they don't understand what is going on. There should always be tongues and interpretations so that people will know what God is saying to the congregation. Amen? It is amazing how pragmatic God is. He is really practical.

He says in 1 Corinthians chapter 14, verse 12,

> 12 Even so ye, forasmuch as ye are zealous of spiritual *gifts,* seek that ye may excel to the edifying of the church.

That's where we've missed it. Too many times we have people who want a gift so they can be somebody, rather than seeking a gift to edify the church. If you're going to seek gifts, maybe you ought to be praying, "God, I want to be used in a gift. What gift is missing in that church?" Let that come forth, and ask, "What does the church need?"

You don't say, "What is the most exciting gift? I want a gift of healing; I want a gift of working in miracles, or something like that." Believe me, when you start asking for the gift of miracles, guess what's going to happen? You will have to start stepping out and taking the chance of looking stupid.

That is why you seldom see the "gift of the working of miracles" in the church, because the working of miracles is not the gift of miracles. It is the "gift of the working of miracles." That means you have to work it. That means you have to do something to make it happen.

In Acts chapter 3, the Apostle Peter reached out to the man, and he told him, "Stand up and walk. Rise up. Jesus Christ has made you whole." He took him by the hand, and it says, "He lifted him up." Notice that

© 2012 Curry R. Blake – John G. Lake Ministries

he lifted him up first, and then, after he lifted him up, "…immediately, his feet and ankle bones received strength."

Notice, he didn't jump up first. Peter lifted him up. Now, what if he'd grabbed him, lifted him up, and turned loose? The man would have fallen right back down. Peter was stepping out and taking a chance of looking stupid. That is why you don't usually see people step out in church; nobody wants to take that chance.

Most people like the gift of faith, which means you stand still and watch the salvation of God. That's what Moses was operating in at the Red Sea when he told them, "You shut your mouths and watch what God is going to do today," and then the sea opened up.

This seminar appears to be turning into a seminar on gifts. The gift of faith operates in a way that usually is in the form of provision or protection. God either provides for you or protects you. Moses operated in miracles for 40 years. They would go into the desert, and they would need food. Pheasant or manna would fall from heaven. Nobody had to go and grow it; nobody had to do anything; it just fell. What they needed just showed up. Their shoes didn't wear out; their clothes didn't wear out. Now, those were maintenance gifts. Those things were miracles.

When they got to the Red Sea, they had this army coming upon them. The first thing Moses said was, "Why are you crying?" They were all crying, "Why did you bring us out here to die?" Moses said, "Shut up! Stand still and watch the salvation of God!" He said, "The Egyptians you see today you will never again see."

Then, he turned around to God and said, "God, You have to do something about these Egyptians." The first thing God said was, "Why are you crying to Me?" You can imagine that about that time Moses was sweating. "What do you mean why am I crying to You? This is the time to cry to You. I've got a Red Sea in front of me and I've got an army behind me. Something has to happen here. This is the time to cry." God said, "No. Why are you crying to Me? What is that in your hand?" Moses said, "It is the rod of Your authority." God said, "You stretch out your hand and part the water." He didn't say, "You stretch out your hand and I will part it." He said, "You do it!"

When He first called Moses He told him, "You will be like God to the people. They will look to you like you are God." Yet Moses remained the most meek and humble man on the face of the earth, even if he had to say so himself, which he did. He wrote that. He was so humble that he could even write that about himself. All he did was stick his hand out and the sea parted.

The gift of faith operates in protection and in provision. It either protects you or provides for you. He says in verse 13,

> 13 Wherefore let him that speaketh in an *unknown* tongue pray that he may interpret.

If you speak in an unknown tongue, you should pray that you can interpret. He doesn't make any distinction here about you praying in a congregation, or speaking in an unknown tongue in a congregation, or alone. Why? That's because it's the essence of the same gift operating. It is the same Spirit.

> 14 For if I pray in an *unknown* tongue, my spirit prayeth, but my understanding is unfruitful.

If he was praying in an unknown tongue, who was praying? He said, "My spirit." His spirit was praying. Did you hear that? It was his spirit. It didn't say it was the Spirit of God. He said, "My spirit prays."

We understand that it is the Spirit of God in your spirit that allows your spirit to speak the words of God and to pray, but it is your spirit doing the praying, which means that it is you. You are a spirit. You don't have a spirit; you are a spirit. You are doing the praying!

© 2012 Curry R. Blake – John G. Lake Ministries

Even if you stood there saying, "I don't have a sound. I've got nothing. The Bible tells me I will pray in other tongues, so I will say, 'Blah, blah, blah.'" I know that's the way it sounds many times, but if you start speaking that out, you watch and see if all of a sudden that doesn't turn into a language, and then you will be surprised. Why? That's because you are praying. You are deciding to pray in an unknown tongue. You start saying that out loud and then the Holy Spirit jumps into it, takes hold, and runs with it.

Smith Wigglesworth used to say, "I may start with the flesh but I end up in the Spirit." He said, "If the Spirit doesn't move me, I move the Spirit." A lot of people thought it was sacrilegious for him to say that. However, since it was Smith Wigglesworth who said it, most people would agree with him now, because they know of his results.

I always used to say, "Everybody loves these guys because they are dead. When they were around, nobody liked them." Everybody was afraid of them. It was like when I was around Dr. Sumrall. It was amazing. When I walked into his office at his church, I always expected a line of people to be at his door. There was nobody there. That whole building was empty except for Dr. Sumrall and his secretary.

He would be sitting there, writing. There were no people lined up at the door to talk with him and get his wisdom. That's because everybody was afraid of him. Why? He was mean.

I have a lot of video tapes of Dr. Sumrall. I saw him on a video tape when He was at the Mabee Center in Tulsa, Oklahoma doing a service there. He preached and then when he finished he said, "Alright, I'm going to pray for you. If you need prayer, come down front and line up." People started lining up. He said, "Anybody else? Does anybody else need prayer? Come now." A couple more people came up, and then he said, "All right, now stop! Nobody else comes. That is it. You've had your chance. If you need healing, you should have gotten in line. If you are not in line, don't get in line. That's it. You've had your chance."

He started praying at one end. The camera was way back and you could see this woman sneaking into the line. She didn't think he was serious. She was standing there. He went down the line, praying for people, and he got to her and asked, "Where did you come from?" She said, "Well, I just got into line" "After I told you not to come?" "Yes." "Go, sit down." She was standing there looking around. He said, "I am not going to pray for you. I told you, 'Go and sit down.'"

The weirdest thing happened. I was watching this video tape, and I could feel the atmosphere in the room change. One minute he was this saintly God's General and everybody was looking at him thinking, "Wow! I hope he is going to lay his hands on me." The next minute everybody in the room was mad at this mean old man. It changed just that quickly. It was amazing. He stopped like he had heard what they were thinking. I know what I was thinking; it was like he heard it. I'm sure everybody there was thinking the same thing, but it was like he heard what we were thinking.

He turned around and said, "If you are not serious about getting healed, I am not going to be serious." He said, "I told you, 'If you want it, come up and get it.' If you are that slow, you're not serious. If I had said that in Africa, you would have come running, but I said it here and you have to think, 'Let me decide.'" He said, "If you want to decide, sit there and decide and I won't pray for you." He said, "It's my prayer. I get to decide who I pray for and who I won't." You can't really argue with that logic. After that, I wouldn't have wanted him to pray for me.

In verse 14 he said,

14 ...but my understanding is unfruitful.

Verses 15-17,

> 15 What is it then? I will pray with the spirit, and I will pray with the understanding also: I will sing with the spirit, and I will sing with the understanding also.

> 16 Else when thou shalt bless with the spirit, how shall he that occupieth the room of the unlearned say Amen at thy giving of thanks, seeing he understandeth not what thou sayest?

> 17 For thou verily givest thanks well, but the other is not edified.

Notice, he said, "You give thanks well, you're doing a good thing, but people aren't edified."

> 18 I thank my God, I speak with tongues more than ye all:

He keeps building up tongues. I don't know how people can tear down tongues. Everything he says about it is good. Everything he says about it is positive. He was telling them, "Just do it the right way."

> 19 Yet in the church I had rather speak five words with my understanding, that *by my voice* I might teach others also, than ten thousand words in an *unknown* tongue.

He didn't say don't speak in tongues; he just said that he preferred his words have understanding in the Church. Now, in his private life, I guarantee you he preferred to speak ten thousand words in an unknown tongue.

> 20 Brethren, be not children in understanding: howbeit in malice be ye children, but in understanding be men.

Get ahold of this. Don't be stupid. Wise up.

> 21 In the law it is written...

What was he quoting? He was quoting Isaiah chapter 28.

21 ....With *men of* other tongues and other lips will I speak unto this people; and yet for all that will they not hear me, saith the Lord.

22 Wherefore tongues are for a sign, not to them that believe, but to them that believe not: but prophesying *serveth* not for them that believe not, but for them which believe.

23 If therefore the whole church be come together into one place, and all speak with tongues, and there come in *those that are* unlearned, or unbelievers, will they not say that ye are mad?

24 But if all prophesy, and there come in one that believeth not, or *one* unlearned, he is convinced of all, he is judged of all:

25 And thus are the secrets of his heart made manifest;

The purpose of prophesying in this way is to bring out things and say, "This is what's going on in your life. This is it." We would call this a word of knowledge. If God is revealing the secrets of His heart, we would call it word of knowledge, but here Paul calls it prophesying, because he lumps all spiritual wording in the Church under the guidance of prophecy. When we are talking about prophecy, it's not just prophecy. It has to do with word of knowledge, word of wisdom, and all of these vocal gifts.

25 And thus are the secrets of his heart made manifest; and so falling down on *his* face he will worship God, and report that God is in you of a truth.

26 How is it then, brethren? when ye come together, every one of you hath a psalm, hath a doctrine, hath a tongue, hath a revelation, hath an interpretation. Let all things be done unto edifying.

In other words, "When everybody comes together don't say, 'Well, it's my turn. Let me speak.'" "No. We've heard enough tonight.

Everybody doesn't have to speak. We've heard this and we've heard that, and that's good, but it is enough. You can speak next time. Everybody doesn't have to say something."

> 27 If any man speak in an *unknown* tongue, *let it be* by two, or at the most *by* three, and *that* by course; and let one interpret.

He says, "If any man speak in an unknown tongue, let it be by two, or at the most by three, and that by course," or in order, "and let one interpret." It doesn't say, "Let everybody interpret." Basically, he was saying that you ought to be able to look around and say, "I really feel like I've got this message and I want to give it out in tongues. I am supposed to give out, but I don't see Brother So and So, and nobody else here interprets that I know of, so I'll hang on to it."

God doesn't say, "Oh, I've this going on, and I've got to take over this service." No, it's usually someone getting excited in the Spirit. Usually their emotions grab hold of their spirit and bring out that tongue by emotion. It's not necessarily God wanting to do it. Sometimes you say it and it's just God speaking to you. You just heard some teaching, you got excited, and you just wanted to speak in tongues.

He says in verse 28,

> 28 But if there be no interpreter, let him keep silence in the church...

Notice, he says, "If there is no interpreter, let him keep silence," but to keep silence, you first have to know there was no interpreter. He didn't say, "If there is no interpreter, go ahead and give the tongue and then see if there is an interpreter." That's what goes on in churches. Somebody gives a tongue and they wait to see if anyone interprets it. It shouldn't be that way.

It should be that if there is an interpreter then he can give it, and if not, stay quiet. That means you have to know who can interpret. It's showing a community working together, not just somebody walking in and saying something. They knew what was going on.

> 28 ... and let him speak to himself, and to God.

> 29 Let the prophets speak two or three, and let the other judge.

He can't just speak and that's the way it is. No. It has to be judged.

> 30 If *any thing* be revealed to another that sitteth by, let the first hold his peace.

> 31 For ye may all prophesy one by one, that all may learn, and all may be comforted.

> 32 And the spirits of the prophets are subject to the prophets.

> 33 For God is not *the author* of confusion, but of peace, as in all churches of the saints.

God doesn't interrupt Himself.

> 34 Let your women keep silence in the churches: for it is not permitted unto them to speak; but *they are commanded* to be under obedience, as also saith the law.

He is not saying women shouldn't speak. He is saying, "Let things be done decently and in order." He says,

> 35 And if they will learn any thing, let them ask their husbands at home:

You have to remember that in the early days of the church, the women sat on one side and men sat on the other. It's still that way in many countries around the world.

When someone would be teaching, the wife would yell to the husband and say, "Is that right? That's not what you said. When we talked about it, you said something else." Don't do that. Take it home, and talk about it at home.

What it also tells you is that husbands and wives are supposed to be talking about the Bible at home. They are not supposed to just be coming to the church to listen to the message. They are supposed to be discussing it at home.

Then, he says,

> 35 ...for it is a shame for women to speak in the church.

It is talking about speaking out and causing confusion. We know that Philip's daughters began to prophesy. We know that the first woman to ever report Jesus' resurrection or the first evangelist was a woman, so it's not wrong for women to speak. As a matter of fact, Galatians tells us that there is neither male nor female. Paul even lists several women as co-apostles with him and that they were co-workers with him, and he gave them equal honor. This is not a put down for women, saying, "Women should not do anything in church."

Now, it does say, "Don't let a woman usurp authority over man in the church." We've had people say, "Well, how are you going to do that?" In the old days, women could only teach Sunday school or maybe a women's class somewhere. The fact is that it doesn't say women can't teach. It just says, "Don't let a woman usurp authority."

If a woman comes to me, and she has a gift in teaching or is knowledgeable in teaching and wants to teach a class, and I say, "Yes, that sounds good. Teach a class." Then, a man comes in and says, "What's she doing teaching a class?" "Well, I told her she could teach a class." "Well, you shouldn't let her usurp authority. I am not going to sit under her." Okay, that's your choice. She is not usurping your authority, and she is not usurping my authority. I gave her the authority.

Now, if I was teaching something, and she was meeting someone over in the corner saying, "Oh, what he is saying is wrong," that would be usurping authority. I would deal with that. I can, as a man, sit under a woman's teaching without her usurping my authority, if usurping means taking it away without my permission. If I decide to sit under her teaching, she is not usurping my authority; I am submitting to her teaching. Why? That's because I recognize that the Spirit of God in her can teach me something. I am not looking to her as the teacher, but to the Spirit of God.

That's what Paul was talking about in 1 Corinthians 1:12 when he said,

> 12 Now this I say, that every one of you saith, I am of Paul; and I of Apollos; and I of Cephas; and I of Christ.

Who were they? These were all ministers of God in whom the Spirit of God was coming through. The key was what they were teaching, and not who was teaching. "There is neither male nor female."

As far as JGLM is concerned and as far as what we do, if you can do the job, you can have the job. Now, you've got to do the job. If you are a man and you don't want to sit under a woman, don't go to her class. Do something else. Probably the main reason she's teaching is because you wouldn't step up and do your part.

Cho said, "If you want to start a church, send a woman because she will get things done." That's true because they get men to do things for them. A man will go in and say, "Listen, we need help," and all the guys will say, "Yes, you surely do need help." They will sit around, twiddle their thumbs, watch football, drink beer, and then go to church and talk about how spiritual they are.

Now, if you tell a woman that, she will say, "Yes, we need a piano." She'll go to a man and say, "We need a piano," and he will say, "Okay, I'll get you one." She will get the piano.

He says in verse 36,

> 36 What? came the word of God out from you? or came it unto you only?
>
> 37 If any man think himself to be a prophet, or spiritual, let him acknowledge that the things that I write unto you are the commandments of the Lord.
>
> 38 But if any man be ignorant, let him be ignorant.
>
> 39 Wherefore, brethren, covet to prophesy, and forbid not to speak with tongues.

Did you hear that? It said, "Covet (or desire earnestly) to prophesy, and forbid not to speak with tongues."

> 40 Let all things be done decently and in order.

"Decently and in order" is how the leadership of a church decides things are supposed to be done. If someone had walked in off the street, and had seen all of us praying in tongues like we were just a while ago, they would have said, "That's chaos." To the unlearned it would have looked like chaos, but if they had been in here and had seen that we were moving people into this, they would have seen that it was not chaos. Everybody knew what they were doing. They were doing it under authority and were doing it the right way.

What is "decent and in order" is based on who is leading. As long as I'm okay with it, and I am the one leading then it is "decent and in order." Now, if I let you get wild and crazy, and stupid things start happening, then that's my own fault and I will answer to God for that.

"Decent and in order" does not mean dead and quiet, although that is the way it is usually translated.

I'm going to give you a couple of things here, and then I'm going to move you into this. It's not going to take very long. I'm going to take you through, step by step, just to get you moving in it.

How many of you would say, "I am fluent in speaking in tongues?" In other words, "I can do this, and I can go on." How many of you would say, "I speak in tongues, but it should be more fluent?"

What I want to do is take those of you that say, "I am fluent," and I want to partner you with the people that say, "I'm not very fluent and would like to be more fluent." At this point we're not going to be laying hands on people; there's no need for that.

We're just going to stand next to each other. It will be like two tuning forks. Since we are all of the same Spirit, then with two tuning forks, if one tuning fork starts to vibrate, the other one, being next to it, will vibrate. If you are not very fluent, you will become fluent because you are near somebody who is fluent. It is the same Spirit in both of you and the Spirit in the one will cause your spirit to activate more.

When I get around Bill Hamon and around other prophets operating, it is amazing. When prophecies start coming out, and words of knowledge start coming out, all kinds of things start to happen. It's amazing to watch. If I keep it stirred up, it's good, but if I am not careful about it, I will let it die out. When I get around them again, I can say, "Oh, yes, this is good." It goes back and forth. Lately, I've seen it more and more; I am keeping it stirred up because I recognize it.

When I was raised up in some of the Word of Faith circles, nobody taught this. Honestly, I don't know if I have ever seen a seminar on tongues, in and of itself. There are a couple of people that had a few things here and there, but usually it was very shallow, with very little depth to it. Basically, it just says, "Okay, let's just pray in tongues. There is no reason behind it and we don't understand it, but we are going to pray in tongues." That is one of the reasons why we are having this teaching on tongues now.

Almost every major miracle that we've seen in our lives was preceded by an extended period of praying in tongues. When I started looking at that, I put two and two together and said, "Wow, if I pray in tongues for a long period of time, that means one of two things is taking place: number one, I am praying in tongues and therefore the miraculous is activated or, number two, I am praying in tongues and it draws calamity. It is one of the two." That's pretty much the way I figured it out. I believe that it activates miracles, so I am going down that road.

Years ago, we lived up in the Denison/Sherman area. I was working on a construction job here in Plano, Texas. I helped do the groundwork for Collin Creek Mall, and my dad actually worked there for a while, also. He drove a bulldozer and I did belly-dumping, if you know what that is. We helped do the groundwork before the mall was ever there. We lived across the street, over on 15th Street, down the road a little bit in an apartment complex with my first daughter before she passed away. That tells you how long ago that was.

Even before that, I was working on a construction job. We would pick up in Sherman and drive down to Plano. We were doing siding on a building. We had built some scaffolding and we had to climb up that and put up siding.

I was between the second and third floor, halfway up between the two. I was a lot younger, a lot more agile, and a lot quicker. I could climb like a monkey. It was just very easy for me to climb, so they would always send me up the scaffolding. The scaffolding was so rickety that if the wind blew, it would move. It had boards across it, but they were not connected.

A friend of mine would ride with us in this van with all of these construction workers. Every morning we decided that we were going to start witnessing to them and getting them saved. We said that we were going to start praying in tongues, because we figured the best way to get them saved was to let them see the power of God.

The only way we could know the power of God and demonstrate it was to pray in other tongues and explain to them, "We are speaking in tongues, because the Spirit of God is in us," and so we'd pray in tongues all the way down. They would look at us like we were crazy, yet we would do it and keep on with it. It kept them quiet because most of the time, they were telling dirty jokes or cursing, so we figured it would at least keep them amused and they wouldn't be telling the dirty jokes. We prayed in tongues all the way down there.

My friend was back by the truck watching as I climbed up the scaffolding. I was up on the scaffolding, facing the building when I felt a slight shake. The next second I was turned the opposite direction, facing outward, but on the ground. I had fallen two stories, straight down, and landed on my feet. I had no recollection of falling. I had no recollection of landing. One second I was up on the scaffolding and the next second I was there on the ground, turned around, and all of the scaffolding was lying around me.

It was just before lunch, and we had been praying in tongues for about four hours. We had done that pretty much every day for close to a week. As soon as I hit the ground, I was standing there, and then I realized I was on the ground. Brad came running toward me asking, "Are you okay? Are you okay?" I said, "Yeah," but I was still trying to figure out what had happened. I was kind of shocked, not ready to preach, necessarily.

All of these guys came running over to see what was going on. Brad turned around, slapped his hands together very loudly, and said, "THAT'S THE POWER OF GOD! RIGHT THERE! YOU SAW IT!

NOW, WHO NEEDS TO GET SAVED?" I mean, he was quick. I said, "Yeah! You're right! Let's do it!"

Right after that, that whole job shut down, and we were out of a job. We have had these things happen and then God would move us; He would move us into something else, every time.

One time we were coming back from a revival in Henderson, Texas. It's a long way from Plano, and we were on a back road. My dad at that time was Chief of Police in Tatum, Texas, so we lived out in Tatum.

I am trying to put in details, because some day, somebody is going to write all of these things down, and people are going to read about them. I know as a historical researcher, I like details. When they copy these things down, and write them out, and put them in a book, they will have the details. They'll say, "Thank God he told details." You may not care, but they will.

Amazing things happened during that time. We were praying in tongues a lot. Anyway, we were driving back after we went to this revival. It was starting to turn cool outside. It was after midnight. We had our kids in the back seat. That's back when kids didn't have to have seat belts or car seats. You just laid them out on the seat. If you had too many, you just laid them out on the seat, and in the floorboard. The one in the floorboard got the hump to lay their head on. They don't remember it, but they were all laid out and going to sleep on the way back.

As we were driving down this back road, through this country area, it was getting colder outside. It was after midnight. My wife turned to me and said, "We need to pray in tongues." I said, "Okay," so we started praying in tongues. There we were, both praying in tongues, driving through that dark, cold area.

About five minutes after we started praying in tongues, we turned this corner. This was a back road; it was a Texas back road. There was about a foot of space between the road and the fence. It was barbed wire fence all the way down the side of the road. There was nowhere to go except down the road. As we turned this corner, my lights hit a herd of cattle lying across the road. Now, cattle don't line up neatly. They don't leave space for cars; they just lie on the road. The reason they were on the road was because it was getting cold outside and the road was still warm from the day. They would lie down on the road to stay warm.

As I turned this corner, we were praying in tongues, and there was no time to do anything. I didn't even have time to say, "Jesus." We were already praying in tongues, so we just stepped it up a notch and prayed in tongues a little louder and stronger. To this day, I don't know what happened. All I know is that the next second after seeing those cows, we were on the other side of them.

We stopped, got out, and looked at the cows. The cows were looking at us like, "What was that?" We just stood there looking at them. There was no explanation. I didn't swerve. I basically just locked my elbows and waited for the crash, but the next second we were on the other side of the cows. We had been praying in tongues a lot, but there was just that five minutes of praying in tongues just before that happened.

I will give you another example. We were in Sulphur, Louisiana helping to start a church down there. I was working at a construction job. One Friday night I walked from our house to a 7/Eleven store to get a soft drink. As I was walking up to this 7/Eleven, there was a car full of teenagers. As the car with these teenagers was backing out, I was walking toward them. The car was wide, and as they backed out, all I could see was the keyhole on the trunk, and the car coming right toward me.

I had spent almost eight hours at work that day praying in tongues. My job just entailed me to go around picking things up, so I had been praying in tongues all day long, just constantly. I saw this car coming toward me. I was standing right in the center of the back of the car. One second they were backing up right into me and the next second I was standing beside the rear door of the car. I was just standing there and they were all looking at me like, "Whoa, where did you come from?" Then, they put it in drive and peeled out.

There was no way, with that car backing up, that they missed me and I ended up at the side of the car. I don't know how I got there. All I know is one second I was about to get hit and the next second I was standing beside it.

I could go on and on. These are just some of the miracles that have happened and every time, we had spent some amount of time praying in tongues. We've seen the miraculous, over, and over, and over again. What I'm saying is that there is something to that.

Years ago, back in the early '80s there was the old Word of Faith Family Church over in Farmers Branch, Texas, and Robert Tilton was the pastor.

They had these little seminars they would do every month and they would do them by satellite. We would drive down from Sherman for those seminars.

On this particular night, T.L. Osborn was speaking. It was in February, and it was cold and icy out. We were going through Van Alstyne, and my kids were asleep in the back seat. We had just started praying in tongues. I didn't have a vehicle but a friend of mine had a car. We were in his car but he wanted me to drive. I was driving along, we were all praying in tongues, and we hit a patch of ice going over an overpass and the car just started spinning.

The weird thing was that I was in one lane and the car moved to the middle of the two lanes and started spinning over the overpass. If we had stayed in the lane we were in, we would have hit the side rail. The car moved to the middle while spinning, went over the overpass, and kept spinning. We were praying in tongues, again; we were praying loud and strong. Every time we would go around, all of the cars following us got closer. We could see them getting closer as we were spinning in circles. We were praying in tongues and just spinning.

We got to the other side of the road and the car started spinning in the right direction, went to the side of the road and stopped. We got out, looked around, and nobody was hurt. My kids were sound asleep and didn't even wake up. We got excited about what had been going on. We started praying in tongues even more. We jumped back in the car and we went on down to Dallas because then, we had a testimony.

I could go on and on about all of the things that have happened. We have so many different testimonies.

I've told you before how many times my Mom would wake me up in the middle of the night. Even if it was three or four o'clock in the morning, she would come and get me and say, "Curry, wake up. We've got to pray for your dad. Something is wrong." We had no clue what it was but we would get down on our knees. Even though I had to go to school the next day, I would be there with her, half asleep. She would start praying. Within a couple of minutes we would get a phone call from the Police Department.

I remember December of 1972, we were praying for my dad, not knowing what was going on. The phone rang and she answered it. They told her that my dad had been shot in the hand which sounded like they said, "In the head." It shocked her and she dropped the phone. Then I picked up the phone and they said, "No, it's in the hand. We have a car waiting to pick you up and bring you to Parkland Hospital," so we went. She had awakened me ahead of time to pray for him before we ever got the call. That happened numerous times.

What I'm trying to get across to you is that you take the initiative to begin praying in the Spirit. Don't wait until you need it. Pray and be ready so that when you do need it, you'll have a testimony instead of a tragedy. Amen?

PRACTICAL APPLICATION

This section incorporates actual directions to a real audience. Readers are encouraged to do the same.

"Father, we thank You. We thank You for that blood that cleanses us from all unrighteousness. Father, we praise You, right now, in the name of Jesus."

Everyone give Him thanks and praise right now.

"Father, we thank You."

Come on. Lift your voices. Appreciate Him for a moment.

"Father, we thank You for Your presence, for Your Spirit, for being willing to inhabit us and change us into the likeness of Your Son. Father, I thank You for that. In the name of Jesus, right now we accept forgiveness, we accept cleansing, we accept this walk of the Spirit and we thank You for it in the name of Jesus. Amen. Amen."

The next step is very simple. If you have not received the Baptism of the Spirit, and you are His child, you just ask Him and He will give it. Just like with everything else, once you do that, you have to believe that you receive it and act like you've got it.

That's all faith is: asking, receiving, and then acting like you've got it. We're going to do that. Even if you have received before, then thank

Him for that gift. If you have not received and you are His child, just ask Him. Say, "You said that if I ask, You'll give me the Holy Spirit. I am asking right now and I thank You for it in the name Jesus." It's that simple.

Forget about everyone else around you and just begin to communicate with God Himself. This is between you and God. Right now, just begin to do that. You can do it quietly or with your voice; you decide.

"Father, we thank You for Your Spirit, and that Your Spirit abides within us and that You have filled us with Your Spirit. Father, I thank You that we are able to remain filled with Your Spirit by speaking to ourselves in psalms, hymns, and spiritual songs, and that we are connected with Your love and filled with your Spirit in the name of Jesus. Father, we thank You, even now; You said in Your Word that when people were filled with the Spirit, they began to speak with other tongues, as the Spirit gave them the utterance. Father, we thank You for that utterance. Right now, we will begin to pray with our spirit and Father, we thank You that You speak through us in other tongues."

Now is the time to build up your tongues and maintain those tongues.

TONGUES FOR PERSONAL EDIFICATION - MAINTENANCE TONGUES

Those of you who have received your Baptism in the Spirit with other tongues, begin to speak in other tongues, even now.

These are maintenance tongues. These are just steady and not too loud, just a kind of maintenance. It's for edification; it is to work with you. Just keep it going; it will be a constant flow. It's just one river of many rivers.

Begin to pray in the Spirit, in the name of Jesus, right now. Pray in the Spirit, quietly there to yourself; then get a little bit louder. Let's move a little bit louder, take it up just a notch; we don't want you getting really loud, not yet; just bring it up a little bit.

TONGUES FOR THE UNBELIEVER

I want you to pick someone, preferably someone in your family, someone who needs the Spirit of God to infill them, save them, deliver them, and change their life. You know the Spirit of God needs to work in them to change things. Pick that one person now. Right now, there's somebody coming to your mind, in your family, who needs God. Right now, I want you to direct your tongues toward them in intercession. I want you to think of them and connect with them, by the Spirit, and then speak in other tongues and direct it to them, in the name of Jesus.

Right now, think of that person. They're unsaved; they need God. That means that they do not know God; they need help; they need to know God Himself; they need to meet Him. Right now, begin to pray for them. Pray earnestly and pray seriously. Pray out of the very depths of your belly. Let it come forward. Begin to intercede for them. Now get strong with it; get serious with it. Push that out.

There you go; that's it. That's it right there; that's it; that's it. There you go, right there. Now keep that going; keep that going. There you go. That's good.

"By the Spirit of God, we decree them to be saved, to be healed, and to be delivered. We decree even now, to call them into God and to make the way for them to receive Christ, even now to save that life."

Now, move into thanksgiving. In your tongues, begin to thank God for the result of what you've been praying. Thank Him. They are going to come to God; they're going to know Him. Workers are going to go across their paths. Their lives are going to be changed; the Spirit of God is going to move upon them; He will draw them.

Keep it going. Begin to thank and worship God for their salvation. Bring it forward.

I want you to put your hands on your belly, not in the center of your belly, but a little lower. That's out of your belly. That's where these rivers of living water are going to pour out.

Now, I want you to think about that loved one again, but this time I want you to move into actually birthing them in the Spirit. This is where you start to travail for them. I want you to know that we're going to push this thing through. We're going to fight for their lives. We're going to fight for their lives in tongues. Begin to take it in tongues. Direct it toward them; you can picture them but direct it toward them.

There you go; let that travail come forth. "Father, we thank You for the Holy Spirit working through your people."

That's it! Keep it going. In the Spirit of God, bring it forth. Bring it forth. Bring it forth. That's it! You put the enemy to flight. You put the enemy to flight.

"IN THE NAME OF JESUS, BIRTHING, BIRTHING INTO THE KINGDOM OF GOD. LIVES CHANGE BY THE SPIRIT OF GOD, CHANGE IN THE NAME OF JESUS."

RIGHT NOW, IN THE SPIRIT, PULLING THIS FORTH; BRING IT FORTH. THAT'S IT, RIGHT THERE. RIGHT THERE IN JESUS'

NAME, RIGHT THERE. BEGIN TO TRAVAIL BY THE SPIRIT OF GOD. IN THE SPIRIT OF GOD BRING IT FORTH;

"LET THERE BE BIRTHINGS INTO THE KINGDOM OF GOD, NOW! LET THERE BE BIRTHINGS INTO THE KINGDOM OF GOD, NOW! LET THEIR LIVES BE CHANGED. LET THEIR DESTINIES BE CHANGED. IN THE NAME OF JESUS, ABSOLUTE FREEDOM FOR THEM."

Keep it going a little bit more and a little bit more. Focus on your loved one. Focus on them.

There are things that you want to bring forth in the Spirit, so bring it forth in "groanings that cannot be uttered." Let Him come out of you in "groanings that cannot be uttered." This is not so much speaking in tongues; this is right now in your spirit. You feel what the Spirit feels and that groaning comes out, so go there. Go to that same place. It's right there in the belly, rivers of living water, and let that groaning come out. It is just inside you, right there; you let that groaning come forth.

It's like a birthing that takes place, but it is inside. It is not words; it's not even speaking in tongues. Let the "groanings that cannot be uttered," come forth. Even now, right there, you just let it come forth; let it come up. It's not an emotional thing. It's not a made up thing, but it is in the Spirit. Right now, just let what is in you come forth with "groanings that cannot be uttered."

You ask, "What does that sound like?" I don't know what your groanings sound like. That's you; it is your spirit. It's the Spirit of God groaning within you, working with your spirit.

"Even now, right now, Holy Spirit, begin to move among Your people. They've opened, they've accepted this, so in the name of Jesus right now, begin to move within them, to bring forth the groanings. Holy

Spirit, You said that You desire to work within us, to make intercession for us."

This will be more for you than it is for anybody else, so let Him do this for you. Let Him bring it forth. There it is, inside. It's almost like a tightening of the stomach, but it's not just physical, it is spiritual. That's it, right there; let it come forth. Bring it out; push it out, straight forward. There you go, just push right there in the Name, by the Spirit of God. That's it. This is a little different than speaking in tongues; it's a little unfamiliar, but that's okay. This is training and activation.

"In the name of Jesus, 'Holy Spirit, work that which is for our good. Work that which is for our good, even now in our spirits, in the name of Jesus.'"

All right, now turn it into a slight song; turn it into a melody. Turn it into a melody. I just want you to take it on into a song. Begin to sing with the Spirit. Sing, but keep it low; don't bring it up loud, but just keep it low. It's almost like humming within yourself, but let it be a worship to Him. Let it be a worship to Him.

Now, bring it up a little bit louder, a little bit stronger with a little bit of push. That's it. Just let it come forth.

I'm just trying to take you through all the stages, so that you break that flesh thing that doesn't want to do that.

"Holy Spirit, bring forth revelation, and understanding, and wisdom. Bring it forth, right now, Father. Let the doctrine that's gone forth take hold. Let them understand that the eyes of their understanding are being opened. Let it be enlightened so that they can grasp the doctrine and it becomes a part of them so that they can understand it and the enemy cannot steal it. Father, I thank You for it, even now. Holy Spirit we, thank You for Your presence."

TONGUES FOR PERSONAL EDIFICATION – BUILDING UP

Now, we're going to go back into edification. Begin to speak in tongues at mid-level for edification. We are going to bring it up. Begin to speak in other tongues for edification. Edify, and make it strong. That's it. Just bring it forward.

"Right now, in the name of Jesus, we command it to be so."

Now, we're going to do a little turbo charge with it, so we're going to kick it up. Kick it up, bring it up; get it strong. Get it loud, get it forceful! Pray it like you mean it. Pray it like you mean it. Bring it forth! HIT! Hit with your words in the name of Jesus, right there. That's it. Strong! Strong! Strong! Right now bring it forth. Bring it forth, bring it forth; that's it. That's it; keep it strong. That's it right there. Keep it going; don't let it drop, keep it going. Keep it up. Keep it up. Pray forcefully; that's it. In the Spirit you are forcing things through and pushing things through. There you go. That's it.

Now, I want you to fight with it. I want you to FIGHT with your words. Strong! Forceful! Hit! Fight with it. Bring it up. That's it; there you go. Bring it up. Let's go. That's it.

"In the name of Jesus, by the Spirit of God! Strong! Strong! OUT OF YOUR BELLY, RIVERS! RIVERS OUT OF YOUR BELLY, in the name of Jesus!"

Strong. That's it, there you go. Strong! Good, good, good. That's good.

TONGUES FOR PERSONAL EDIFICATION – WHILE MOVING

Alright, let's take it down for a second. Listen. You can keep going, but keep it very low for a second; keep it where you can hear my voice.

Now, I'm going to show you a difference; you've been doing it while staying stationary. Don't worry about what this looks like, just forget about what it looks like. We're going to start moving.

Start moving. Go clockwise and start praying in tongues. Now, pray in tongues. Go ahead; get it started. Bring it up, just bring it around, just bring it around, bring it around. Pray in tongues. Now, you're focusing on walking and your tongues are lower. Get the tongues up louder; bring them up louder. There you go. Okay, now bring it in. That's it. Now, begin walking a little faster. Walk faster. Pray faster.

Walk faster. Pray faster. Get it loud, get it loud; bring it up, bring it up. That's it. Get it loud, get it strong. Pray it like you mean it. There you go, strong and loud. Strong and loud. Get it strong, out of your belly, in the name of Jesus. There you go, out of your belly.

Now speed it up a little bit. Speed up the walking, and speed up the tongues. Speed it up. Louder and stronger. Come on.

Okay, women and men keep walking, but I want the women to pray in tongues and not the men. Men keep walking but stop praying. Keep walking, but stop praying. Women keep praying. Keep praying and get it loud and strong. Loud and strong. There you go. Watch, you'll get to where you like to walk and pray. Walk and pray. That's it, there you go.

Okay, now women stop praying and men start praying. Men, pray out loud; pray strong. Let's go. Come on, the women are a lot louder than that, come on, let's go. Come on men, pray out loud. Out loud.

Come on, kick it up. Pray like you mean it. There you go, serious and strong. Serious and strong. That's it.

All right, now everyone pray. Everyone pray. I just want you to get used to praying in different positions and in different modes. Okay, you can start going back to your seats, but keep praying. Keep going. Keep praying. Keep it loud. Keep it strong.

TONGUES AND INTERPRETATION

We're going to do one last thing before we finish here. We said earlier that we were going to take people who are fluent and put them with people who are not. If you would say that you are fluent in your tongues, I want you to come down front. Fluent is where it just flows, where you don't have to force it so much. Once you get it started, it just flows, and it's not broken up. It just flows, almost like a conversation.

Those of you who are not fluent come down and get near one of these people that are fluent, preferably men with men and women with women, so you can stand in front of each other. You can shake hands if you want to, but you don't have to touch if you don't want to. Go ahead and start praying. Start praying; start praying together.

Praying together, that's it, praying together. That's it. There you go, praying together, work with one another. There you go. That's it. Keep it going. That's it; there we go. Keep it going; just let it flow. Let it flow. Just for a few minutes. That's it.

Okay, now bring it down. Bring it down; begin to stop. Bring it down. Everybody stop. I know it usually takes a while to stop. Bring it down, everybody stop. Listen carefully. Everybody stop.

I want you to look at the person in front of you that you've been praying with. I want you to take turns, and I want you to bless them in your known language, as if you are interpreting what you've been praying, because that's what is going to take place.

You can start by saying just some scriptures you know, some of the things that God has said, but then let it go on and let things start coming out and flow. Take turns. Begin to bless them. Bless them with the things you know the Bible says about everybody and then take it from that into specifics that the Spirit of God will bring out.

Begin to bless them with life, with health; bless them with healing. Bless them with operating in the gifts and all of the things that have been given to them. Bless their life. Bless their marriage, if they're married. Bless their house, their cars, and their things. Bless their property. Bless their ministry. Begin to bless them; begin to speak the will of God into their life. Begin to bless them; that's it.

After you've done that, you can switch off and let the other one do it. You don't want to do all of the blessing. You get blessed and you give blessing. Bless them. Begin to speak well of one another.

Now, begin to thank God for that person. Thank God for their life, for their blessing, and for the Spirit of God dwelling within them.

Everybody, bring it down. Stop. I know it's hard to stop, but bring it down.

Ask each other if there is something that needs to be prayed for, specifically. When they tell you, you're not going to pray for them—you're going to bless them. They're going to say, "I need prayer for this..." Then you're going to bless them with the answer for what they need.

"I need healing." "All right, I bless you; be healed." "I need a job." "In the name of Jesus, I bless you with a job. The job you need, you will find and it will be a blessing, and you will prosper." Whatever need they give you, you bless them with the answer. We're not going to pray to God for it, we're going to bless them with the answer. Go ahead and ask one another if there's a particular need.

Everyone turn and face this way, because I want you to detach from that person you've been praying with. If you continue to face them and don't purposely make a motion, you'll tend to stay attached, or connected to them. I want you to break that attachment, that connection. That's because I want this to go to you and not be shared between you.

What I mean is this: I am going to bless you and speak the same way with all of you and put that blessing upon you. Now, you've already been blessed with every spiritual blessing in heavenly places, so there's nothing new that I can give you, but I can call for those things to be activated and fulfilled in your life.

Here's the key: I want to make sure that you understand that all of this is not just a seminar; it is the beginning of your life. This is the way that you're going to live. You start incorporating this into your daily life. This is not the end; this is the beginning. This is an activation. This is when it starts, and you have to keep it going by going home and doing this on a regular basis.

We are going to pray that this is going to be sealed within you and then worked out in your life. All I am going to do is bless you with that and what I want you to do is to make a decision to accept that and to see that work out in your life.

Let us pray:

"Father, we thank You. We thank You for Your Spirit that is upon us, within us, with us everywhere we go, all the time. Father, I thank You that we have been blessed with every spiritual blessing in heavenly places. Father, we thank You that we are not receiving anything new but we are receiving activation and fulfillment of what You have already given us.

"Father, right now, in the name of Jesus, we release, open, activate, make fully functional, all of the spiritual blessings that You have given us. Right now, in the name of Jesus, we release those blessings. We cease to allow the enemy to hinder these from being activated in our lives.

"In the name of Jesus, first and foremost, I break any spirit of fear and any spirit of timidity. Father, we thank You that the righteous are as bold as a lion and that our righteousness is of You. These people are righteous and therefore, they are bold. Right now, Father, we thank You for boldness in every life. We thank You Father for the fulfillment of Your will in their lives.

"Father, right now, we release giftings, operations, and callings into these lives. Right now, these giftings, these callings, these operations, and all of these things, by Your Spirit, we release and we activate. We seal this, so that this will come to pass in their life. In the name of Jesus, right now, we say, BE BLESSED, in the name of Jesus. BE BLESSED in the name of Jesus. You are to walk as the blessing in this land. We are the salt of the earth and that salt must now become the salt of the earth. Go into the earth and bless the earth.

"Father, I thank You that this salt that's going forth into the earth, that the blessing will be upon them and work its way through them and that those around them will receive of the blessing, as an overflow in the actual abundance of life that You have given us. I thank You for this abundance in their lives, in every area, spiritual, physical, emotional, social, and financial; in every area there is an abundance of the life of God. There is no lack; there's abundance. We say there shall be abundance throughout their lives.

"Father, we thank You that there are no longer to us generational curses, but we have generational blessings. Father, I thank You that right now, we decide to accept and believe that our blessings will be generational to our next generation and on to the next generation, and that we will not forget to tell those of the future generations about the wonders of our God and that we will let them know what He has done. We will not forget to tell our children and our children's children and the generations after that of the goodness of God and the blessing of God.

"Father, we thank You that this will become a generational blessing that we will see fulfilled in our families. There will be health where there has been sickness; there will be prosperity where there has been poverty.

"Father, we thank You that our families, our households and those of our bloodlines, being through the blood of the Son of God, going through our children and our children's children, that they will receive the Spirit of God. We thank you that they will be saved, that they will be blessed, that they will be prosperous, that they will know the Lord and that they will know Him in their hearts, and function in their calling.

"Father, we thank You that the Spirit of the living God is covering this land and Father, we thank You that the knowledge of the glory of God will fill this land. Father, we thank You even now, that the tide of the enemy has not only been stopped but is being driven back. This land will once again be a land that shines as the land of the free and will be a land that will be known as the land of God, that God has blessed this people.

"Father, I thank You. I thank You Father that people will look to the people in Your house and say because they are there, we are blessed. Father, we thank You for protection. We thank You, that Your blessing is upon us and that Your glory resides upon us. Father we glorify You, and Father we say we desire to shine as lights in this world, representative of the God that we serve and the God who is our Father.

"Father, we thank You. We thank You right now, that even our blessings will make those of Abraham jealous and want to come to You. We thank You that those blessings will make those of Ishmael jealous, and that they will want to come to You and to know You and know what Spirit they are to be of.

"Father, we thank You right now, that those in authority that have been charged with our safety know and hear, by the Spirit of God, the plans of the enemy and that those plans will be discovered, and Father, that they cannot make a plan that will not be discovered. Every plan they make will be discovered, sought out and brought down, so that no weapon formed against us shall prosper.

"Father, we thank You even now, that your blessing is upon us and because we are here, therefore, Your blessing is upon America; it's upon every nation in which people live who call upon the name of our God and upon His Son, Jesus Christ. Father, we bless this land. We bless this land and we say, 'Let it return to God in the name of Jesus.'

"We bring to Jesus those He died for. We bring them to Him and say these are the crowns that we will lay at Your feet. We thank You for allowing us to be witnesses by Your Spirit. Even now, in the name of Jesus, we will keep the Spirit of God stirred up within us and functioning within us."

Repeat this after me:

"Father, I thank You for the truth of Your Word. I am filled with your Spirit. I thank You for a spirit language. I thank you for communication between You and me. Father, I commit to You to keep this gift stirred up. I will keep the gift stirred up, in the name of Jesus, and I will burn brightly for You. In the name of Jesus, I make this commitment. Holy Spirit, I totally commit to You the right to remind me of this commitment. Father, I thank You for it in Jesus' name. Amen. So be it. Amen. Amen."

This is a start. This is not the end. Keep it going. Amen.

JGLM TRADEMARKED NAMES

All derivatives of JGLM names are Copyrighted trademarks:

Divine Healing Technician(s)
John G. Lake Ministries
John G. Lake Healing Rooms
John G. Lake's Divine Healing Institute
Dominion Life International Apostolic Church
Dominion Bible Institute

All derivatives of these names are Copyrighted trademarks and may not be used without the express written permission of:

John G. Lake Ministries
P. O. Box 742947
Dallas, Texas 75374
www.jglm.org

Please advise JGLM if you come into contact with anyone using the following names without authorized permission:

John G. Lake Ministries
John G. Lake's Divine Healing Institute
John G. Lake Healing Rooms
Divine Healing Technicians Certified
DHT

APPENDIX A: HISTORICAL INFORMATION

1. The information presented in this book is for historical purposes only. References to people, organizations, professions, etc., are presented for the sole purpose of giving an accurate overall understanding of the prevailing viewpoints of particular groups, religions, denominations, and movements of the time periods referred to in the seminar.

2. Each reader is expected and required to make personal comparisons and decide for themselves which viewpoints to accept and endorse.

3. The material presented and its successful application is predicated upon the viewpoints of those during the time periods in which they lived.

4. Curry R. Blake and John G. Lake Ministries are in no way responsible or liable for the successful application of the material or for future re-presentation of the materials presented in this book.

APPENDIX B: PRACTICES CONCERNING MEDICINE OR MEDICAL TREATMENT

1. All information presented is not to be construed as advice or instruction in activities or practices concerning medicine or medical treatment.

2. The author of this book is not in any way a trained medical or psychological professional.

3. Any ministry services are being rendered from a position of compassion and mercy and are not to be construed as medical treatments or as substitutions for medical treatments.

4. No one can present themselves or anyone under their guardianship for ministry, without relinquishing and waiving all legal recourse that would or might be the end state of such person and/or anyone they present for ministry.

5. Anyone using this material cannot hold JGLM liable or responsible for their personal practice of ministry.

Appendix C: Rules For Reproduction Of JGLM Materials

1. The physical material in this book is and shall remain the property of the presenter and the JGLM organization they represent. All material in this book shall belong to the author.

2. No reproduction of the material in this book is allowed without express written permission from the author of this book.

3. Any material and/or information in this book or gained during the seminar or from audio/video material from the host organization, if presented to others at any time, shall be presented in its entirety as it is presented in this seminar, without change, adaptation, omission or addition.

4. Prior to the presentation of this material to any other persons, groups, and/or organizations, reader will contact and inform the presenting organization of personal intentions in writing. If told not to present the information, such person(s) are not to present it.

5. In the event said person is given permission to present information, they are to provide the host organization with an audio/video recording (in its entirety) of the material presented.

APPENDIX D: NON-MEDICAL ADVICE

1. The information presented in this book is in no way intended as advice or instruction concerning the use of medicine, medical treatment, or the avoidance thereof.

2. Each person is responsible to investigate all methods of remedy they are contemplating.

3. No one has a right or responsibility to make your decision except you.

4. Any reference to medicine or medical treatment is solely for historical or informational purposes.

The Teaching That Birthed A Legend Is Now Raising An Army.

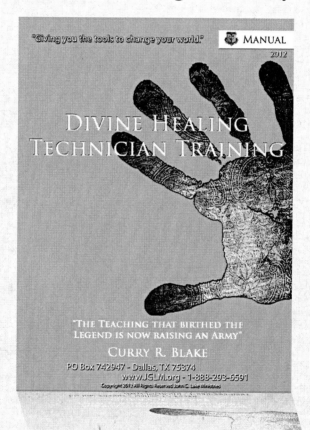

New Man
This Changes Everything...

The Primary focus of the DHT seminar is to train believers to biblically and effectively minister healing. The purpose of the New Man seminar is to reveal to believers what was accomplished by Jesus for us through His death, burial, and resurrection. The New Man Seminar reveals what you are (in Christ) not what you will some day become. It also reveals how to begin being who you are rather than emphasizing waiting for the next "Christian Fad".

DOMINION
BIBLE INSTITUTE

TRAINING THE NEXT GENERATION OF GOD'S GENERALS

SIGN UP TODAY!
dbi@jglm.org